*Light of Truth
and Fire of Love*

Light of Truth and Fire of Love

A Theology of the Holy Spirit

GARY D. BADCOCK

William B. Eerdmans Publishing Company
Grand Rapids, Michigan / Cambridge, U.K.

02 01 00 99 98 97   7 6 5 4 3 2 1

Library of Congress Cataloging-in-Publication Data

Badcock, Gary D.
    Light of truth and fire of love: a theology of the Holy Spirit /
Gary D. Badcock.
        p.   cm.
    Includes bibliographical references.
    ISBN 0-8028-4288-7 (pbk.: alk. paper)
    1. Holy Spirit. 2. Holy Spirit — History of doctrines. 3. Word of God
(Theology). 4. Word of God (Theology) — History of doctrines. I. Title.
BT121.2.B23 1997
231′.3 — dc21   96-53941
                                                                      CIP

*to Susan
and Hannah*

Contents

Introduction:
The Holy Spirit in Christian Theology

THE PLEA for a revitalized theology of the Spirit who "blows where he wills" is a recurring theme in theology. It has been prominent in theology in recent times, but the recognition that the Spirit is, on the one hand, a relatively neglected theme in Christian theology, and yet, on the other, the essential basis of Christian faith and life is much older, appearing regularly in the theological tradition. This is not, of course, to say that such a recognition appears everywhere and at all times; many a theologian past and present appears too secure in the knowledge of God to admit to poverty in the spiritual life. Or, to put the same point in another way, the experience of God — which is, I shall argue, the primary point at issue in all talk about the Spirit, however it is defined — has not always been integrated in any meaningful way into systems of theology.

There is to this extent a pronounced pneumatological deficit in Christian theology over against, for example, its enormous elaboration of the doctrine of Christ. Clearly, Christian theology is inherently christocentric, oriented as it is to the mystery of God in Jesus Christ, the "one mediator between God and humankind" (1 Tim. 2:5). Following both the Pauline theme that the Spirit is the Spirit of Christ, and above all the discourse of Jesus in John

1

14–16, the work of the Spirit has generally been understood to be somehow hidden beneath that of Christ, with the result, however, that the former has not received the degree of sustained treatment in the history of theology that the latter has been given. The hiddenness of the Spirit has been accentuated, moreover, for historical reasons involving the reaction of the church to radical spiritual movements such as Montanism, or the radical Reformation; this has resulted in the doctrine of the Holy Spirit being closely tied — in Western theology especially — to the doctrines of church and Scripture. There is clearly a strength in this, for it functions as a defense against the wilder excesses of those who, as Luther so aptly put it, believe they have "swallowed the Holy Spirit, feathers and all."[1] The question of discernment is always central in all claims to experience of the Spirit, but the risk of domestication of the Spirit to the structures of christology or to the preaching and sacraments of the church in all of this also needs to be borne in mind. The weakness of such attempts to control spiritual experience is that the Lordship of the Spirit can all too easily be compromised, and all too often has been compromised, not so much because the link with christology and ecclesiology is itself inappropriate, but rather by default, as the question of the doctrine of the Spirit *as such* is insufficiently emphasized and clarified theologically.

Pneumatology requires an organic link both with christology and with ecclesiology, or else it easily degenerates into something that is by definition unrelated to Jesus Christ and that has no place in and is of no use to the church. On the other hand, to be linked to christology and ecclesiology does not necessarily mean to be dominated by them; a pneumatology in which we are concerned supremely with the Holy Spirit as "Lord and Giver of life" cannot be adequate where it is conceived merely as a function of christology or, worse still, of ecclesiology. One of the central arguments that will be developed in what follows is that there is a more subtle, reciprocal relation between christology and pneumatology, and between Spirit and church, than is generally allowed. The Spirit is free to blow where he wills, quite apart from the high theologies of the Word, and even of the Word incarnate, or of the church and

1. Martin Luther, *Against the Heavenly Prophets*, 1; *WA*, 18:66.

its sacraments, which the theological tradition likes to impose on all things pneumatological. The link between pneumatology, christology, and ecclesiology is still to be acknowledged, but it is often present in theologically unexpected ways and places.

All the basic problems of theology are centered on the fact that in it, we are concerned with God and the world, and with their relations. This is true not only in traditional systems of doctrine but also, in a sense, in those recent theologies or antitheologies in which the objectivity of God is denied, for here, too, the question of the God-world relation regulates everything, even if only negatively. In pneumatology, there are, accordingly, two poles between which the doctrine of the Holy Spirit is developed: the doctrine of the person of the Spirit, on the one hand, and the doctrine of the work of the Spirit, on the other (which includes the element of human experience of the Spirit). In the former, we are concerned with developing the theme of the divine status or nature of the Spirit. Because in the Christian revelation this introduces the question of the relation of the Spirit to God the Father and to Jesus Christ his Son, this question takes a trinitarian form. This is sometimes very explicit in particular theologies and sometimes only implicit, but it is always the case. On the other hand, from the standpoint of human beings, the *locus* of pneumatology is the realm of faith and ecclesial life, the experienced realm of life lived in faith under the gospel of Jesus Christ. Here we are concerned with the doctrine of reconciliation to God and its outworking in human experience, where the correlate of the Christian doctrine of the Spirit in its most general sense is Christian life, including such things as worship, ethics, and spirituality. Since the doctrine of the Spirit's person and work go together, this, too, generally assumes a trinitarian form: we come to the Father through the Son, in the Spirit.

This second point suggests that Christian pneumatology might perhaps not be as insubstantial as is sometimes alleged. The spiritual life cannot itself be said to have been neglected in the Christian church, and while it does seem that, historically, the tide of interest in spirituality ebbs and flows to some extent, the quest for spiritual meaning has always been alive and well, and is even as alive and well in the contemporary context as it has ever been. Perhaps our problem in pneumatology is not so much the lack of a theology of the Spirit as an incapacity to see the work of the Spirit where it exists and, in particular, an inability or an unwillingness to integrate that work of the Spirit into the basic structures of our theological thought. The theology of prayer is a case in point; whereas praying is basic to the religious life and presumably also to all theology in the true sense of the word, and while prayer can readily be understood in pneumatological terms (Rom. 8:26-27), it is rarely treated in any detail or with any depth in systems of theology.

The effects of this on Christian theology are clear. First, the frequent neglect of the spiritual life in theological systems is impoverishing, for such theologies can only be incomplete and largely irrelevant to the life of the church. The predominance of the ideal of rationality or *logos* in the bulk of Christian theology may help to explain why the perhaps somewhat a-logical, unpredictable, indefinable work of the Spirit in the world has not been made theologically thematic, but it cannot excuse that fact. Without the "source experience" that the Spirit brings, as Noel O'Donoghue has written, the whole theological enterprise either hardens into intellectual or moral puritanism, or else tends too radically to humanism.[2] If theology ceases to be really related to the God who is the source of life, in other words, then it is no longer *truly* theological.

Second, where the pneumatological reality of faith as lived is not taken up into theology, then life itself is robbed of theological depth. This does not mean that life in the Spirit has not been lived, but only that it has not always been properly thought through. The need, clearly, is both for theological reflection to be spiritually deepened and for Christian spirituality to be deepened by theological reflection. This need may be readily perceived in various places. In the Protestant tradition, where the Spirit tends to be seen as an adjunct of the Word, there is a degenerate tendency to restrict the work of the Spirit to the gift of faith in the Word; therefore, where experience of the Spirit does not arise in connection with listening to sermons or reading the Bible — to caricature the position only

---

2. Cf. Noel Dermot O'Donoghue, "Vision and System," in *Heaven in Ordinarie* (Edinburgh: T. & T. Clark, 1979), p. 149, and his "Mystical Imagination," in *Religious Imagination*, ed. James P. Mackey (Edinburgh: T. & T. Clark, 1986), pp. 186-205.

slightly — there is no experience of the Spirit at all. What is especially lacking here is an awareness of the Spirit's presence, not merely in the sacraments and the fellowship of the church, and wherever love is found, but also in darkness and doubt, and in the difficult carrying of the cross.

Third, pneumatological reality has long gone unrecognized as something of pneumatological importance. When, for example, theologians past and present decry the neglect of the doctrine of the Spirit, one needs to ask if they are not to some extent looking for pneumatology in the wrong place. There is a basic question here that needs to be asked but that is almost universally overlooked: What, after all, would constitute an adequate pneumatology if one were to be developed? Could it ever be even *conceived* in terms of the rational categories of conventional theology, bound up as it is with the ideal of *logos,* intelligence, discourse, and so on, or would it perhaps not have to be developed rather as a function of *love,* or of will and practical reason, to use the classical Augustinian and Kantian terms? This would certainly not make such a theology any less meaningful. Perhaps even the term *pneumatology* needs to be reconsidered, since it enshrines in our theology the idea that *logos* and *pneuma* are entirely compatible, or even one and the same, in the sense that to know the Spirit is to have a *logos* of the Spirit, a doctrine of the Spirit. Can one speak rightly of a *logos* of *pneuma,* or might we perhaps better speak in our theology of the Spirit in terms of love, and so, for example, of a love of the Spirit, a *pneumatophilia?*

Such an approach would at least allow us actually to make sense of what ought everywhere to be taken for granted in theology: that an illiterate peasant farmer can in fact know God better than the scholar, however learned and well acquainted with the standard written sources and issues of theology. One needs also to recall here that the first and great commandment is to love God, not to know him; in religion, it is the moral, relational dimension that is of primary importance. This does not mean that the intellectual enterprise of theology is necessarily undermined, but it does seem to imply that it will be through the love of God that it is given its real value. Theological knowledge alone can be dead and barren, but enlivened by love, it is a living and fruitful thing indeed.

Perhaps it was this that Karl Barth, the modern theologian of the Word *par excellence,* realized only at the end of his life when he wrote of the potentially positive contribution of liberal Protestantism, and especially of Schleiermacher, to the future of theology. In an essay entitled "Concluding Unscientific Postscript on Schleiermacher," he speaks frankly of the possibility of a theology, unlike his own, that would be a theology "predominantly and decisively of the Holy Spirit." "Everything," he wrote, "which needs to be said, considered, and believed about God the Father and God the Son in an understanding of the first and second articles might be shown and illuminated in its foundations through God the Holy Spirit, the *vinculum pacis inter Patrem et Filium.*"[3] Although his own characteristically christocentric approach is presented here as something that was primarily directed against the *subjectivism* of Schleiermacher and the liberal tradition, Barth argues that the new theology of the Spirit of which he speaks could be conceived as a rehabilitation of Schleiermacher's theology, although within the terms of his own christological corrective. The contribution of Schleiermacher is seen to lie in his analysis of the lived experience of faith on its subjective side.

In fact, all Christian theology that is worth the name must have at its heart the question of the human being who lives in relationship with God and neighbor, for it is just this that is central to the teaching and example of Jesus. Barth's own fear that liberalism's adaptation of this theme effectively relinquished the divine pole in the divine-human relationship needs to be faced squarely, but it is also important for us to note that this is an extreme judgment to which the liberals themselves would by no means have acquiesced. Certainly, we ourselves need not accept it uncritically. To accommodate one's theology to the legitimate insights of both Barth and the liberal tradition means only that the life of faith under the grace of God must itself be a proper subject for theological discussion. In particular, where — as in much contemporary theology — God is conceived in trinitarian terms as the Father who

3. Karl Barth, "Concluding Unscientific Postscript on Schleiermacher," in Barth, *The Theology of Schleiermacher,* ed. Dietrich Ritschl, trans. G. W. Bromiley (Edinburgh: T. & T. Clark, 1982), pp. 277-78.

makes a place for human beings in his own life through the reconciling and glorifying work of Christ and the Spirit, the human reality
thus brought into view can hardly be ignored. This is not anthro-
pocentrism, but simply good theology.

The following pages present a theology of the Holy Spirit that
draws on both old and new theological insights. First, we will
examine a number of crucial episodes and questions that have
emerged in the field of pneumatology in the history of Christian
thought; then, toward the end, a contemporary theology of the
Holy Spirit will be developed. This will be closely, but by no means
uncritically, related to the theological enterprise that Barth himself
initiated earlier in this century, and that characterizes so much of
theology today: the return to the doctrine of the Trinity as the
framework for Christian reflection. If, in short, the *locus* of pneumatology is the life of faith, the outworking in the individual and
in the church of the divine outreach that comes from the Father,
through the Son, and reaches completion "in the Holy Spirit,"
then the question of the ground of faith and of ecclesial life in the
triune God is clearly of real importance. Thus the two poles of
pneumatology are held together: its *locus* in the experience of
reconciliation in the most general sense, and its grounding in the
being of God himself, the God who reaches out to the world in
truth and love.

As we shall see, the doctrine of the Trinity enables us to see
the work of the Spirit as something more than an inconsequential
"extra" tacked on to the doctrine of the person and work of Christ.
The trinitarian dimension also enables us to comprehend the work
of the Spirit in terms adequate to the reality with which we are
concerned. The Holy Spirit as the "light of truth and fire of love"
is the Spirit of the Father and the Son, the Lord and Giver of life;
and conversely, it is precisely because the Spirit is the Spirit of Father
and Son that he is the Giver of life, the source of faith and love in
the lives of human beings.

1. Spirit in Biblical Perspective

ONE OF THE most striking things encountered in the whole of the theology of the Holy Spirit is that God should be said to have or to be Spirit at all. The basic meaning both of the Hebrew *ruach* and of the Greek *pneuma,* which are rendered into English as "spirit," is "air" or perhaps "moving air," that is, wind or breath. However, it is not immediately obvious why either or both should be susceptible to theological usage. Indeed, this is one of the particular problems of the doctrine of the Spirit. In Christian theology, for example, the fact that Holy Spirit, the personal name given to the third person of the Trinity, is nonpersonal — and, in particular, unlike the names Father and Son in this respect — has created difficulties for exponents of the doctrines of the Holy Spirit and of the Trinity from the beginning. Why did the ancient Jews adopt the word *ruach,* and with it the notion of breath and wind, into their theological vocabulary, and why did the theological notion of *ruach* persist beyond the confines of their own religious tradition to become such a prominent concept in New Testament theology and in the Christian religion?

One clue to this question can be found in the language of prayer in the Old Testament, in particular in the Psalms, where *ruach* is used to speak both of the human relationship with God and of creaturely dependence upon God:

8

Create in me a clean heart, O God,
and put a new and right spirit within me.
Do not cast me away from your presence,
and do not take your holy spirit from me.
Restore to me the joy of your salvation,
and sustain in me a willing spirit.

(Ps. 51:10-12)

Or again:

O LORD, how manifold are your works!
In wisdom you have made them all. . . .
Yonder is the sea, great and wide,
creeping things innumerable are there,
living things both small and great. . . .
These all look to you
to give them their food in due season;
when you give to them, they gather it up;
when you open your hand, they are filled with good things.
When you hide your face, they are dismayed;
when you take away their breath [*ruach*], they die,
and return to their dust.
When you send forth your spirit [*ruach*], they are created;
and you renew the face of the ground.

(104:25-30)

We see here a profound awareness of the continuity of creaturely life with God, both in the moral and religious sphere of human existence and in the sphere of creatureliness as such and even life as such. And yet the *discontinuity* between the two is also clear in such talk about the *ruach* that God and his living creatures share, for on the one hand, the Spirit of God is holy, and on the other hand, the Spirit is that upon which creatures depend for their very existence, and not something they possess by permanent right.

We might also derive a little help at this point from comparative religion, for spirit as a *religious* concept is not unique to the

Jewish or Christian traditions.[1] The special significance of spirit —
or, more correctly, "breath" — in the vocabulary of the religions
of the world appears to derive from the associations between breathing and living and between life and the sacred. In many languages,
the words for life and breath are the same; and in the ancient
cultures from which these languages derive, the sign that indicates
the presence of life in animals such as ourselves is not the pulse or
the brainwave, as in modern medicine, or even physical movement
or consciousness, but more often than not the presence of breath.
To have breath or spirit is quite simply to be alive, and to be alive
is to be in receipt of that life from God. We see this theme plainly
in various places in the Old Testament, in such texts as Job 12:10
("In his hand is the life of every living thing and the breath of
every human being"), Ezekiel 37:5 ("I will cause breath [*ruach*]
to enter you, and you shall live"), and in the "breath of life" texts
of Genesis 6:17; 7:15; and 7:22.

The biblical concept of Spirit can therefore be seen to be
rooted in biblical anthropology and even in the biblical understanding of the animate creation in general. By implication, however, this level of discourse affects what is meant in talk of *God* as
having Spirit or, more rarely in the Bible, as being Spirit; in the
same way that human beings are alive because they have spirit, so
God also is designated as the living God when he is characterized
as having Spirit. The living God is the God who is actually present
in human affairs, and it is, it seems, at least partly for this reason
that so many biblical references to the Spirit have to do with divine
activity in the world. Furthermore, since for human beings the
capacity to breathe — the presence of life, in other words — carries with it conscious life in its emotional and intellectual aspects,
to speak of God as Spirit is to speak of God as having an analogous
life of his own. That God can be grieved or angered, that God
can love and take pity, or that God can know and plan certain
things is simply assumed throughout the Bible, although, paradoxically, it is set alongside a polemic against making God in our
own image.

---

1. J. Bruce Long, "Life," in *The Encyclopedia of Religion*, ed. Mircea Eliade
(New York: Macmillan, 1987), vol. 7, pp. 541-47.

All of this, however, can be expressed in the simple observation that God has Spirit. This does not mean, of course, that God literally breathes, or that God has the physical prerequisites for inhalation and exhalation. God is sometimes spoken of in the Bible as having nostrils and a mouth, but none of this can be taken literally. In the same way, to say that God has breath is to say something that is undoubtedly theologically significant, but its significance, like so much else in theology, cannot be derived from the literal meaning of the words we use.

In examining the doctrine of the Spirit of God that emerges from the pages of the Bible, therefore, we need to be aware that we are dealing in the first instance with analogy. Although God is himself much more than analogical, and although the Spirit of God is more than an analogy — above all in the Bible, as we will see shortly — all that we can say initially presupposes that our language about the Spirit, whether this is the Spirit of God, the Spirit of Yahweh, the Holy Spirit, or the Spirit of Jesus Christ, begins in the same way that our language about the nostrils or mouth or face or hands of God begins. Having noted this, we can then move on to discover something of the distinctiveness of what the Bible has to say about the Spirit.

The Old Testament

To begin at the beginning of the Old Testament's theology of the Spirit, we have to start, not with the relatively late Genesis 1:2, which by something of a historical accident appears at the beginning of the Bible, and which speaks of the Spirit of God *(ruach elohim)* sweeping over and countering the primeval chaos waters, but with the deeper roots of Hebrew religion. In some of the oldest identifiable traditions of the Old Testament, dating perhaps from the ninth century B.C., the Spirit of God is spoken of in the context of the activity of nameless groups or schools of early prophets. These groups seemingly lived under the direction of a leader and were collectively known as "sons of the prophets." We learn of their existence only in passing, since the narratives are mainly concerned with other things. Nevertheless, what we do learn in the narratives and what we can reconstruct from them are of considerable interest. In 1 Samuel 10, for example, in fulfillment of the words of Samuel, who spoke of the Spirit of the LORD *(ruach yahweh)* coming upon Saul, Saul meets a procession of prophets, at which point the Spirit of God *(ruach elohim)* rushes upon him, so that he prophesies with the prophetic band. From parallel texts such as 1 Samuel 19:23-24, where again Saul prophesies as a result of the *ruach elohim,* but this time naked, lying on the ground for a day and a night, we can deduce that this form of prophetism was anything but coolly rational and composed. The term "ecstatic prophetism" is rightly used to describe it.

It is often argued that such early Hebrew prophetism as a cultural phenomenon derived from Canaanite religion, and that the very phrase *ruach elohim* (which thus antedates the phrase *ruach yahweh*) itself reflects these cultural ties.[2] The word *elohim* stems from the common Semitic "El," which appears in Canaanite religion as the high god *el elyon,* "God Most High."[3] Although the derivation is indirect, *elohim* is morphologically a plural form of *el,* the Semitism representing in this case anything from a straightforward plurality to an intensification of power to the plural of majesty. The literature of the Old Testament is sometimes in something of a linguistic and theological haze at this point; witness, for example, the opening of Psalm 82: "God *[elohim]* has taken his place in the divine council *['dat el];* in the midst of the gods *[elohim]* he holds judgment."

The claim that early Hebrew prophetism took its rise from, or that it arose in relation to, the prophetic traditions of Israel's neighbors is partially supported by the early links in texts such as 1 Samuel 10 between the concept of *ruach* and the theologically ambiguous term *elohim.* Our sources are fragmentary, however, and even with the biblical and archaeological evidence that suggests that polytheism was the norm rather than the exception in early Israel,[4]

2. E.g., H. C. Schmitt, "Prophetie und Tradition," *Zeitschrift für Theologie und Kirche* 74 (1977): 255-72.

3. Helmer Ringgren, *Israelite Religion,* trans. David Green (London: S.P.C.K., 1969), pp. 67-68.

4. Mark S. Smith, *The Early History of God: Yahweh and the Other Deities in Ancient Israel* (San Francisco: Harper & Row, 1990).

the fact is that we know almost nothing of these prophets. *If* the narratives concerning prophets such as Samuel, and, later on, Nathan, Elijah, and Elisha, could be taken as an interpretative key to the question, then we could reliably rule out such a connection. In the case of Elijah in particular, an emphatic distinction is drawn between the prophet of Yahweh and the prophets of Baal (1 Kings 18), but here, as indeed already in 1 Samuel 10:6, it is the *ruach yahweh* and not the *ruach elohim* that is in view. This indicates that these traditions may well come from a different theological source.[5]

What is more certain is that later in Israel's history, many of the classic Hebrew writing prophets actively dissociate themselves from these early prophetic traditions. Amos is the most obvious case in point: "I am no prophet, nor a prophet's son," he protests (Amos 7:14). But equally significant and surprising is the fact that in the preexilic writing prophets, the Spirit is not generally appealed to as the source of prophetic inspiration. (Isaiah 32:15-20 anticipates the postexilic prophets who speak of the renewal of Israel by the Spirit, but this is exceptional.) It seems, therefore, that the early conception of the Spirit as inspiring the ecstatic prophets of Saul's era became discredited because of various abuses, in all probability related to the links between such prophetism, the *ruach elohim,* and the religious traditions of the surrounding Canaanites. Jeremiah, the arch foe of infidelity to Yahweh, may well be referring to these prophets and to this prophetic tradition when he counsels, "The prophets are nothing but wind [*ruach*], for the word is not in them" (Jer. 5:13). By contrast, it is to Jeremiah that the *word (dabar)* of Yahweh is given (Jer. 1:9). The prophetic tradition survived, but largely, it seems, in a way that bypassed a great deal of the early tradition of ecstatic prophetism — just as it also bypassed, to a very great extent, other central religious institutions of kingship, priesthood, and temple cult. Furthermore, although Ezekiel and the postexilic writing prophets see prophecy again as the work of the Spirit (e.g., Neh. 9:30; Ezek. 2:2; 3:24; Zech. 7:12), even this does not represent the only theological view avail-

---

5. The same applies to the narratives of the judges, where again it is the *ruach yahweh* and never the *ruach elohim* that is in question: e.g., Judg. 3:10; 6:34; 11:29; 13:25.

able at the time. Over against these later prophets, the Deuteronomist responds to the tragedy of the exile by emphasizing the role of the Law in Israel's religious life. The theological phrase *ruach elohim* does not figure in the Deuteronomistic history, while prophecy as a religious institution, and in particular prophetic activity analogous to that of the surrounding nations, is seen as something to be strictly controlled, or even positively discouraged (Deut. 13:1-5; 18:9-22).

It is clear, therefore, that a question mark is placed over the work of the Spirit in these Old Testament traditions, in particular in relation to prophecy. The Spirit's activity, however, is not restricted *simply* to prophecy. Saul's experience of the Spirit resulted initially, at least, in his prophesying, but the real reason for the gift of the Spirit related to the kingship. Echoes of the Judges narrative therefore appear in 1 Samuel 11:6, where the *ruach elohim* (but not the *ruach yahweh,* as in the Judges parallels) falls upon Saul so that he rescues the city of Jabesh from the Ammonites. David, for his part, similarly receives the Spirit, only in this case the *ruach yahweh,* in anticipation of the kingship (1 Sam. 16:13). In the early Hebrew theology of kingship, therefore, the king appears as the one anointed by the Spirit, who by virtue of that anointing is God's instrument in bringing blessings on his people. Historically, of course, national blessing was not forthcoming, and corrupt kings led to disillusionment. Yet it is precisely in this context of religious disappointment that the messianic expectations of the later Old Testament make sense: One day, there will be an ideal king, endowed with the Spirit in an ideal way, who will usher in the earlier expectation of national blessing (e.g., Isa. 11:2). It is not just the messianic king who will be endowed with the Spirit, but his subjects as well; the giving of the Spirit to the Messiah will usher in the giving of the Spirit to Israel.

Other biblical texts likewise provide evidence of a considerable widening of the role of the Spirit beyond prophecy alone. For example, in a relatively late priestly text, the Spirit is said to endow workmen with the requisite technical skill to construct the tabernacle (Exod. 31:3; 35:31). In the Hebraic Wisdom tradition, the Spirit is said more generally to endow human beings with understanding (Job 32:8; Prov. 1:23) — a theme that will be extended in Hellenistic Judaism, where the theological category of wisdom and the ancient notion of Spirit are closely aligned (Wis. 7:22; 9:17). While these do not measure up to the more profound associations made between the Spirit and the ethical and spiritual renewal of Israel in the postexilic writing prophets, they are nevertheless significant in opening up the activity of the Spirit to the wider realm of human existence; it is not just the ecstatic prophet who has the Spirit, or the king, but also the ordinary man or woman who fears God.

It is in the image of the Spirit as the agent of ethical renewal, however, that the Old Testament's theology of the Spirit finds its highest expression; it is the *holy* Spirit, in short, that is the instrument of God's purpose in creation and in history. The elusive image of the Lord's Servant in Second Isaiah, for example, is that of a bearer of the Spirit who will bring justice and righteousness to the earth (Isa. 42:1ff.). In the exilic era again, the prophet Ezekiel speaks of a new relationship between Israel and the Spirit that will come to pass, and so both vindicate Yahweh's holiness and give Israel a new heart and a new obedience.

This new confidence — we might even say, this new faith — in the Spirit as the principle of renewal and new hope, which characterizes so much Hebrew thought in the exilic era, is clearly one of the greatest watersheds in the development of the theology of the Spirit. First of all, it is here that the Old Testament theology of the Spirit is most profound, for here the work of the Spirit is related to the deepest sources of human ethical and spiritual life, not only in Israel, but in all humanity. Second, on the basis thus laid, the Old Testament's theology of the Spirit moves creatively in the direction of the eschatological hopes that are so characteristic of later biblical Judaism. Here, as in Ezekiel's vision in the valley of dry bones, the theme of *ruach* as the life-principle that comes from God and the theme of eschatological renewal are fused in the prophet's hopes for the future of Israel, risen from the grave and restored to the land. Moreover, a new relationship between Israel and the Spirit is spoken of, bringing with it a new heart and a new obedience to Yahweh's laws and commands (Ezek. 36:24ff.). The holiness of Yahweh will thus be vindicated in the newfound holiness of his people, newly possessed as they will be by his Spirit.

In Second Isaiah a similar vision for the future is developed, only in this case in connection with the mysterious figure of the Servant:

> Here is my servant, whom I uphold,
>   my chosen, in whom my soul delights;
> I have put my spirit upon him;
> he will bring forth justice to the nations.
>
> (Isa. 42:1)

The vision of Ezekiel is here expanded, so that the activity of God through the Spirit is seen as offering promise to the whole of the earth. The Servant, who in Second Isaiah represents at the literal level the corporate entity that went into exile, sold into slavery because of its sins, and who also represents at a more profound level Israel's messianic hope for deliverance, is one of the theologically richest of all the biblical bearers of the Spirit, for here we find the image of Christ — anointed, suffering, liberating, and exalted.

Finally, the prophecy of Joel, cited by Peter in his Pentecost sermon in Acts, extends the promised blessing of the Spirit to all of God's people, and not just to the prophet or king:

> I will pour out my spirit on all flesh;
> your sons and your daughters shall prophesy,
>   your old men shall dream dreams,
>   and your young men shall see visions.
> Even on the male and female slaves,
>   in those days, I will pour out my spirit.
>
> . . . Then everyone who calls on the name of the LORD shall be saved.
>
> (Joel 2:28, 31; cf. Acts 2:17ff.)

Rather than the Spirit being withdrawn from the world, the world being unworthy of the Spirit's presence, what is promised is a universal gift — a gift open to all who will receive it. The principle of life and energy in God, the instrument of his purpose in creation and history, and the agent of ethical renewal thus become the present possession of all those who call upon the name of the Lord.

What can theology make of this? Several issues still central to the theology of the Holy Spirit emerge, which shows that the Old Testament discussion is not simply locked in the past. First of all, there is the fact that *ruach* as a theological category in the Old Testament cannot simply be defined in impersonal terms as wind or breath. In fact, the Old Testament understanding of *ruach* or Spirit involves the idea of life in general, and particularly the idea of personal life in its emotional, voluntary, and intellectual aspects. To say that human beings have *ruach* is to say that they are the living beings they are; to say that God has *ruach* is similarly to say that God is the living God who acts, who makes plans, who is saddened and angered, and so on. This relates closely to one of the central questions of the theology of the Spirit: Are we justified in calling the Spirit a "person" in the trinitarian sense?

Second, there is a clear and close relation between Spirit and Word in the Old Testament; this link is sometimes present only in an indirect way, as when Jeremiah argues that the (old) prophets are nothing but wind and that the word of Yahweh is not in them, but even this shows that the link between the two categories is recognized. Among others, the Joel text brings the connection to more positive expression: "Your sons and your daughters shall prophesy." Here the older relationship between the gift of the Spirit and the prophetic word is reintegrated into the mainstream of Old Testament theology. This, of course, ties in with a variety of central themes in theology — with the doctrine of the inspiration of Scripture, for example.

Third, experience of the Spirit has from the beginning been regarded as theologically ambiguous. Much of the Old Testament seems actually to go so far as to deny the legitimacy of all experience of the Spirit, in order to tidy up religious and theological confusion. The shift in so many of the biblical texts from the *ruach elohim* to the *ruach yahweh* is almost certainly related to this internal debate in Old Testament theology: Was there perhaps at some point an attempt to define authentic experience of *ruach* in terms of one rather than the other? Whatever the answer to this question, the issue continues into the present. How do we define what authentic experience of the Spirit and authentic spirituality are?

Finally, however, the connection between Spirit and religious experience in the Old Testament remains clear. Despite what might sometimes seem to be the best efforts of theologians past and present to empty theology of religious depth by leaving little or no room for religious experiences of faith, prayer, renewal, and so on, the Old Testament presents us with something different, which serves as a permanent barrier against over-rationalization and over-systematization of the realities of faith and the content of theology. "Deep calls to deep in the roar of your waterfalls," says the Psalmist with astonishing simplicity (Ps. 42:7, NIV). Or, as we might paraphrase, Spirit calls to spirit and they answer one another in the human encounter with God.

Paul and Luke-Acts

The New Testament, too, speaks openly about experience of the Spirit. Paul, in fact, echoes much of what has just been said in a number of places. In 1 Corinthians 2:6-16, for example, an astonishing series of claims are made concerning the Spirit. First of all, there is the claim that "we" — that is, Paul and his group, but by implication at least *some* Christians generally — speak of a secret divine wisdom that is hidden from the powers that be in the world, but that is revealed to "us" by the Spirit. Paul then goes on to explain that, just as no human being knows the secret thoughts of another, but only that person's spirit within, so no one can know the thoughts of God, but only the Spirit of God. This is the very Spirit, however, that is given to Paul and to the Christian church, in order that divine illumination might be given. Paul goes to the extraordinary lengths of apparently overturning two separate sayings from Isaiah regarding the incomprehensibility of God and his ways, juxtaposing them with statements concerning the new revelation that comes by the Spirit. First, to Isaiah 64:4, "What no eye has seen, nor ear heard, nor the human heart conceived," Paul's response is, "these things God has revealed to us through the Spirit" (1 Cor. 2:9-10). The Isaianic text, it seems, applies only to the rulers of this age who crucified the Lord — that is, to the human being who lives by the principle of the flesh; under the new principle of life in the Spirit, all this is changed. Second, to Isaiah 40:13, "For who has known the mind of the Lord so as to instruct him?" Paul responds with the astonishing, mysterious claim, "But we have the mind of Christ."

The characteristically Pauline conception of the gift of the Spirit as the down payment *(arrabon)* made by God toward the final fulfillment of his promises (2 Cor. 1:22; 5:5) lends support to this reading of 1 Corinthians 2:6-16. The Spirit in Pauline theology is the eschatological gift, the gift ushering in the age of fulfillment. If 1 Corinthians 2 permits us to say that there is some sort of kinship between the human spirit and the divine Spirit, echoing Old Testament conceptuality,[6] then the clearly eschatological sense in Pauline pneumatology compels us to say that his theology also moves well beyond this, for something radically new and utterly distinctive, something that breaks the continuity between the natural person and the spiritual person, is what Paul has in mind.

In order to make sense of this new experience of the Spirit, in particular against the background of Old Testament expectation, we need first of all to remind ourselves that the movement from the promise of the Spirit in the Old Testament to its perceived fulfillment in New Testament thought is at least as subtle as the movement from Old Testament messianic expectation to New Testament realization. Certainly, the Old Testament expectation of the outpouring of the Spirit upon all people comes to full expression in the New. The ways in which this is fleshed out in New Testament theology, however, in relation to Christ himself, for example, and in relation to the doctrines of church, baptism, and salvation, which are the context of New Testament pneumatology, are diverse. Several major and relatively distinct strands of New Testament pneumatology need to be distinguished. To begin with, there is the Pauline tradition, to which we shall return shortly, but there is also the synoptic witness to Jesus as the anointed one, the bearer of the Spirit. According to the first of the evangelists, Mark, the beginning of the gospel of Jesus Christ is marked by the story of

---

6. C. F. D. Moule, *The Holy Spirit* (Oxford: Mowbray, 1978), pp. 7-17.

John the Baptist, who preached a baptism of repentance for the forgiveness of sins, and who pointed forward to the coming one who would baptize with the Holy Spirit. It is not clear whether this second baptism was understood by Mark to have been accomplished through the ministry of Jesus in his own lifetime, or something that the ministry of Jesus made possible but that the evangelist himself does not speak about in his Gospel — perhaps church baptism. In Luke-Acts, however, this unclarity has been overcome, as the evangelist's clear pneumatological interests reveal that what is decisively important about Jesus is intimately related to the Spirit's presence in him and in his church after Pentecost.

Luke-Acts not only repeats the story of Jesus' baptism from Mark, but returns to it again in the context of the continuation of Jesus' ministry after the resurrection (Luke 3:16; Acts 1:5). At the beginning of Acts, we see the fulfillment of the saying of John the Baptist, "he will baptize you with the Holy Spirit and fire," in the Pentecost narrative. More clearly than Matthew and Mark, Luke-Acts is able on this basis to leave room for the time of the church and the ingathering of the Gentiles between the ministry of Jesus and the time of final fulfillment; this "time between the times" is the period of the Holy Spirit's activity. What Paul sees as the down payment of the Spirit, in anticipation of the final consummation, Luke-Acts sees in more salvation-historical terms as the empowering of the church for its appointed mission: "you will receive power when the Holy Spirit has come upon you; and you will be my witnesses," the risen Christ promises in Acts 1:8.

There are a number of central themes in the New Testament theology of the Spirit; power and wisdom are two of them, and both are found in Acts. The connections between Spirit, word, and witness are clear enough, being grounded firmly in Old and New Testament theology; the question of power is perhaps more confusing. The popular Jewish and Gentile mentality of the New Testament era involved the conviction that the world is occupied not only by human beings, animals, vegetables, and so on, but also by invisible superhuman forces, both good and evil. According to a wide spectrum of early Christian theology, the sinful world, maddened and led astray by evil spirits, needs to be set free from its captivity to evil; as late as the flowering of patristic theology in the fourth and fifth centuries, this would still underlie the *main-stream* understanding of the work of Christ.[7] The gift of the Spirit, too, is interpreted as the gift of power to deal with the realm of evil spirits and with their malignant influences upon humanity at large. The mission of the church is thus a two-sided one: first, to witness to Christ crucified and risen, but also to combat the spirits. Exorcism was an important part of the life and faith of the New Testament church and the primitive church down to the third century and beyond; just as Jesus cast out the demons, so do the apostles in the story of Acts, and so will the primitive church. The rival realm of the Holy Spirit is thus set over against the realm of the demons, against which it is victorious.[8]

Furthermore, as a function of the power of the Spirit committed to the apostles by the risen Christ in Luke-Acts, miracles, signs, and wonders are presented as normal events. Although linked also with the word of Jesus and sometimes with the name of Jesus, it is clear that it is by the power of the Spirit that the apostles act. This feature of the primitive Christian gospel is seen not only in Acts, which may or may not exaggerate the situation in this respect, but also elsewhere. The apostle Paul, though one of the champions of a cerebral Christianity, is quite capable of linking the presence of the Spirit with the performing of miracles, not only in the celebrated discussion of the spiritual gifts in 1 Corinthians 12 and 14 but also in Romans, among other places:

> In Christ Jesus, then, I have reason to boast of my work for God. For I will not venture to speak of anything except what Christ has accomplished through me to win obedience from the Gentiles, by word and deed, by the power of signs and wonders, by the power of the Spirit of God, so that from Jerusalem and as far around as Illyricum I have fully proclaimed the good news of Christ. (Rom. 15:17-19)

7. Cf., e.g., Gregory of Nyssa's *Great Catechism,* found under the title *Address on Religious Instruction* in *Christology of the Later Fathers,* ed. E. R. Hardy and C. Richardson (Philadelphia: Westminster Press, 1954), pp. 268ff.

8. Adolf von Harnack, *The Mission and Expansion of Christianity in the First Three Centuries,* ed. and trans. James Moffatt, 2nd ed. (London: Williams and Norgate, 1908), pp. 125ff.

The preaching of the gospel, according to this text — and others such as 1 Corinthians 2:4-5 — intrinsically involves for Paul a demonstration of its power, for to be in Christ is for Paul to have a share in the eschatological Spirit, which makes all this possible.

The movement forward from Jesus to Spirit, from expectation of the Spirit to fulfillment, is clear in all of this. Another important characteristic of New Testament pneumatology, however, must also be noted, and that is the attempt to trace the present experience of the Spirit in the church back into the history of Jesus. Many New Testament scholars argue that the connection between the Spirit and Christ that appears in Luke-Acts has its earliest expression in a pre-Pauline formula cited in Romans 1:3-4, where Christ is described as "descended from David according to the flesh and . . . declared to be Son of God with power according to the spirit of holiness by resurrection from the dead."[9] The Spirit's presence, it is claimed, was initially associated with the resurrection and the birth of the church, rather than with the whole of the life story of Jesus. Just as the general tendency of contemporary New Testament scholarship is to trace belief in Jesus' divine Sonship back from its origins in the resurrection through Jesus' life until finally we arrive at a clear preexistence doctrine, so also scholars argue that, over time, the primitive christology associated with the resurrection and represented in Romans 1:3-4 was gradually pushed further and further back into the history of Jesus. Mark, the earliest of our Gospels, reflects the stage at which Jesus was understood to be Son of God according to the Spirit (*kata pneuma*) at his baptism; Matthew and Luke both independently attribute Jesus' divine Sonship to his special relationship to the Holy Spirit from his conception (see especially Luke 1:35b).[10]

The results of recent New Testament scholarship in this respect are of real importance for theology, for they affirm an intimate connection between christology and pneumatology in the New

9. Joseph A. Fitzmyer, *The Gospel According to Luke (I–IX)* (Garden City, NY: Doubleday, 1981), pp. 340ff.; Raymond E. Brown, *The Birth of the Messiah* (London: Geoffrey Chapman, 1977), pp. 311-16; and James D. G. Dunn, *Christology in the Making* (London: SCM Press, 1980), pp. 34-35, 136-49.

10. C. K. Barrett, *The Holy Spirit and the Gospel Tradition,* 2nd ed. (London: SPCK, 1966), pp. 5-24; Brown, *The Birth of the Messiah,* pp. 108, 156.

Testament. It is less certain, however, whether the claim that pneumatic christology originated with the resurrection and was subsequently traced farther and farther back into Jesus' history can be sustained. First of all, the writers of the New Testament were surely well aware of the specific connotations of the term *Messiah*. If Jesus had not possessed the Spirit from the beginning of his ministry, then his ministry itself could not properly have been conceived as messianic. The formula used in Romans 1 cannot, therefore, be understood to assert without further ado that Christ did not possess or was not closely associated with the Spirit until the resurrection. In fact, this is probably the least plausible interpretation of these words. Second, even in Luke-Acts, where we arguably have the most thoroughgoing development of this particular theme in the whole of the New Testament, Jesus is variously said to receive the Spirit at his exaltation to the right hand of the Father (Acts 2:33), during his ministry (Luke 4:14), at his baptism (Luke 3:22), and in some sense at his conception (Luke 1:35). The evangelist himself certainly sees no contradiction between these different texts. Jesus is made the Messiah after the resurrection (Acts 2:36), yet clearly not in a way that conflicts with his being the Messiah before (e.g., Luke 9:20); accordingly, his reception of the Spirit can take place across time in a way that is not self-contradictory. The evangelist, in short, sees no need to omit the account of Jesus' baptism, for example, once he has given his account of Jesus' conception. Rather, Luke-Acts has a rather more dynamic and sophisticated view of the relation between Christ and the Spirit than the commentators are able to grant. This suggests that the concern for stages of theological development, so beloved by contemporary scholars, may well be quite foreign to the New Testament.

In the Pauline literature of the New Testament, similarly, pneumatology and christology are closely related. Although Paul, for example, can argue that the Spirit is the Spirit of God that searches the deep things of God (1 Cor. 2:10), his more characteristic mode of expression is to say that the Spirit is the Spirit of God's Son (Gal. 4:6), the Spirit of Christ (Rom. 8:9), or the Spirit of Jesus Christ (Phil. 1:19), so that the Spirit is also the Spirit of sonship in the religious life of the believer (Rom. 8:15; Gal. 4:6). In the crucial Pauline pneumatological texts 2 Corinthians 3:17

and 1 Corinthians 15:45, furthermore, what is generally regarded
as a Pauline version of Spirit christology appears: The Spirit is here
the earthly presence of the exalted Lord, in the sense that in the
Spirit the resurrected Lord is active and manifested in his resurrection power.[11]

A single phrase occurring in 2 Corinthians 3:17, "the Lord is
the Spirit," is of particular interest at this point, as a text that is
sometimes regarded as the key to and a summary of the relationship
between Christ and the Spirit in Paul. Scholars contend that this
text identifies the *pneuma* with the risen Christ; "Lord" here, as
in the whole of the passage from 2 Corinthians 3:1 to 4:6, where
Paul defends his apostleship against those who challenge his authority, refers to Christ.[12] The phrase "the Lord is the Spirit" in
3:17 therefore appears to mean that the life-giving Spirit, who gives
Paul his apostolic authority and who glorifies and liberates the
church in Corinth, is none other than the resurrected one. The
point is that, in reference to the experience of Paul and the
Corinthian church, Christ is the Spirit, and the Spirit who is at
work is Christ, so that both the authority of the apostle and the
glory of the New Covenant derive immediately from the risen Lord.

A second Pauline expression in 1 Corinthians 15:45, "the last
Adam became a life-giving spirit," can be similarly understood.
According to James Dunn, Paul again here equates the risen Lord
with the Spirit.[13] The phrase describes both the mode of existence
of the risen Jesus and the character of the Spirit itself, the point
being once again to define the character of Christian experience as
something rooted and grounded in the crucified one. After the
resurrection, we might say, Jesus becomes the definition, in some
sense, of the Spirit's activity in the life of the church, for with the
resurrection, Christ's existence is *as Spirit:* The preexistent Spirit
of the Old Testament has taken on the character of Christ, and vice

---

11. Ernst Käsemann, "Geist und Geistgaben im NT," in *Die Religion in
Geschichte und Gegenwart,* ed. H. F. von Campenhausen et al., 3rd ed. (Tübingen:
J. C. B. Mohr, 1958), col. 1274; Ingo Hermann, *Kurios und Pneuma* (München:
Kösel-Verlag, 1961).

12. Hermann, *Kurios und Pneuma,* pp. 17-25.

13. James D. G. Dunn, *Jesus and the Spirit* (London: SCM Press, 1975),
p. 322.

versa. According to Dunn, the chief reason for this is christological: as Jesus is the eschatological revelation of God, so all the Old Testament words for the revelatory activity of God — Wisdom, Word, and Spirit — must take on his character. Since, for Paul, the Spirit is the basis of the new life, the eschatological life of the resurrection, and thus the fulfillment of the promise of God, the character of that life must be determined by Jesus.

This kind of treatment of Pauline pneumatology follows in an older tradition of thought represented by Albert Schweitzer, whose *Die Mystik des Apostels Paulus* (1930) understands the Spirit in Paul as a field of divine power that determines the life of the believer.[14] Schweitzer's work was part of a wider reaction earlier in this century to the liberal-idealist tradition of the nineteenth century, which understood Spirit as that which gives the dual capacity for self-consciousness and for a rational penetration of the world of experience, and which interpreted Paul largely along these lines. Schweitzer maintains that this interpretation must be broken down in face of the fact that for Paul, and for primitive Christianity in general, "Spirit" means the divine energy of miracle and ecstasy.

The claim at stake here is this: For Paul, being "in Christ" is to be understood eschatologically as a corporate solidarity of believers with Christ and with one another, through baptism, and ultimately as a corporate sharing in the event of the resurrection. For Schweitzer, therefore, Paul's "mysticism" is a "Christ-mysticism" and not a "God-mysticism," the participation in the eschatological event of salvation rather than a Hellenistic sharing in the divine life.[15] The Spirit of Christ, in keeping with this, is the principle of the state of existence characteristic of the resurrection. Life in the Spirit is thus entry into this new mode of existence, as opposed to the life of the "old person" in the flesh, and thus the beginning in the here and now of the process of resurrection.[16] It is for this reason, according to this view, that the end-time gift of the Spirit

---

14. Albert Schweitzer, *The Mysticism of Paul the Apostle,* trans. W. Montgomery (London: A. & C. Black, 1931), pp. 425-26, 433.

15. Schweitzer, *The Mysticism of Paul the Apostle,* pp. 5-25.

16. Schweitzer, *The Mysticism of Paul the Apostle,* pp. 160, 167.

follows the resurrection of Christ — a fact that is otherwise not immediately self-explanatory.

There is no doubting the exegetical and theological strengths of this argument. For example, it makes clear connections between Jesus, the resurrection, the Spirit, and the new life of the church, thus presenting the Pauline theological vision as a coherent whole. What is especially evident on this view is that, after the coming of Christ, the Spirit cannot be understood apart from its relation to him, for the canon of authentic experience of the Spirit is defined christologically by Paul, precisely because the new existence in Christ is something pneumatological. If there is a weakness in this view, however, it lies in the unclarity that emerges concerning the status of Christ and the Spirit: Are they two or one? Some commentators are strangely unprepared to tackle this issue head-on,[17] plainly ignoring both the fact that Christ does not fill the whole sphere of deity in Paul's thought and the fact that a plurality of *some* sort in Paul's God, and certainly in Paul's religious experience, must be admitted. The Spirit within and the risen Christ beyond are not one but two. That Paul adopts a trinitarian formula in the benediction of 2 Corinthians 13:13, for example, is significant in this respect in that he sees no need, after 2 Corinthians 3:17, not to mention the Spirit because he has already mentioned Christ. Furthermore, the importance of 1 Corinthians 2:10 needs to be borne in mind: "the Spirit searches everything, even the depths of God." It has been argued that the "depths" of God referred to here are exclusively summed up in Christ crucified,[18] but this conclusion is artificial. Pauline theology is quite capable of treating the Spirit in terms that take us beyond the crucified one alone to God (cf., e.g., Rom. 8:26-27). In theological terms, we may say that for Paul, the Spirit is as much the Spirit of the Father as he is the Spirit of the Son.

---

17. E.g., Dunn, *Jesus and the Spirit*, pp. 319-26.

18. Eduard Schweizer, "ΠΝΕΥΜΑ, ΠΝΕΥΜΑΤΙΚΟΣ," in *Theological Dictionary of the New Testament*, ed. Gerhard Friedrich, trans. G. W. Bromiley, vol. 7 (Grand Rapids: Wm. B. Eerdmans, 1968), p. 425.

John

The Johannine tradition presents a doctrine of the Spirit that is at least as powerful as that of the Pauline epistles. The consensus, however, is that something new can be seen here as well. Unlike the Pauline epistles, the presupposition of Johannine pneumatology is the death of the first Christian generation and the clear conviction that the early *parousia* of primitive expectation was not to be.[19] In response to this problem, the fourth evangelist, rather more consistently than Paul who went before, presents the work of the Spirit as the initial installment on the church's eschatological hope. The doctrine of the Spirit or of the Paraclete that thus emerged resolved the theological anguish of the Johannine community in two ways: first, the apostolic witness continues after the apostles' death through the presence of the Paraclete in the church; and second, Jesus has already returned in the persona, as we might rightly say, of the Paraclete.[20] Though the *parousia* is as yet somehow incomplete, the religiously impossible task of straining constantly toward the heavens in the hope of the coming of the Son of man is overcome. The synoptic hope of the coming kingdom of God is thus supplanted by eschatological experience of the Spirit.

Although this view represents a broad scholarly consensus and does some justice to the theology of the Fourth Gospel, I wish to suggest that, seen purely in these terms, the Johannine theology of the Spirit is at best incomplete. What happens in the Fourth Gospel is not only that the Spirit comes to the fore as the solution to the problem of unfulfilled eschatological expectation, as the Johannine community looked into the future, but also that the doctrine of the Spirit itself comes to be developed in terms of past events in the story of Jesus. This is of great theological importance, for the real question, not just of Johannine pneumatology but of Christian pneumatology generally, is not why the doctrine of the Spirit emerged, but how the new presence of the Spirit in the

19. C. K. Barrett, "The Holy Spirit in the Fourth Gospel," *Journal of Theological Studies*, new series, 1 (1950): 1-15.

20. R. E. Brown, *The Gospel According to John (xiii–xxi)* (New York: Doubleday, 1970), pp. 1142-43.

Christian community flows from Jesus. Or, to put the matter another way, the question is in what sense Christian existence present is related to Christ-event past.

We have already seen how recent Pauline scholarship has provided an answer to this question as far as Pauline theology is concerned; Paul understands the Spirit both as the power of the resurrection, the mode of existence now enjoyed by the risen Jesus, and as the principle of Christian existence. Whether the latter is qualified as *en christo* or *en pneumati* therefore makes no difference, for these amount to precisely the same thing. Jesus in his resurrection became life-giving Spirit, the very life-giving Spirit at work in the Christian community, proclaims Paul in 1 Corinthians 15:45; to be in Christ or in the Spirit in the Christian community is thus to have an anticipatory share in the powers of the coming age, the powers, as Schweitzer puts it, of the resurrection. In Paul, according to this view, there is a movement forward from christology to pneumatology, though this movement presupposes a close link between the two. The Johannine treatment of the relation between Jesus and the Spirit is rather more subtle, in that there is not only a movement *forward* from the story of Jesus to the era of the church, in which the Spirit dwells, but in that there is also a prior movement in which the theology of the Spirit is itself handled, as in the synoptics, by means of a *backward* movement toward the story of Jesus. The Spirit, in short, is given to the community through the glorification of Jesus in his passion, but the Spirit could not in fact be what it is in the life of the Christian community without or apart from the glorification of Jesus in his passion.

Of particular significance here is the first mention of the Spirit in the Fourth Gospel, which appears, not in the context of any of Jesus' discourses, but in what might be called the Johannine baptism narrative:

> And John testified, "I saw the Spirit descending from heaven like a dove, and it remained on him. I myself did not know him, but the one who sent me to baptize with water said to me, 'He on whom you see the Spirit descend and remain is the one who baptizes with the Holy Spirit.' And I myself have seen and have testified that this is the Son of God." (John 1:32-34)

At first sight, this text appears to be inconsistent with the overall vision developed in the Fourth Gospel of the relation of the Spirit to Christ. Bultmann states the problem succinctly:

> The evangelist has clearly not thought out the relation between the Spirit which Jesus receives in his baptism and his character as the Logos; in the rest of the Gospel Jesus appears not as the bearer but as the giver of the Spirit. The imparting of the Spirit to Jesus is taken from the tradition and has, in the evangelist's interpretation, no longer any importance for Jesus; it is significant for the Baptist only as a sign of recognition.[21]

At a deeper level, though, the claim of inconsistency or even of incoherence cannot easily be defended. To begin with, the Johannine baptism narrative, as I have called it, is presented as an account of the testimony of John the Baptist concerning Jesus. This testimony is of significance in the Gospel because of the program outlined in the Prologue earlier in the same chapter, which says of John that he was sent by God to bear witness to the light that the Logos is (John 1:6-8). A number of factors need to be considered here: the sheer proximity of the Johannine account of Jesus' baptism to the Gospel Prologue, for example, coupled with the pneumatological interests of the evangelist and the fact that the only significant strand of synoptic and particularly Markan tradition that could be developed pneumatologically by the fourth evangelist was the tradition of Jesus' baptism, together with the Baptist traditions concerning the coming baptism with the Spirit. Taken together, these factors make it implausible to suggest that the evangelist should have treated this question so carelessly. It is precisely the one upon whom the Spirit descended and remained to whom the Baptist bears witness: this one, he says, is the Son of God. From this point of view, Bultmann rather curiously appears to be part of that long and unfortunate tradition of utterly orthodox thinking which has consistently and persistently refused to admit anything genuinely pneumatological into the christological question. We

21. Rudolf Bultmann, *The Gospel of John*, ed. R. W. N. Hoare and J. K. Riches, trans. G. R. Beasley-Murray (Oxford: Basil Blackwell, 1971), p. 92, n. 4.

shall have occasion to return to this problem repeatedly in the rest of this book.

Bultmann's basic argument is that John 1:32-34 is irrelevant to the evangelist's view of the relationship between the Spirit and Christ, in that there is an inconsistency between Jesus' character as the Logos and his reception of the Spirit. However, the argument that the Logos doctrine precludes that the Son should be understood as the bearer of the Holy Spirit appears to involve a misreading of Johannine christology. While on the one hand the capacity to give the Spirit is clearly appropriated to Christ, there is on the other hand nothing at all incoherent in the idea that the Spirit should have been received by Christ from the Father. The fourth evangelist is able to make the theologically extraordinary point that to see Christ is to see the Father, but the basis for this claim lies in the Johannine theme that the authority exercised by Christ is none other than the authority of the Father committed to him. An impressive array of "gifts" from the Father to the Son can be cited from the Fourth Gospel. Bultmann himself supplies the following list:

> everything 3.35; 13.3; (17.7); his name 17.11; [glory] 17.22, 24; [authority over all flesh] 17.2; [to have life in himself] 5.26; works, or the work 5.36; 17.4; words 17.8; the [judgment], or the [authority] for the [judgment] 5.2, 27; everything that he asks for 11.22; the believers 6.37, 39; 10.29; 17.2, 6, 9, 12, 24; 18.9.[22]

Although Christ is thus presented as dependent on the Father, and indeed obedient to him, it is still truly he who acts: the dead, according to John 5:25-26, will hear the voice of the Son and will live, even though it is from the Father that such authority is derived. According to this logic, Johannine christology cannot possibly exclude the idea that the Son both receives the Spirit from the Father and himself gives the Spirit to the world. Indeed, what would be highly inconsistent with the christology of the Fourth Gospel would be that the Spirit the Son gives were *not* the Spirit he first receives, in the same way that he receives everything else. From this point

22. Bultmann, *The Gospel of John*, p. 165, n. 1.

of view, the witness of John the Baptist to Jesus appears far less as an aberration from the Johannine christological norm and far more as the Johannine christology framed in the Baptist's pneumatological categories — categories that the evangelist himself wishes to develop and to extend.

We turn now to consider those Johannine texts that speak of the giving of the Spirit to believers in Jesus rather than to Jesus himself. The Fourth Gospel in fact speaks in a variety of ways about this. While in the Baptist discourses of chapter 1, it is Jesus who will baptize with the Spirit, this is strangely not mentioned in chapter 3 in the account of new birth, despite its connections with Christian baptism. In chapter 4, however, Jesus says to the woman at the well that he will give to the one who asks living water, a saying that may be related to the baptism theme of chapter 3. In the bread of life discourse, the words Jesus speaks are *pneuma* and *zoe*, Spirit and life (6:63), but the sense of this is left undefined. In John 7:37-39, however, those who come to Jesus to drink are promised living water, which here for the first time explicitly refers to the gift of the Spirit that was to come after Christ's glorification. The Spirit is then not mentioned again until the farewell discourse, where the gift of the Spirit is variously described as coming from the Father at Jesus' request (14:16), as being sent by the Father in the name of Christ (14:26), as being sent by Christ from the Father (15:26), and as being sent by Christ (16:7). In his dying act, Jesus "handed over the Spirit" *(paredoken to pneuma)* (19:30, my translation), which is at least a plausible rendering, and in John 20:22, the risen Lord breathed upon the assembled disciples and said, "Receive the Holy Spirit." The picture that thus emerges does not uniformly involve the giving of the Spirit by Christ, although this can be fairly described as on balance the view that emerges.

Most interesting of all is the saying of John 7:39, according to which the gift of the Spirit to the Christian community was to be made possible through Jesus' glorification in death. This is in fact a much clearer motif in the Gospel than the theme that it is Jesus himself who gives the Spirit, being confirmed again in 16:7 and through the postresurrection gift of the Spirit, if not also through the Johannine treatment of Jesus' death itself, and being contradicted nowhere. Indeed, it is arguably a much more important theme in John than this other, first because the idea of the glorification of Christ in his death is of crucial importance in the theology of the Fourth Gospel, and second because a variety of eschatological events are ushered in for Johannine theology by the death of Christ, the giving of the Spirit being but one of them.

In John, we see the realization of eschatological hope in relation to the cross in a number of ways. Eternal life, for example, is the present possession of those who believe, certainly, but specifically the possession of those who believe in the one who was lifted up (John 3:14-15), and of those who eat his flesh and drink his blood (6:54). Judgment similarly takes place in the historical mission of Jesus, through, for example, the light that has come into the world in him (3:19), in the words he speaks (12:48), but above all in his death (12:31-33). The Spirit is likewise presented as the eschatological gift given to the world by the self-giving of Christ in his cross.

Seen in this way, the gift of the Spirit in the Fourth Gospel takes on a certain unexpected character. Just as in the case of judgment, for example, where we find that instead of the elements being consumed by fire or the last trumpet's sounding we have the crucified Lord of the church and the summons to faith, so we have in the gift of the Spirit nothing other than something centered decisively upon the Johannine Christ, who loves his own to the end. It is well known that the Fourth Gospel is silent on the ecstatic experience of the Spirit described, for example, in 1 Corinthians 12; Johannine pneumatology is no less ecclesiological than Pauline pneumatology, and certainly no less mystical, but it is even more clearly christological than the Pauline doctrine of the Spirit. In the Fourth Gospel, the *locus* of the gift of the Spirit is ultimately the crucified Jesus, who gives his life for the church, from whose dead body there flows water, symbol of the Spirit (John 19:34), and who is glorified in order that the Spirit might come.

It is clear from all this that, as in the synoptics, the notion of Christ as the baptizer with the Spirit persists in the Fourth Gospel beyond chapter 1, even if it is not again explicitly mentioned. In the link established between Christian baptism and the gift of the Spirit in chapter 3, in the frequent return to the theme that Christ will give to believers living water, in the farewell discourse, where the Spirit is said to be either given by the Father at the risen Christ's request or sent directly by Christ from the Father, and in the breathing of the Spirit upon the disciples by the risen Christ in John 20:22, it reappears, perhaps indirectly, but nevertheless emphatically. The sense of the Baptist saying that what is important about Jesus is that he will give the Spirit is thereby drawn out in Johannine christology. It is, however, only through his passion and resurrection that Christ achieves this goal.[23]

Certain important consequences for what we might call Johannine spirituality follow. When the evangelist speaks of living water, welling up to eternal life, or of drink that will suffice for all thirst, he is clearly speaking eschatologically, with reference to the Spirit as both within and beyond present experience. Through all of this, however, the reference to the crucified and risen Jesus is clearly implied. The spring of water that wells up to eternal life cannot be artificially detached from the glorification of Jesus. The theology of glory, in other words, which seems at times to emerge from the Fourth Gospel, contains within itself the theology of the cross.

Finally, this helps us to understand the Johannine theology of the Paraclete. It is often argued that the Johannine Paraclete, as the Spirit of truth, is the Spirit of Christian *paraclesis* — of Christian teaching and preaching, in other words — and this is no doubt true

23. It is interesting in this context to note that the Baptist saying of chapter 1 concerning Jesus as the baptizer with the Spirit is framed by two Baptist references to Jesus as the Lamb of God (1:29, 35). Although there is no clear causal connection between these theological motifs, there is a clear theological association between them that takes us to the heart of Johannine pneumatology. In the Fourth Gospel, it is because Jesus is the Lamb of God — we might say, the one whose glorification is his passion — that he is also the *locus* of the Spirit. There is no Spirit as far as the church is concerned before Jesus is glorified; all the eschatological gifts — eternal life, judgment, Spirit — are focused in this single decisive event and take on its revolutionary character. Thus in Johannine theology as much as in Pauline theology, Christian existence, characterized by the Spirit, necessarily takes on the character of Jesus; love and lowly service, together with the task of bearing witness to the Lord who was crucified, are its hallmarks. What the evangelist is saying through the mouth of the Baptist is that it is *this* one, this crucified and risen one, in whom the Spirit is found.

in its way. It is, however, at best a half-truth, insofar as it appears to restrict the Spirit to the rather prosaic task of inspiring and confirming what is preached by the church. There can be little doubt that the theology of the Paraclete is developed with a view to the theology of the Christian community: Christ is still present, the *parousia* is not a vain hope, the apostolic witness continues. But the Paraclete is also to be understood in relation to the gift of the Spirit as the eschatological gift of the rest of the Fourth Gospel, which comes through none other than the crucified one, and as the one who brings none other than the crucified one into the midst of his community. In this sense, the Fourth Gospel offers a profound vision of what the Spirit is in the life of the Christian community. The latter's witness is something more than a formal ministry of the Word, for it can never be dissociated from the realization of the promise of living water, since both spring from the one source. In John, the ministry of witness must be integrally related to a spiritual life and experience, grounded in the crucified one and realized in an experience of the Spirit he gives. This is one of the more liberating features of the Fourth Gospel, for not even theology, which is at every level a proclamation of the Word in its way, can be isolated in a purely theoretical existence; rather, its roots must reach deep into God, and this can provide it with a vitality and relevance without which the theological enterprise cannot be sustained.

2. The Patristic Consensus

The Shape of Patristic Pneumatology

One might suppose that the enthusiasm with which New Testament writers gave voice to their newfound experience of the Spirit would have persisted beyond the apostolic age into the era of the early church. By popular consent, as it were, we are accustomed to seeing early Christian history as the time of glorious faithfulness to the gospel, the age of the martyrs and the time of the church's first expansion amid persecution. Along with this perception, it is generally assumed, not least by theologians who wish to return to primitive church practice, that the early church era was particularly rich in the spiritual sense. The New Testament's confidence in the presence and power of the Spirit is thus taken to have continued beyond the apostolic age. Unfortunately, the literature that has come down to us from subapostolic times does not support this view, at least as far as the doctrine of the Holy Spirit is concerned. Whereas we find in the New Testament an extremely rich mine of pneumatology, many of the distinctive themes of the doctrine of the Spirit in the New Testament appear to have simply disappeared by the second century. The Holy Spirit did not fade entirely from view — as we shall see, the second-century church and the patristic church generally continued to speak of the Spirit's presence and activity — but there is no evidence in the second century of the pneumatological excitement found in the New Testament.

For the Christian writers of the early second century, collectively designated the apostolic fathers on the grounds that they claim to have been in touch with the apostles themselves,[1] the outpouring of the Holy Spirit on the church remains one of the central presuppositions of the doctrines of the church and salvation. However, the power with which this conviction is expressed, and the depth of understanding of its significance, is much diminished in comparison with the writings of the New Testament. This is in keeping with the rest of their work, for it must be said in general that the apostolic fathers are not men of brilliance or penetrating theological insight; rather, their central contribution lies not in their elaboration of the faith but in their call for obedience to the ecclesiastical hierarchy, their warnings against heresy, and their simple commendation of the faith, even in the face of martyrdom. There is no doubt that a man like Polycarp, for example, was a great Christian leader and a great man of faith, but a great theologian he was not.

The basic claims made regarding the Spirit at this time are few and easily grasped. Clement of Rome, who died around 100 A.D., speaks in his letter to Corinth of how a rich outpouring of the Holy Spirit had come upon the church there, and that a profound peace and unity had been granted to the church in response to their faith in Christ crucified and their longing to do good.[2] It is unclear, however, whether Clement refers here to the Pauline era or to his own. Though this presence of the Spirit is seen as threatened by the envy that has arisen in Corinth, it is still presupposed in the bulk of the letter's practical moral exhortation to the Corinthian church. In the letters of Ignatius of Antioch, where again practical exhortations to church unity are the primary theme, the one ref-

---

1. This circle includes Clement, Ignatius, Polycarp, and perhaps Hermas. Unless otherwise indicated, all translations of the Greek Fathers in this chapter are my own, based on the *Thesaurus Linguae Graece*. Full bibliographical details can be found in Luci Berkowitz and Karl A. Squitier, *Thesaurus Linguae Graece Canon of Greek Authors and Works*, 3rd ed. (New York and Oxford: Oxford University Press, 1990).

2. *1 Clement*, 2.

erence to the Holy Spirit that is of interest concerns the prophetic utterance made by Ignatius when he was among the Philadelphians.[3] The Spirit, he says, proclaimed, "Do nothing apart from the bishop, keep your flesh as the temple of God, love unity, flee division, be imitators of Jesus Christ as he is of his Father." The *Martyrdom of Polycarp,* for its part, mentions the Spirit only twice: Polycarp prays before his death, praising God for his hope for a portion, with the martyrs, in the cup of Christ, the resurrection, and the incorruption of the Holy Spirit; and he concludes his prayer with a trinitarian ascription of glory.[4] Finally, in the *Shepherd of Hermas,* much is said of the Spirit, but little that is clear. In at least two places he identifies the Holy Spirit with the Son of God.[5] Yet, paradoxically, he also presupposes the Old Testament sense of continuity between the Spirit of God and the human spirit, though, unlike most of the Old Testament, he is much preoccupied in this context with the problem of the moral struggle between the Holy Spirit and the evil spirits. At one point he speaks beautifully of how the Holy Spirit is "delicate" and unaccustomed to dwelling with evil; the Spirit therefore departs from the impure.[6]

From the later second century on, a number of central pneumatological themes recur. The Spirit is repeatedly said to have inspired the Scriptures of both Old and New Testaments, over against Marcion and other Gnostic heretics who held that the Old Testament — and some of the canonical New Testament — was the work of an inferior deity, a god other than the God and Father of Jesus Christ. While the office of prophet seems for the most part to disappear as a living one in the church, the Spirit is still related to the moral life of the Christian, and specifically to Christian holiness. The seal of the Spirit in baptism is an important theme here, since baptism initiates the Christian life. On the whole, however, the importance of the Spirit in Christian theology in the early patristic era is overshadowed by the emerging christology of the Logos.

We can see this, for example, in Justin Martyr's *First Apology,*

---

3. Ignatius of Antioch, *Epistle to the Philadelphians,* 7.
4. *The Martyrdom of Polycarp,* 14.
5. Hermas, *Similitudes,* 5.6; 9.1.1.
6. Hermas, *Mandates,* 5.1-3; 2.6.

written around the middle of the second century. In his attempt to defend the new faith against charges of superstition and barbarism, Justin's central emphasis is that in the Christian faith, the true Reason (*logos*) of God is revealed and known. Even in his account of the rite of baptism in the *Apology*, where Justin could most obviously have been expected to develop the role of the Spirit more positively, we find nothing of pneumatological importance. Rather, the washing of baptism is described as an illumination *(photismos)*, an image that suggests the insight that instruction in Christian doctrine brings.[7] The baptismal theme of repentance and cleansing from sin is present, but it is not expressly related to the Spirit.

Elsewhere, it is fair to say, Justin does assume the presence of the Spirit in the Christian community; indeed, in his later *Dialogue with Trypho the Jew*, he speaks openly at one point about the abundance of the gifts of the Spirit among Christian believers.[8] Justin here responds to the objections of Trypho regarding the conflict between the church's belief in the preexistence of Christ and the New Testament accounts of the descent of the Spirit upon him; the latter, Trypho argues, implies a certain need of the gift of the Spirit on the part of Christ, whereas the former suggests that he has no need of anything. Justin's answer is instructive and points the way ahead for so much of the Christian tradition. According to him, Christ indeed had no need of the Spirit, just as he himself had no need of the cross; it was rather for our sake that he received the Spirit. It seems that his point is a double one: The descent of the Spirit upon Jesus was on the one hand a sign to the world that Jesus is more than a carpenter, and on the other a sign to the world that the power of the Spirit rests upon him. Justin denies, however, that the descent of the Spirit at the Jordan added anything to Jesus' consciousness of God or to his intrinsic power, for as the Logos he possessed all of this and the Spirit, too, from birth. The implication is that in Christian baptism, in which we imitate Christ, the power of the Spirit that is his comes upon those who believe. On the whole, however, this is not a major theme in Justin's theology of the Spirit; rather, the main role reserved for the Spirit in Justin is the inspiration of Scripture: The Spirit spoke by the

---

7. Justin Martyr, *First Apology*, 61.
8. Justin Martyr, *Dialogue with Trypho the Jew*, 87-88.

prophets, and his word has been fulfilled in Jesus Christ. Since it is Jesus Christ, the Logos of God, who is the primary focus of Justin's theological interest and attention, his central pneumatological preoccupation is accordingly with what we might call the Spirit's service to the Logos.

The relation between the Spirit, the Son, and the Father also emerges as a question of crucial significance from a very early stage in patristic theology. One of the great rivals to the emerging Logos christology of the great church was the Spirit christology of the Ebionites, a group of early Christians geographically concentrated east of the Jordan and having their origins in the Jewish-Christian tradition. The theology of the Ebionites is notoriously difficult to reconstruct, since our sources are partial and mainly indirect, but at least two versions of their position have been put forward. On one reading, the Ebionites held that Jesus, the human son of Mary and Joseph, perfectly fulfilled the Law of Moses and as a result of his obedience was consecrated Messiah and endowed with the power of God through the gift of the Spirit at his baptism.[9] He was thus equipped for his messianic office as the new lawgiver and the eschatological Son of man. Another view follows the statements made concerning the Ebionites by early patristic sources; according to Tertullian and Epiphanius, the Ebionites held that at the baptism of Jesus, an archangel named Christ descended upon him, as he had earlier upon the prophets.[10] Although Jean Daniélou argues that the angelic theme is genuine,[11] it is perhaps best to say that it represents a late Ebionite doctrine in which the preexistence of Christ is asserted, but in which a creaturely status is asserted of him over against the claims of Logos christology. The other view is likely the more primitive, and authentic, version of Ebionite theology, since it is more clearly rooted in the Jewish tradition.

Spirit christology also appeared in Christian theology in the Gentile world, its main representatives being Theodotus the cobbler,

9. Hans-Joachim Schoeps, *Jewish Christianity*, trans. Douglas R. A. Hare (Philadelphia: Fortress Press, 1969), pp. 59-73.

10. Tertullian, *On the Flesh of Christ*, 14; Epiphanius, *Against Eighty Heresies*, 30.16.3-4.

11. Jean Daniélou, *The Theology of Jewish Christianity*, ed. and trans. J. A. Baker (London: Darton, Longman & Todd, 1964), pp. 55-64.

a Byzantine layman who was active in Rome around 190, and Paul, bishop of Samosata from around 260 to 268. Again, the destruction of original texts and the polemics of the orthodox make the positions of these men difficult to reconstruct. However, both appear to have taken the view *(a)* that the dominant Logos christology of the church left insufficient room for the biblical theme of the messianic anointing of Christ, and *(b)* that this Logos christology, with its related notions of the divinity of Christ and incarnation, was unacceptable because it compromised divine transcendence.[12] That the power of God, conceived as an influence rather than as God himself, should rest upon Jesus was, from the point of view of pagan Greek culture, more acceptable than the more radical doctrine of incarnation that was emerging in the great church. It was this presupposition that found its way into the thinking of Theodotus and Paul of Samosata, and it was precisely this that made their theological claims such a pervasive problem in the early patristic era.

One of the most unfortunate things to happen in the history of the doctrine of the Holy Spirit occurred as an indirect result of the expulsion of the likes of Theodotus and Paul of Samosata from the church and the proscription of their views. The exclusion of their versions of Spirit christology in favor of the emerging Logos christology amounted to a deliberate choice of Logos christology rather than Spirit christology, which meant that subsequent attempts to develop the pneumatological aspects of christology would inevitably be regarded as suspect. The success with which Spirit christology of any real sort was excluded is remarkable. In fact, the Christian theological tradition is almost completely silent on the question of the relation between the Spirit and Jesus as it is presented to us in the synoptic Gospels; or perhaps more accurately, the tendency to play down the significance of the anointing of Christ means that traditional christology makes nothing of the pneumatological theme of anointing. The very possibility that a christology could be legitimately developed in this way, even in conjunction with a christology of the Logos, was actually condemned in the course of the Nestorian controversy in the fifth

---

12. J. N. D. Kelly, *Early Christian Doctrines,* 5th ed. (London: Adam & Charles Black, 1977), pp. 115-19.

century, through which Logos christology reached its clearest and most definitive expression. Although there is little evidence that Nestorius himself wanted to develop a strong Spirit christology — he fails, at least, to mention the theme in his final defense in his pseudonymous *Bazaar of Heracleides* — the fact that his theology was perceived to be open to such development was one of the grounds for his condemnation. Cyril of Alexandria, his arch-foe, complained that Nestorius's theology involved the erroneous notion that Christ needed the Spirit in order to carry out his saving work; according to Cyril's ninth anathema against Nestorius, Christ cannot have had need of the Spirit, for the Spirit was already his as the Lord Jesus Christ, the incarnate Logos.[13] What, then, becomes of the baptism narratives of the Gospels, one might ask? Cyril's response is identical to that of Justin Martyr: The Spirit descended upon Jesus at his baptism, not for his sake, but for ours.[14] There is undoubtedly an important and legitimate theological point in this, for the Spirit cannot be divorced from the Son, as if the Son has no connection with the Spirit except by grace, but it must also be said that it effectively denies that the Spirit is of strictly christological significance — which is, to say the least, a questionable claim in view of the synoptic witness to Jesus.

On the question of what the Holy Spirit does in the matter of salvation, and how central the Spirit's work is in salvation, opinion differs. The greatest Christian theologian of the third century, Origen (c. 185-254), speaks at times of how the Holy Spirit dwells with the saints alone; unlike the Word and the Father, who are always at work in the just and the unjust alike, the Spirit's activity for Origen seems to be restricted to the worthy.[15] Origen appears to ground his views here on two arguments. On the one hand, since it is by the Spirit that people confess the faith of Christ, and since not all confess that faith, not all can as a matter of fact presently possess the Spirit; indeed, Origen argues, the Holy Spirit is specifically said in Scripture to be given only to some through the laying on of hands. On the other

13. Cyril of Alexandria, *Epistles to Nestorius,* 4; *Epistles,* 17.
14. Cyril of Alexandria, *Commentary on Luke,* Sermon 11, trans. R. Payne Smith (Oxford: Oxford University Press, 1859), p. 47.
15. Origen, *On First Principles,* 1.3.5-8.

hand, though in a similar way, since the distinctive ministry of the Holy Spirit is to purify and sanctify, the impure and the unsanctified cannot possess the Spirit.

Origen's views are of interest for a number of reasons. First of all, the Platonic background of his thought involves the notion that rational creatures participate in the divine Reason, the Logos, and the view that everything that exists, without exception, participates in the Father himself as Being itself and the source of all being.[16] Since not all are holy, not all participate in the same way in the Holy Spirit. Does this mean that the role of the Spirit in the God-world relation is less important than that of the Father and Son? From one perspective, this seems undeniable. Yet Origen also argues that it is through holiness that rational creatures exist as God wishes them to be, that is, without sin, and through holiness alone that they can attain to union with God. Thus from another perspective the Holy Spirit is uniquely important in Origen's theology. This fact is, once again, related to the theology of baptism, which is ordinarily the moment when the Spirit is received, and which is strongly connected in Origen's theology with moral transformation. The sacrament, according to Origen, does not operate automatically — even on the authority of the divine word — for the free response of the creature is constantly required in the economy of salvation.[17]

Second, an important point relating to Origen's tendency to subordinationism needs to be considered. Origen teaches that the Father is greater than the Son, and that the Son in his turn is greater than the Holy Spirit, for the Son has his (eternal) origin in the Father, and the Spirit in the Son.[18] Scholars differ on the question of how this is to be interpreted — an important question, since Origen's theology would eventually be condemned, in large measure for its subordinationist tendencies. At one point, for example, Origen appears to teach that the Spirit came to be — in the sense of John 1:3

16. Origen, *On First Principles,* 1.3.5-8.

17. Origen, *On First Principles,* 3.5.8. On the theology of baptism in Origen generally, cf. Henri Crouzel, *Origen,* trans. A. S. Worrall (Edinburgh: T. & T. Clark, 1989), pp. 223ff.

18. Origen, *On First Principles,* 1.3.5.

— through the Son, but whether this represents his final word on the nature of the Spirit is questionable.[19] What we can say in general is that, measured against the standards of orthodoxy in the third century, there is nothing controversial in Origen's view of the Trinity. In fact, the whole of the Christian theological tradition before the Arian crisis was subordinationist to some extent. What is also clear is that Origen's subordinationism refers first and foremost to the divine approach to the world, the Father's successive outreach by means of his Word and Spirit, and that his subordinationism consequently structures the world's approach to God; whereas no one has seen the Father, he is made known through the Son, in the Spirit. The regular view of the pre-Nicene fathers on the doctrine of salvation is mirrored in Origen's theology at this point. It may be the case that all rational creatures participate in the Logos, as Origen says, but the fact of sin means that this participation is marred and, so to speak, ineffective in concrete existence. Without the grace of the Holy Spirit, without a moral transformation, and without purity of heart, in short, no one can see God. Thus the role of the Spirit, even for the Origenist doctrine of participation in God the Father and Son, is crucial, for without it there is no salvation. The role of the Spirit as the third term in the descending order of the divine outreach can therefore be seen to be necessary in Origen's thought, rather than artificially imposed, for it is equally the starting point in the long struggle for salvation that is at the heart of Origen's theology. Without the Spirit there is no gospel, for without the Spirit, the problem of sin remains.

It is not clear from Origen exactly how the Spirit makes human beings holy, but the fact that the Platonic word "participation" is used in this context shows that Origen has in mind something of both moral and metaphysical significance. A real sharing in the nature of God by means of the outreach of the Father and Son in the Holy Spirit is therefore in view. Scholars often allege that Origen effectively has no pneumatology, or that his pneumatology is subservient, as one recent commentator has written, to an "imperial" doctrine of the Logos.[20] Because of the all-pervading role of the

19. Origen, *Commentary on the Gospel of John*, 2.6.
20. Kilian McDonnell, "Does Origen Have a Trinitarian Doctrine of the Holy Spirit?" *Gregorianum* 75 (1994): 23ff.

Logos in Origen's theology, in short, little is left to the Spirit, while what remains — for example, the age-old notion of the inspiration of Scripture — can as easily be attributed to Logos as to Pneuma.[21] From what we have seen, however, this does not in fact appear to be the case. Although the role of the Spirit is not developed in the same way as that of the Logos in Origen's theology, it underlies his whole theological vision and program. Henri Crouzel, in his magnificent study of Origen, has emphasized such themes as Origen's concrete pastoral concern for the church, his spirituality, and the content of his preaching.[22] One cannot, in fact, ignore all of this in assessing Origen's theology, in particular because it bears so immediately upon the role of the Spirit in his thought. Insofar as Origen sees himself as serving the church in his work, in short, he sees himself as serving God in the place where the Spirit is uniquely active. His concern for moral and spiritual growth in this connection is not merely an implicit but — given what he actually says about the role of the Spirit — an explicit pneumatology. We need to recall here the fact that, in seeking a theology of the Spirit, we need to look in the right place; no theology of the Spirit will correspond to a theology of the Word. Origen's may be an imperial doctrine of the Logos, but Origen's own basic theological starting point in his doctrine of participation in the Trinity precludes the possibility that Logos can do everything in the divine outreach and in the human approach to God.

This is not to say that Origen's pneumatology is entirely adequate; most obviously, for example, he appears to have little in the way of a doctrine of the Creator Spirit, at least insofar as this bears upon the question of the Spirit's presence in nature. In this context, the judgment is undoubtedly just: "The absence of a relation to the creating act, together with the decision to tie the Spirit to the worthy delivered pneumatology to interiority."[23] However, Origen fails to take up and develop not only the Old Testament

21. See the references cited by McDonnell, "Does Origen Have a Trinitarian Doctrine of the Holy Spirit?" p. 23.

22. Crouzel, *Origen.*

23. McDonnell, "Does Origen Have a Trinitarian Doctrine of the Holy Spirit?" p. 32.

theme of the Spirit as the principle of life but also such central New Testament themes as the relation of the Spirit to the resurrection of Christ. Even the scope of his understanding of the Spirit within the bounds of the Christian community and faith is therefore restricted. Once again, we find a failure in patristic theology to capitalize on the multidimensional picture of the Spirit that emerges from the New Testament. It is a failure that will often be repeated.

The Deity of the Holy Spirit

Despite its weaknesses, the patristic consensus on the doctrine of the Holy Spirit must be taken seriously, most obviously because it has served as the theological norm for those concerned with the doctrine throughout most of Christian history. The greatest achievement of the patristic era in pneumatology was, of course, the definition of the divinity of the Holy Spirit at the Council of Constantinople in 381, from which we have received what is traditionally called the Nicene Creed. Even here, however, a realistic assessment of the patristic consensus is needed. The definition arrived at in 381 came about only following a series of long-running theological controversies, while the final theological definition reached, as we shall see, falls somewhat short of what in fact the greatest theologians of the period had desired.

The prime mover in the development of the doctrine of the divinity of the Holy Spirit in the fourth century was, ironically, the presbyter and arch-heretic Arius, who started a controversy in Alexandria around 318 by teaching that the Logos is a creature who is obedient to his Creator's (i.e., the Father's) will. From the beginning of his existence, according to Arius, he was the Son of God and a creature of enormous power and glory, but not God in the strict sense. Arius was in fact trying in this way to exclude one of the great heresies of the preceding century, modalism. His procedure was to take up third-century subordinationism in a new way and use it to rebut the modalists. In the third century, the standard orthodoxy of the church was that the Father has his Logos and his Spirit, by which he relates to the world in creation and redemption. Third-century trinitarianism is basically economic, in other words, or concerned with the *oikonomia*, the dispensation of God toward his creation. Whereas in himself the Father is unknown and unapproachable, the world of creatures has access to him through his Logos and Spirit.

The modalist alternative to this was to say that Father, Son, and Holy Spirit are merely successive manifestations to us of the *one* God, and that the three names refer to the successive characters or masks under which God appears to us in history. The different names do not, therefore, denote any real distinctions in God. The strength of this was its clear affirmation of the full deity of the three, and its avoidance of the conceptual difficulties associated with the Christian doctrine of God as one and yet three. Its main difficulties, however, are not hard to perceive; we read in the New Testament that Christ prays to the Father, whereas modalism would appear to be committed to the view that Christ, in praying, is making a petition in his humanity to his own divine nature. Furthermore, modalism stumbled, for its third-century opponents, at the point of the cross, for the modalists had to maintain that in one sense, the same God as God the Father, and not his mediating Logos, was in Christ in the events of the passion. For the orthodox, the claim that the mediating Logos was the one in Christ in his death was more palatable than the modalist implication that God the Father was.

In responding to the modalist claim, Arius adopted an extreme version of the standard orthodoxy of the third century, pushing its subordinationist tendencies to what he saw as their most obvious conclusion. According to Arius, "The essences *[ousiai]* of the Father and the Son and the Holy Spirit are separate in nature . . . and are estranged, unconnected, alien . . . , and without participation in each other. . . . They are utterly dissimilar from each other with respect to both essences and glories to infinity."[24] In other words, whereas the orthodoxy of the third century as represented, for example, by Origen saw the distinctions of the three mainly in terms of three levels of the divine outreach to the world, and so in terms more of what God does than of what God is, Arius saw the distinctions in terms of a radical metaphysical discontinuity, where

---

24. Arius, as quoted by Athanasius, *Orations against the Arians*, 1.6.

the subordination of Son to Father and Spirit to Son was pressed to the hilt. Arius thus defined his position quite sharply, though he possibly thought that he was merely clarifying the logic of what had always been said in order finally to refute the modalists. In fact, of course, when he asserted that the Logos is separated from the Father by an infinite difference of substance, controversy erupted. Third-century trinitarianism was subordinationist, but it was not subordinationist in *this* sense. There is no doubt that Arius's position would allow no compromise with modalism, but in the final analysis it was not in keeping with the great tradition of the church.

Arian theology had a profound impact on the development of Christianity, both positively and negatively. Positively, Arius and Arianism had powerful, articulate supporters, both theological and political; the history of the first half of the fourth-century church is largely theirs. Negatively, the Arian preoccupation with differences in the divine *ousia* forced the eventual Nicene definition of the identity of substance of the Father and the Son, and generated an even more powerful and articulate theological response from the orthodox. It is with this second aspect of Arianism that we are concerned here. The central questions facing us are these: Why did the great church reject the theology of Arius, and how did this subsequently affect the shape of the doctrine of the Holy Spirit?

In a recent work, two scholars, Robert Gregg and Dennis Groh, have argued that the metaphysical aspects of Arian theology outlined above were also undergirded by a basic soteriological concern.[25] Although theirs is largely an argument from silence — for we have no Arian texts that explicitly press the soteriological point — there is a certain plausibility in their thesis. First of all, so few Arian texts have survived that *all* arguments concerning Arian theology are arguments from silence to some extent, but second, soteriology is such a central theological theme that it seems unthinkable that it did not function as a decisive pole in Arian thought. What we can say with certainty is that the problem its opponents saw in Arianism was that since the Arian Christ is a creature, he cannot save us from sin and death; only God can save, so if Christ

25. Robert C. Gregg and Dennis E. Groh, *Early Arianism* (London: SCM Press, 1981).

is savior, then he must be God. The claim of Gregg and Groh, who extrapolate backwards from this positive anti-Arian argument, is that Arius himself must have taken the view that salvation comes about by imitating Christ. As the first and most perfect of the Father's creatures, he is the model of perfect creaturehood who shows us the way of salvation by example.[26] Christ's Sonship is therefore like ours, a moral sonship, so that Christ for Arius was one among many brothers.

It is difficult to say whether or not the Arian position was so well developed; nowhere is there surviving textual evidence for the claims made by Gregg and Groh. What is better attested is the Arian view that the Son is a creature, that the Father alone is God in the unqualified sense, being by nature immutable, and that the Son is divine, but not in the same way as the Father. From the anathemas that the Council of Nicea issued, we know that Arius and his followers held that there was a time when the Son did not exist, that he was created *ex nihilo,* and that he is by nature mutable since his substance is other than the Father's (though by the exercise of his will the Son retains a certain qualified, semi-divine immutability).[27] Another "exemplarist" Arian soteriology has therefore been proposed, over against that postulated by Gregg and Groh. This soteriology seeks to take account of the Arian preoccupation with theological ontology, and specifically highlights the fact that Arianism wanted to find in the Logos a semi-divine, semi-creaturely intermediary between God and the world. According to this view, which has recently been advanced by R. P. C. Hanson, Arius and Arianism sought in this way to take the scandal of the cross seriously by acknowledging God's involvement in the shame of the cross — only at the inferior level of the divinity of the Son.[28] Arian soteriology was exemplarist, therefore, in the sense that it understood the incarnate Word as (a second) God suffering as humans suffer. The Arian Christ thus reveals that we have not been abandoned.

26. Gregg and Groh, *Early Arianism,* pp. 43ff.
27. Socrates, *Ecclesiastical History,* 1.8.
28. R. P. C. Hanson, *The Search for the Christian Doctrine of God* (Edinburgh: T. & T. Clark, 1988), pp. 121-22.

It may be the contemporary disposition toward a theology of divine suffering as much as anything that underlies Hanson's theory, but whatever the reality, the opponents of Arianism, most notably Athanasius, argued against it on both biblical and theological grounds. Of the theological arguments, the most important was that the human situation is far more problematic than the Arian view presupposes, that as we are the prey of sin and death, the one solution to our dilemma is that God himself should intervene in and ontologically transform the human situation by means of incarnation. Therefore, the logic of the gospel as the message of salvation — represented as divinization — requires that the incarnate one also be true God.[29] This was and remains a profound argument, and represents one of the central convictions underlying classical orthodox christology.

The central christological points made in the creed produced by the Council of Nicea were specifically designed to exclude the Arians. The second article of the creed runs as follows:

> [We believe] in one Lord Jesus Christ, the Son of God, begotten of the Father, Only-begotten, that is, of the substance [*ousia*] of the Father; God of God, Light of Light, Very God of Very God, begotten not made, of one substance with the Father, by whom all things were made, both things in heaven and things on earth; who for us and for our salvation came down and was incarnate, was made man, suffered, and rose again the third day, ascended into heaven, and is coming to judge the living and dead.[30]

That the Son is of the substance of the Father definitively rejects the idea that the Son is a creature, a point hammered home by the clause affirming that the Son is of *one* substance with the Father, which is an explicit denial of Arius's claim (as reported by Athanasius from Arius's *Thalia*) that the substances of the Father and the Son are infinitely different. The significant language that the creed uses is not language about the work of the Son — for though this is

---

29. Athanasius, *Orations against the Arians* and *On the Incarnation,* passim.
30. Socrates, *Ecclesiastical History,* 1.8.

also included, it is uncontroversial — but about the being or *ousia* of the Son in his relation to the Father.

In speaking in this way, the Creed of Nicea shields the doctrine of salvation from the implications of the deficient ontology of Arian christological theory. What is also interesting and important — in fact, of decisive importance for the development of the doctrine of the Trinity — is that in order to do *that,* the fathers at Nicea were forced in their creed for the first time to define a christological standpoint in which something was said about the ontological relationship between the Father and the Son. They had, in short, to define the relation in terms of the divine *ousia,* and in terms of nothing less than the divine *ousia* — in other words, to say something about God in himself — in order to exclude Arianism.

Earlier Christian thought, as we have seen, had been mainly concerned with the economic approach of God to the world, and so the trinitarian speculations of the third century, for example, were mainly concerned with the Son and Spirit as agents of the Father in the world, agents that mediate between the Father, who is utterly transcendent, and the world that he has made. The Council of Nicea, however, constituted the decisive step in a general movement from economic to immanent trinitarianism that took place in fourth-century Christian thought. The fourth century saw the Nicene *homoousios* applied to the Son-Father relation in 325, and also extended to the Spirit-Son-Father relation through the writings of the theologians up to and after the Council of Constantinople in 381. By this means, the question of the being of the Trinity in itself came to the fore in theology; one illustration of the extent to which this happened is the sense the words *theologia* and *oikonomia* came to bear in the course of the fourth and fifth centuries: *Theologia,* theology, came to mean simply the doctrine of the immanent Trinity; *oikonomia,* economy, came to mean everything else that the Trinity does in relation to creation.[31]

At Nicea, the christological problem thrown up by Arius was in theory resolved; the christological clauses of the Creed of Nicea were actually designed to exclude the Arians. What, then, of the Holy Spirit? Unfortunately, Nicea did not arrive at or even attempt a similar

31. C. M. LaCugna, *God With Us* (San Francisco: Harper, 1991), pp. 37ff.

clarification of the Spirit's status, even though Arius, according to Athanasius, had explicitly denied the divinity of the Spirit together with that of the Son. Over against the elaboration of christology in its creed, and indeed, over against the massive step taken at the Council of Nicea in the direction of the internal relations of Father and Son as the basic affirmation of the gospel, all the Nicene theologians thought it necessary to do — or all that they felt themselves able to do — with reference to the Spirit was to append to the second, christological article of the creed a third, which affirmed that we believe also "in the Holy Spirit." In other words, no attempt was made in 325 to defend the deity of the Holy Spirit in the highly explicit terms used in connection with the doctrine of Christ.

In fact, it took almost half a century for the implications of the new way of understanding the relation between the Son and the Father that the Nicene *homoousios* represented to sink in within Christian theology generally. Initially, Nicea sent a shock wave through much of the church. There was, first, the unresolved problem of the Holy Spirit: Should the Spirit be defined as of one substance with the Father or not? Of more immediate concern in the first half of the fourth century, however, was the following problem: If Father and Son are of one substance, which means roughly that they have one identical being (at least, this is the sense that the Nicene *homoousios* came to bear within the orthodox camp), then how are they different? One needs to remember at this point the innate conservatism of theological establishments and, above all, of ordinary Christians, and the fact that, at that time, the canons of Nicea represented theological innovation in the church. To make matters worse, many good Christians were horrified at the conclusions reached at Nicea because it looked to them as if the idea that Father and Son are of one identical *ousia* implied modalism. That was certainly how the Arians saw things, and they made the most of the opportunity afforded by conceptual unclarity on the part of their opponents. How one differentiates the Father and Son in the light of the Nicene *homoousios* was destined to become the great problem of mid-fourth-century theology.

Since the Holy Spirit was ultimately to become part and parcel of the second problem of differentiation, we turn first to the question of the development of the doctrine of the deity of the Spirit.

We have seen already that the Creed of Nicea was content to affirm, "We believe in the Holy Spirit," after the lengthy definition of the person and work of the Son that it provided. We have also seen that there was no clear understanding of the status of the Spirit in the third century; although it is fair to say that the Spirit belongs to the sphere of the divine from the earliest times in Christian theology, what this means is never officially defined before 381. What was it, then, that led to the development of the doctrine of the person of the Holy Spirit as it came to be defined? The answer, once again, can be found in the by-now familiar story of Arianism.

After 325, Arianism continued as a formally excommunicate religious movement, and in fact it thrived at various times: Even Constantine, who is sometimes said to have been responsible for the key Nicene phrase "of one substance with the Father," wavered on the Arian question in the years after Nicea, and was prepared in 336 to see the troublesome Athanasius excluded and Arius welcomed back into the fold.[32] The Arians produced a number of counterblasts to Nicea themselves, as well as leading figures to challenge the likes of Athanasius. They also produced counter-creeds of their own to use in their liturgy and to submit to the emperors to show that they were good Christians after all. These frequently manage to say more about the Spirit than the Creed of Nicea does. For example, around 360 an Arian named Eunomius reproduced what is perhaps a creed written by Arius himself in his *Apology*,[33] according to which

> We believe in one God, the Father almighty, from whom are all things; and in one only-begotten Son of God, God the Word, our Lord Jesus Christ, through whom are all things; and in one holy Spirit, the Counsellor, in whom is given to each of the saints an apportionment of every grace according to measure for the common good.[34]

---

32. Socrates, *Ecclesiastical History*, 1.23; Hanson, *The Search for the Christian Doctrine of God*, p. 264.

33. So Basil, *Against Eunomius*, 1.4.

34. Eunomius, *Liber Apologeticus* 5, in *Eunomius: The Extant Works*, ed. and trans. Richard Paul Vaggione (Oxford: Clarendon Press, 1987), p. 39.

One is struck by the similarity between this and third-century theology. However, the key question that arises in the context of the specific claims of Arianism, in its theological ontology, is whether what is said here is enough. The strength of their position is that the Arians were arguably reflecting the language of Scripture and tradition in their creedal formulations, which after all do use divine titles for the Father that they do not use for Christ, and for Christ that they do not use for the Spirit. It is a notorious fact that the New Testament does not call the Spirit "God." Were the Arians right, therefore, to refuse to speak of the Spirit as God, and simply to refer to the fact that the Spirit is the Spirit promised by prophets and by Christ himself, and the Spirit that the New Testament church received?

After many years of anti-Arian struggle — not all of which left his reputation unblemished[35] — Athanasius came, it seems, for the first time upon this problem. Athanasius, of course, had been the champion of the Nicene cause after 325. His theology had been instrumental in the development and elaboration of the Nicene faith. He had also suffered considerable persecution from Arian politicians over the years. Not until decades later, however, did he turn to the question of the doctrine of the Holy Spirit. Probably between 359 and 360 in Alexandria,[36] his colleague Serapion, bishop of a neighboring city, had a group of converts from Arianism to the Nicene faith in his church; these converts accepted the *homoousios* in the case of the Son, but as far as the Holy Spirit was concerned continued to hold that he was a creature.

Athanasius responded to Serapion in a number of letters that are among the most important sources for the doctrine of the Holy Spirit in the whole of Christian theology. What Athanasius does in his *Letters to Serapion* is to use the doctrine of the person of Jesus Christ already developed at the Council of Nicea as evidence in the case of the doctrine of the Holy Spirit; in short, the logic of Nicea's christology is applied by Athanasius to pneumatology.[37] His con-

---

35. J. Quasten, *Patrology* (Westminster, MD: Christian Classics, 1984), vol. 3, pp. 57-59.

36. Hanson, *The Search for the Christian Doctrine of God*, pp. 748ff.

37. See, e.g., the arguments of Athanasius, *Letters to Serapion*, 2-3.

tention is that the Holy Spirit is *not* a creature; the Holy Spirit, according to Athanasius, bears the same rank and function relative to the Son as the Son does to the Father. A number of arguments are used to support this conclusion. For example, Athanasius cites the baptismal formula "in the name of the Father, and of the Son, and of the Holy Spirit," and maintains that since we now know that the Son is God along with the Father, it makes no sense at all to introduce a creature, the Arian Holy Spirit, into the Trinity. The Spirit, he maintains, is a procession from the Father and not a mere creation of the Father, citing John 15:26 — "the Spirit of truth who proceeds from the Father."

The most important of the arguments in defense of the deity of the Holy Spirit in the *Letters to Serapion,* however, is based on the doctrine of sanctification. Sanctification, then as now, was associated specifically with the work of the Spirit. We know, furthermore, that sanctification is an inherent part of the divine economy of salvation: without holiness, nobody will see the Lord. Thus, according to Athanasius, if sanctification is the work of the Holy Spirit, and if sanctification is part of salvation, then the Holy Spirit must be our savior, together with the Father and the Son. Using the same argument that was used to reject the Arians's christology, therefore, Athanasius also rejects their pneumatology: to be our savior, the Spirit must be God; if he were not God, then he could not save us. The argument runs from the work of the Holy Spirit to the person of the Holy Spirit, and is thus rooted in the doctrine of salvation. Here we see the simplicity and strength of the Nicene position, grounded as it is in this soteriological logic.

One of the important features of the *Letters to Serapion* is that the term *homoousios* is used here for the first time after Nicea in connection with the Holy Spirit: The Spirit is, according to Athanasius, *homoousios* with God (i.e., the Father). This claim is found at an advanced stage in the discussion, after a range of arguments for the divinity of the Spirit have already been developed. Athanasius knows that applying the term to the Spirit is an innovation, but that such innovation is necessary. A lengthy explanation, however, is required. Even later on in the fourth century, defenders of the deity of the Spirit such as Basil of Caesarea and theologians of the stature of Cyril of Jerusalem shrank back from using the term, because they knew very well not only that the term *homoousios* is not biblical but also that neither the New Testament nor the church before the fourth century had dared to call the Holy Spirit God in this sense. They were the theological conservatives in this situation, and Athanasius was the radical, moving beyond the letter of Scripture and the content of theological tradition. It seems that his views were received with interest, for he was not declared heretical for them by anyone other than the Arians. At the same time, however, his position did not become the standard one; perhaps because the question of the Holy Spirit had not yet been decided upon, Athanasius could claim that the Holy Spirit is of one substance with God without exciting great opposition, since the question was still pending.

The wider church, however, was not nearly so bold in its pneumatology. We see this very clearly in the development leading up to the Council of Constantinople in 381. A number of important theologians were working on the doctrine of the Holy Spirit between Athanasius's *Letters to Serapion* in 359 and the Council itself in 381. Basil of Caesarea, who has already been mentioned, was one of them. In the 370s he, too, wrote a number of letters on pneumatology, along with his most important single treatise, *On the Holy Spirit*, in which he argues that the Spirit's divine operations mean that he cannot be a creature. The Spirit is of God as the breath of his mouth, and he has the power to sanctify; how can he be a mere creature? Basil speaks effusively of the Spirit as an intelligent substance *(ousia)* of infinite power, unlimited by time or ages, which everything in search of holiness and virtue *naturally* seeks.[38] Although there is a note of ethics here, Basil's thought is primarily metaphysical, for he is describing the Spirit as the divine goodness that permeates the world and that the world somehow shares in; the Platonic philosophical basis of his thought, together with his Christian faith, clearly makes him inclined to see goodness in such metaphysical and indeed specifically theological terms. But Basil does not go to the length Athanasius did in using the term *homoousios* in connection with the Spirit; in fact, he goes out of his

38. Basil of Caesarea, *On the Holy Spirit*, 5.22.

way at times to avoid using it, presumably in order to avoid causing a scandal.[39]

One of his close colleagues, however, Gregory of Nazianzus, did not shrink from public use of the term. Gregory's role in the development of the doctrine of the Holy Spirit began in earnest when he was called to Constantinople in 380 by the emperor. In that year, he gave a number of sermons — effectively theological lectures — in the city on a series of theological themes. One of them, *The Fifth Theological Oration,* was concerned with the key debate of the day, the doctrine of the deity of the Holy Spirit. He begins in a modest way, reflecting the clear diversity of opinion in the church at the time:

> among ourselves, some have conceived of [the Spirit] as an activity, some as a creature, some as God; and some have been uncertain which to call him, out of reverence for Scripture, they say, as though it did not make the matter clear either way. And therefore they . . . take up a neutral position.[40]

Gregory's unambiguous view, however, was that this kind of sitting on the fence while the new Arians were pressing the church hard was not an adequate tactical or theological response. Following Athanasius, it seems, he argues against a division of the divine Trinity into Creator and creature as unfitting and incoherent; there is, he argues in a favorite analogy, one light that comes to us from the Father, through the Son, in the Spirit:

> Light, and light, and light, but one light, and one God. David anticipated this when he said, "In your light shall we see light." But now we have seen and we preach, receiving the light of the Son from the light of the Father, in the light of the Holy Spirit.[41]

This divine outreach cannot be divided up between creature and Creator; the creature receives it, indeed, but the light itself is true

---

39. Hanson, *The Search for the Christian Doctrine of God,* p. 776.
40. Gregory of Nazianzus, *Orations,* V, 5.
41. Gregory of Nazianzus, *Orations,* V, 3.

God. Without this, Gregory reasons, something imperfect is introduced into the Godhead, and something disastrous into Christian theology, for if the Spirit in whom the light comes to me is not himself God, how then can I be saved? "If he is ranked with me, how can he divinise me *[pos eme poiei theon]*"?[42]

Gregory thus goes on to pose the decisive rhetorical question: "What then? Is the Spirit God?" The answer is unambiguous: "Most certainly." He continues, "Well then, is he *homoousios*? Yes if he is God!"[43] He also takes up a range of questions associated with these affirmations, derived, no doubt, in large measure from Arian attacks. On one view, for example, to be of one substance with the Father is to be the Son of the Father. This was the basic argument employed after 325 to explain what the word *homoousios* meant and how it related to the terms Father and Son. The question that arose as a result in the case of the Holy Spirit was therefore this: Is the Spirit also a son? Or alternatively, if, as on some readings of the Father-Son-Spirit relation, the Spirit has his being through the Son, and if the Spirit is of one substance with the Son as the Son is of one substance with the Father, does this imply that the Father has a grandson in the Holy Spirit? Gregory counters this with the assertion that to *proceed* from the Father, according to John 15:26, is the pneumatological parallel to the Son's being *begotten* by the Father, and that consubstantiality with the Father results from both.[44] He also attempts to develop a more sophisticated approach to the problem of the one and the three than his opponents take. They object that the plurality of Father, Son, and Spirit is on the same level as the plurality of "three crabs" or "three men," Peter, James, and John. Gregory's response is to claim that the trinitarian concept of consubstantiality makes such a ridiculous comparison impossible, for the theological usage of *homoousios* is *sui generis*. The fact that the three are consubstantial is affirmation enough of the divine unity, while also making simple numeration along creaturely lines logically and metaphysically inappropriate.

Gregory's argument is dazzling, but there can be no doubt

42. Gregory of Nazianzus, *Orations*, V, 4.
43. Gregory of Nazianzus, *Orations*, V, 10.
44. Gregory of Nazianzus, *Orations*, V, 9.

that his sermon was greeted with alarm by many of his hearers. One important factor too often overlooked in this whole question is that of Gregory's character: He was in fact notoriously unreliable and perhaps too theologically volatile.[45] Having said this, one needs also to note the fact that he goes on at the end of his *Fifth Theological Oration* to give a spoonful of sugar to the medicine offered, and yet even here his claim is unique:

> For the matter stands thus: the Old Testament proclaimed the Father openly, and the Son more obscurely. The New manifested the Son, and suggested the deity of the Spirit. Now the Spirit himself dwells among us, and supplies us with a clearer demonstration of himself. For it was not safe, when the Godhead of the Father was not yet acknowledged, plainly to proclaim the Son; nor when that of the Son was not yet received, to burden us further (if I may use so bold an expression) with the Holy Spirit.[46]

In a situation of controversy over whether the Spirit is God or not, Gregory himself clearly takes the affirmative view, but he recognizes both that other things have been taught in the past, and thus that there were people who cannot be characterized as heretics who had no doctrine of the deity of the Spirit, but also that the progress of theology demands that the *homoousios* now be applied unambiguously to the Holy Spirit in order to settle the matter once and for all.

What then happened? Largely for political reasons — a new emperor wanted finally to rid the empire of Arianism — a new council was called to respond again to the Arians, the Council of Constantinople, which met in the summer of 381. We know very little about it, as neither its acts nor an authoritative account from the time have survived. We do not even know with certainty that the so-called Nicene Creed in fact dates from the Council itself, although this seems to modern scholars to be the most plausible view.[47] We do have, however, a clear expansion in doctrinal defi-

---

45. Hanson, *The Search for the Christian Doctrine of God*, pp. 701ff.
46. Gregory of Nazianzus, *Orations*, V, 26.
47. Hanson, *The Search for the Christian Doctrine of God*, pp. 812ff; J. N. D. Kelly, *Early Christian Creeds*, 3rd ed. (London: Longman, 1972), pp. 296ff.

nition in what is by common consent the Creed of 381, the "Nicene Creed," over against the Creed of 325, the "Creed of Nicea." Whereas the Council of Nicea had been content to affirm simply that we believe in the Holy Spirit, the Council of Constantinople expanded considerably on this doctrinal definition:

> [We believe] in the Holy Spirit, the Lord and the Life-giver, who proceeds from the Father, who is worshipped and glorified together with the Father and Son, who spoke by the prophets. . . .[48]

We can see here on the one hand an improvement on 325, in the sense that at least something positive is asserted of the Spirit. On the other hand, it is also clear that despite the work of Athanasius and Gregory of Nazianzus, who for a time was president of the Council of 381, the innate conservatism of the church prevailed. Though the Nicene affirmations regarding the Son were reaffirmed at Constantinople, no attempt was made to define the doctrine of the Holy Spirit in the terms used of the Son. What the creed in effect affirms can be understood as the equivalent of consubstantiality, and certainly that is how it came to be understood from the fifth century onward, but the Council itself refused to sanction use of *homoousios* with reference to the Spirit.

It seems likely that the language used in the Creed of 381 was framed to avoid controversy with conservatives, on the one hand, who were suspicious of theological innovation, and probably also to some extent with the Arians, on the other — who were, after all, still a powerful group only recently ejected from Constantinople itself, and who were only too eager to accuse the orthodox of imposing on believers a pneumatological conception that was alien to Scripture and unknown in the older tradition. In the event, the Council tried to find a *via media* that would meet both the demand for a clearer definition of the status of the Spirit in the Trinity and the need to avoid further upheaval in the church. It found this, significantly, not in the theologies of Athanasius and Gregory, but in the more moderate position of Basil of Caesarea.

Gregory himself was distinctly unimpressed by the Creed of

48. Kelly, *Early Christian Creeds,* pp. 297-98.

381. Years later, in the first piece of Christian autobiography we possess, *Concerning His Own Life,* Gregory commented disparagingly on what he saw as an anarchic and ill-informed Council:

> The sweet . . . sources of ancient faith, which sprang long ago from the deliberations of Nicaea, which unified the sacred name of the Trinity, I saw being miserably befouled by the brackish inflow of ideas from either side. Those who shaped the powers that be could congratulate themselves on being styled moderates. Open supporters of the extremists might be nearer the truth. They were bishops who were just then in the process of learning about God. Teachers yesterday, pupils again today, initiators into mysteries where they themselves have to become initiators after the event, they infect congregations with their own bad doctrines.[49]

Gregory actually goes to the lengths of describing the bulk of the bishops present at Constantinople as a "mob of traffickers in Christ," which hardly befits the claims of those who exalt the doctrines of the "Nicene Creed" of 381, or for that matter the notion of ecclesiastical Councils as authoritative. It is hard to know if Gregory's comments are entirely sane or if they are simply the thoughts of a difficult man who did not get his way, but they certainly open up a fresh perspective on the Council that produced what became *the* definitive orthodox creed of the Christian church.

What is clear is that, historically, the Eastern emperor Theodosius immediately promoted the decision of the Council in conjunction with his ongoing anti-Arian campaign, and that subsequently the anti-Arian version of the Christian faith defined at Constantinople prevailed.[50] Politically, therefore, the Council of Constantinople was a resounding success; indeed, it continues to affect the Christian church decisively even today. Theologically, however, a series of question marks hang over its creed. The most glaring omission is obviously the refusal to mention the word

49. St. Gregory of Nazianzus, *De vita sua,* in *Three Poems,* trans. Denis Molaise Mehan (Washington, DC: Catholic University of America Press, 1987), p. 124.

50. Hanson, *The Search for the Christian Doctrine of God,* pp. 820-21.

homoousios in connection with the Holy Spirit; that the Spirit proceeds from the Father and that the Spirit is worshiped together with Father and Son was and is susceptible to a variety of interpretations, some of which would have been excluded had the word *homoousios* been used. *De facto,* therefore, the *locus classicus* of the doctrine of the deity of the Holy Spirit is the corpus of writings of the theologians of the Athanasian pneumatological tradition rather than the central creed of the Christian church. Therefore, Gregory, who opposed Constantinople's pneumatology as inadequate, is in this sense more important than Constantinople itself.

At best, we have to conclude that Constantinople's pneumatology is ambiguous and that the felt need to define the status of the Son more clearly than the Spirit effectively highlights the importance of the Son over against the Spirit in Christian theology. This is a questionable view that we have already touched upon, and to which we shall return. Second, it is striking that nothing is said in the creed of the relation between the Son and the Spirit, which again is a major theme in the writings of the theologians of the period, not to mention in the New Testament. Again, as we shall see in the next chapter, this omission would subsequently cause major theological problems for the Christian church. Third, although one has to admit the strength of the beautiful Johannine term used to describe the Spirit, the "Life-giver" (*to zoopoion,* John 6:63), and the fact that any creed must be economical in order to be functional, a great deal about the work of the Spirit — about the relation between Spirit and church, for example — has been left unsaid. Perhaps this is wise, as doctrinal definition is intended to point the way rather than to exhaust all possibilities, but perhaps it also reflects a general uncertainty concerning the Spirit's role in human salvation and in the spiritual life. The dominance of Logos as the central category of Christian thought would continue, while orthodox believers would recite the Creed of 381 long after the event, in good conscience maintaining its implicit subordination of the work of the Spirit and its elevation of the importance of that of the Son.

3. The Filioque Controversy

THE QUESTION of the relation between the Son and the Holy Spirit that was left hanging in the fourth-century debates was addressed in Western theology from an early stage in its history by means of what came to be known as the *filioque* doctrine. This doctrine, which has never been accepted in the Christian East, took its rise from the Latin fathers, and from Augustine in particular, whose pneumatological position came to fruition in subsequent Western medieval theology. The specific "home" of the *filioque* is, of course, the Latin form of the Creed of 381. Originally, the pneumatological article of the creed began (in Latin translation): [*Credo*] *in spiritum sanctum, qui ex patre procedit;* by the beginning of the second Christian millennium, the Latin church had officially added the phrase *filioque* ("and the Son") to this: *qui ex patre filioque procedit:* "who proceeds from the Father and Son." Whether this addition provides us with a pneumatological gain or loss is the central question of this chapter.

The Western Pneumatological Tradition

It was not until relatively late in the patristic era that theologians of the Western church began to match their Eastern counterparts in theological creativity and insight. Even as late as the fourth century,

62

Eastern theologians not only carried the theological burdens of the day but could comfortably do so for the most part without reference to the thought of the Christian West. By the end of that century, however, the West had begun to achieve an authentic theological maturity of its own. The first theologian of note here is Ambrose of Milan (c. 339-397), who took inspiration from the theologians of the East, but who also moved beyond them in a distinctively Western way. Although it is certainly too much to say of him that, in the words of one scholar, "he was the most brilliant man of his time,"[1] he was clearly the most important Western theologian of the fourth century, active against the Arians and in contact with the main Eastern figures on the orthodox side of the controversy.[2] He had, however, received a rhetorical and legal rather than a philosophical and theological training, and his typically Roman practical genius is seen in his eventual ecclesiastical career. Not only did he do much to defend the church against the authoritarian demands of the state, but he was also a genuinely holy figure who distributed much of his wealth to the poor and who made himself available as bishop to the great and the insignificant alike.[3]

Theologically, Ambrose's work derives its main importance from the fact that he successfully mediated the achievement of the Greek tradition to the Latin church. Augustine, who came under Ambrose's influence as a young scholar in Milan at a time of personal crisis, speaks in his *Confessions* of the latter's preaching, of how it taught him that the Catholic Church did not believe the things his Manichean mentors had accused it of teaching, and of how the Scriptures came alive to him through Ambrose's teaching.[4] He tells us that his mother Monica, when visiting Augustine in Milan, hung on the words of Ambrose as on a fountain of living water, since she discovered that Ambrose had turned her son from

1. Berthold Altaner, *Patrology,* trans. Hilda C. Graef (New York: Herder and Herder, 1961), p. 445.

2. Jaroslav Pelikan, *The Christian Tradition* (London: University of Chicago Press, 1971), vol. 1, p. 203.

3. Altaner, *Patrology,* pp. 443-45.

4. Augustine, *Confessions,* 5.13-14; 6.1, 3-5; *Oeuvres de Saint Augustin,* vols. 13 and 14, ed. and trans. Aimé Solignac (Paris: Desclée, De Brouwer et Cie, 1962).

the Manichean heresy: "she loved that man as though he were an angel of God."[5]

Among the works of Ambrose is a treatise entitled *On the Holy Spirit,* written almost certainly in 381 but before Constantinople, and the first Western work devoted exclusively to the subject. R. P. C. Hanson dismisses the book as a "pot-boiler," since it makes such liberal use of the great Greek theologians Athanasius, Basil of Caesarea, and Didymus the Blind.[6] Along similar lines, but rather more charitably, H. B. Swete once commented on the unoriginality of the work, but added that this very fact reveals the author's humility and good sense in making judicious use of the Eastern masters.[7] Such judgments are, however, unfair to Ambrose. It is true that his argument for the divinity of the Spirit is derivative and unoriginal, but it is also true that there is little that *can* be added to the claims of the Eastern theologians of the fourth century on this question; to ask Ambrose to say more is to ask him to do what practically all subsequent theologians of the Spirit have, like him, found either impossible or unnecessary. More importantly, however, Ambrose is a theologian who, unlike most theologians and unlike even the Greek pneumatologists mentioned, is not theologically crippled by an all-consuming doctrine of the Logos. There is to be found in Ambrose, more than in any of his Greek sources, a real sense of the vital place of the Spirit in revelation, history, theology, the church, and the Christian life. In these matters he exceeds in a refreshing way the normal expectation one brings to the reading of patristic theology.

Perhaps the greatest strength of Ambrose's treatment of the doctrine of the Holy Spirit is the range of biblical material and themes upon which he draws. Utilizing the methods of spiritual interpretation he learned from the East, he maintains, for example, that it was the Holy Spirit whom Moses saw in the burning bush, flame being in the Bible a type of the Spirit.[8] Similarly, since the

---

5. *Confessions,* 6.1. Unless otherwise indicated, all translations of the Latin Fathers in this chapter are my own, based on the critical editions cited.

6. R. P. C. Hanson, *The Search for the Christian Doctrine of God* (Edinburgh: T. & T. Clark, 1988), p. 756.

7. H. B. Swete, *The Holy Spirit in the Ancient Church* (London: MacMillan, 1912), pp. 317-18.

8. Ambrose, *On the Holy Spirit,* 1.14; *Sancti Ambrosii Opera,* ed. Otto Faller,

Holy Spirit is light, the light of the Lord's countenance (Ps. 4:6) is none other than the Spirit (1.14). The Spirit's work is seen in the creation of the earth (Ambrose thus moves beyond pure interiority in his theology of the Spirit), and again in the earth's re-creation and regeneration (2.5, 7; 3.10). The Pauline Spirit of adoption also appears in Ambrose's theology, together with the eschatological sense of the gift of the Spirit as initiating in the here and now the final glorification of the children of God (1.5). Throughout the treatise, he speaks of the Spirit alternately as the Spirit of grace and as the Spirit of love *(caritas),* but the Spirit is also the Spirit of knowledge, who reveals to us the Father and Son (2.12). In the case of the anointing of Christ by the Spirit, which, as we have seen, is occasionally mentioned by other theologians but for the most part is undeveloped in patristic theology, we find that, in Ambrose's hands, the anointing of Christ becomes a more significant theological theme (1.9; 3.1). Interestingly, it is not only the Father who gave the Son but also the Spirit who gave him, since there is unity of action in the Godhead, and the Spirit that rests upon Christ also leads him in his mission (1.12).

The importance of the Holy Spirit in Ambrose's theology is nicely summed up in a passage concerning the theme of living water:

> [we] learn that the Holy Spirit has been called not only water but also a river, according to what is written: "Out of his belly shall flow rivers of living water. . . ." Therefore, the Holy Spirit is a river, and a very large river . . . which flows always, and never fails. Not only a river, but also one of profuse stream, just as David said, "The stream of the river maketh the city of God joyful."[9]

The Spirit thus flows from and is itself an infinite source that meets the needs of the whole city of God, so that Ambrose's position on the importance of the doctrine of the Holy Spirit is clear: It is folly

---

in *Corpus Scriptorum Ecclesiasticorum Latinorum* (Vienna: Hölder-Pichler-Tempsky, 1964), 79/9. Subsequent references will be given parenthetically in the text.

9. Ambrose, *On the Holy Spirit,* 1.16, in *Saint Ambrose: Theological and Dogmatic Works,* trans. Roy J. Deferrari (Washington: Catholic University of America Press, 1963).

to ignore or to belittle the Spirit, all the more so because the Spirit is the source of eternal life (2.3). To this extent, Ambrose stands apart from a very great deal of the theological tradition in maintaining the centrality of the Spirit to the whole economy of salvation.

Ambrose's theology of the Spirit is also historically important because of a relatively indirect but nevertheless clear statement made concerning the procession of the Holy Spirit. According to Ambrose, the Spirit "proceeds from the Son" (*procedit ex filio;* 1.11). This is combined in his theology with the more common thesis that the Spirit proceeds from the Father, but its presence in his theology in general and in this significant pneumatological treatise in particular provided theological precedent for what would later become one of the standard features of Western pneumatology: the idea that the Holy Spirit proceeds from both Father and Son. In the case of Ambrose himself, the procession of the Spirit from the Son almost certainly corresponds to the Eastern phrase *dia tou huiou* (through the Son, that is, from the Father through the Son), but in a very real sense this is irrelevant, since it is the linguistic precedent that is important. Ambrose thus goes well beyond the distinct reserve of his Eastern contemporaries on this question — many of whom, after all, were reluctant to speak of the Spirit's procession at all. In the event, of course, the Council of Constantinople stuck to the language of Scripture: The Spirit proceeds from the Father. The Latin West, however, was never entirely happy with this scriptural formulation.

It was the great Augustine (354-430), however, who more than any other provided the theoretical foundation for the Western tradition of understanding the procession of the Spirit from both Father and Son. As a rising young scholar converted to Christian faith under Ambrose's influence (his baptism took place in Milan in the spring of 387), Augustine very quickly assumed a position of responsibility in the church. In 391 he returned to Africa in search of a monastic life, only to be forcibly ordained after being "grabbed," as he himself put it, by the faithful one day in church.[10] By December of 393, while still a priest, he addressed a local council of African bishops in

---

10. Augustine, *Serm.* 355.2; cited by Peter Brown, *Augustine of Hippo* (London and Boston: Faber and Faber, 1967), p. 138.

Hippo.[11] It seems likely that his bishop, Valerius, wished to put him forward for wider recognition. His subject was the substance of Christian faith, as summarized in a current North African baptismal creed (perhaps an early version of the Apostles' Creed), and in his title, *On Faith and the Creed.* After discussing the doctrines of Father and Son in turn, following the structure of the creed, Augustine turns his attention to the doctrines of the Trinity in general and of the Holy Spirit in particular. He begins here by affirming the full deity of the Spirit, arguing that the Spirit can be said to be God by the same logic as that which allows us to predicate "God" of Father and Son.[12] The exposition then turns to a discussion of a series of analogies of the Trinity, drawn from Greek sources. The Trinity, Augustine argues, can be likened to a fountain *(fons)*, a stream *(fluvius)*, and a drink *(potio)*, through all of which the one water flows and can be found; similarly, the Trinity can be likened to a tree in its root *(radix)*, trunk *(robur)*, and branches *(rami)*, none of which is identical with the other, and yet all of which are the one tree and the one wood.[13] Augustine then provides a problematic explanation of what he means: Everybody admits, he says, that three cups filled from the same fountain contain one water. This seems to suggest, not that the Father is the source of the other two persons — as in the Greek tradition on which Augustine is dependent — but rather that some underlying principle is the common source of the three.[14] There is in fact a deep ambiguity in Augustine's theology at this point to which we will have occasion to return.

The pneumatological question that preoccupies Augustine in *On Faith and the Creed* concerns what distinguishes the Holy Spirit from the Father and Son, given that the three are one God. Augustine repeats the by-then established view that the Father and Son are distinguished as the one who begets and the one who is begotten; but, as he rightly points out, there was as yet no clear consensus on what is proper to the Spirit alone at this inner-trini-

11. Augustine, *Retractions,* 1.17; *Oeuvres de Saint Augustin,* vol. 12, ed. and trans. Gustave Bardy (Paris: Desclée, De Brouwer et Cie, 1950).

12. Augustine, *On Faith and the Creed,* 16; *Oeuvres de Saint Augustin,* vol. 9, ed. and trans. J. Rivière (Paris: Desclée, De Brouwer et Cie, 1947).

13. Augustine, *On Faith and the Creed,* 17.

14. Augustine, *On Faith and the Creed,* 17.

tarian level.[15] All that had been said, Augustine reports, is that the Spirit is neither begotten of the Father (for then he would be another Son), nor begotten of the Son (for then he would be a Grandson), but rather that he owes what he is to the Father, for there is only one eternal origin *(principium)* in the Trinity, namely, the Father.[16]

That Augustine in 393 makes no mention of the pneumatological article of the Creed of 381, which had already spoken of the Spirit's procession from the Father — a phrase that was certainly interpreted in the East at that time as what Augustine calls the *proprium* of the Spirit — is related to one of the chief curiosities of patristic theology: namely, the fact that the Creed of 381 is not mentioned by any church father or authoritative ecclesiastical document before the mid-fifth century. What is of greater interest, however, is what Augustine goes on to say positively for himself on this question.

According to Augustine, "some have even ventured to believe" that the Holy Spirit is the communion between the Father and the Son.[17] In fact, the view Augustine proceeds to outline is none other than his own — a brilliant and original attempt to develop a trinitarian doctrine of the Spirit that, as a whole, has no real precedent. Many of the key themes that he will later develop in his *On the Trinity* and elsewhere in his theological works are already present here: the Spirit as the communion between the Father and the Son; the Spirit as gift; the Spirit as *caritas*, and *caritas* as the unifying bond; the gift of the Spirit, which reconciles us to God. The latter theme in particular will become central to the whole Western soteriological system of the medieval era, where justification is in certain decisive respects seen in *pneumatological* rather than — as in Reformation theology — christological terms.[18]

Augustine's argument in *On Faith and the Creed* is rudimentary but daring: The love of God, the Holy Spirit, and the common

15. Augustine, *On Faith and the Creed*, 18-19.

16. Here Augustine correctly represents the consensus of the Greek tradition, but contradicts what has been said concerning the "three cups."

17. Augustine, *On Faith and the Creed*, 19.

18. Cf. Alister McGrath, *Iustitia Dei*, 2 vols. (Cambridge: Cambridge University Press, 1986), vol. 1.

divinity of the Father and Son are identical. Augustine thus rather dangerously seeks to discern the *proprium* of the Spirit not only in the love subsisting between the Father and the Son but also in the one divinity of the two. To say with the Johannine literature of the New Testament that "God is love" and that "God is Spirit" is thus to say the same thing. This is a position that Augustine will later make efforts to transcend, since a confusion of Spirit and the divine substance, which seems to come perilously close to what he has in mind, is something he comes to recognize as inadequate. However, the outline of the mature Augustinian position on the doctrine of the Holy Spirit has already been established; on the basis of his central claim that the Spirit is love, he develops not only a powerful view of the role of the Spirit in the inner-trinitarian life but also a corresponding view of salvation, where the centrality of love in God is matched by the centrality of love in the spiritual life. By love we are reconciled to God; by love we have confidence to preach the truth, since "perfect love casts out fear"; and by love of divine Wisdom *(sapientia)*, by which Augustine means the Logos, we enjoy that Wisdom and abide in it. He then follows this up with an obscure attack on those who would deny what he has claimed on the grounds that love cannot be regarded as a *substantia*, which again unfortunately appears to confuse trinitarian persons and divine substance.[19]

On Faith and the Creed is a theologically immature work that is as yet ambiguous on trinitarian questions; it was a wise move on Augustine's part to cloak his tentative pneumatological suggestions under the heading of what others have said. Most obviously, beyond the matter of persons and substance, it is impossible to reconcile Augustine's argument in the text with his earlier treatment of the Trinity in terms of the traditional analogies of fountain, stream, and drink. The latter are based on an emanationist trinitarian paradigm derived from the Neoplatonism that Augustine certainly knew and respected, whereas his rather clumsy attempt to identify the Spirit with the common divinity of Father and Son has nothing to do with such analogies. However, the work marks out important theological territory that Augustine will later explore, and problems that he will resolve while treading fundamentally the same paths in On the Trinity.

19. Augustine, *On Faith and the Creed*, 20.

Next to his famous *Confessions* and *City of God,* Augustine's *On the Trinity* is perhaps his greatest work. Written over the period from about 400 to 416, *On the Trinity* is a book that laid the foundations for the subsequent development of Western trinitarian theology. By the beginning of the fifth century, the problem was no longer so much to establish the divinity of Son or Spirit — indeed, Augustine could simply assume this from the teaching of the church; instead, the concern was to provide conceptual clarification and to expand the horizons of theological understanding given these presuppositions. Even more than the Cappadocians before him, therefore, Augustine consolidates the Nicene faith and attempts to develop its implications. His main achievement in this respect is finally to move beyond the old emanationist paradigm inherited from the second and third centuries, where the focus was not only on descending levels of divinity but also on the divine outreach to the world, on a trinitarian conceptuality geared to the being of the Trinity in itself. Rather than focusing on what the persons do in creation and redemption, in short, Augustine speaks primarily of what they are from all eternity.

Such a project might strike us as bold, but it needs to be seen against the background of Arianism and the response of the orthodox in the fourth century. In 325 and 381, the church was forced into the position of making statements concerning the Trinity in itself — and that despite the fact that divine incomprehensibility was presupposed *a priori* at the time by practically all concerned. Augustine's project derives its rationale from the set of problems thrown up by the Nicene faith. In particular, like the Cappadocians before him, Augustine has to tackle the question of how the three trinitarian persons are distinct, given that, according to church teaching, "the Father, the Son and the Holy Spirit make known *(insinuent)* their divine unity in an indivisible equality of one identical substance."[20] How, in short, can it be that the Nicene doctrine of consubstantiality does not amount to modalism?

---

20. Augustine, *On the Trinity,* 1.4; *Oeuvres de Saint Augustin,* vols. 15 and 16, ed. and trans. M. Mellet and Th. Camelot (Paris: Desclée De Brouwer, 1955). Subsequent references will be made parenthetically in the text.

Although Arianism was no longer a major political danger after 381, it subsequently went underground and remained a theological movement to be reckoned with for some time. In the middle of *On the Trinity,* we find Augustine addressing a late Arian argument against Nicea:

> Among the many arguments which the Arians habitually raise against the Catholic faith, there is one that seems to them to be the best and the most ingenious. They say that whatever is said or thought of God is said, not of accidents, but of substance. Therefore, to be "unbegotten" pertains to the Father's substance, and to be "begotten" to the Son's substance. (5.3)

The Arians concluded that, as a result, the substances of the Father and of the Son are different and cannot by definition be the same *(homoousios)*. One need hardly point out that this was not the reasoning that led to the distinctive Arian claim concerning Christ; rather, it emerged as a subsidiary argument in their theology, fleshing out their position against Nicea and the orthodox. Nevertheless, it was indeed ingenious. The argument relies on the Aristotelian distinction between substance and accidents: Substance refers to what something is by virtue of its permanent nature and being; accidents are inessential qualities that can come and go without altering the substance of an object. The implicit claim is that God has no accidents, for if he did, then he would be changeable — which for both Arian and orthodox alike was unthinkable. Therefore, the Arians claimed, since everything that can be said about anything must refer either to substance or to accidents, everything that can be said about God must be understood to refer to substance. Thus the standard terms "unbegotten" and "begotten," used to refer to the distinctive personal properties of Father and Son, seem to imply that one is what the other is not in the substantial sense.

Augustine has a twofold response to this claim. First, he replies, if whatever we say of Father and Son refers to substance, then how do the Arians interpret John 10:30: "I and the Father are one"? This provides him with a *reductio ad absurdum* of the Arian argument and suggests the conclusion that even on Arian logic something other than substance and accidents can be known of God. His second and much more important move, however, is to raise the question of what this other means of saying something of God might be — for he agrees that there is nothing accidental in God. The answer he provides is intriguing: In between theological talk of substance and accidents, there is another possibility open to us, and that is to speak of divine relations. According to Augustine, this possibility is unique to discourse about God, for the substance-accident distinction does indeed exhaust the possibilities for speaking about creation (5.5). Augustine argues that in the case of the Father and the Son, however, we are compelled to think in the following way: The Father is not Father with reference to himself — that is, to who he is substantially — but rather with reference to the Son, and similarly the Son with reference to the Father. The terms are mutual and make sense only in such a relational context. The names Father and Son, therefore, refer neither to substance, nor to accidents, but to *relations*. The relations themselves are not accidental (as in the case of human father-son relations) because they are not changeable. Augustine goes on to conclude that to say that the Father is God, and that the Son is God, and that the Holy Spirit is God does not mean that there are three Gods, for these names do not refer to the divine substance, of which there is only one (5.8). The names refer, rather, purely and solely to the relations between the three.

The basic Augustinian insight involved here is that in the Trinity a person is a pure relation. There is, however, a flaw in his reasoning that needs to be faced squarely: Neither the personal name "Holy Spirit" nor the correlative term "procession" (or "spiration") is relational; certainly neither is relational in the same way that the names Father and Son are. Augustine himself, however, recognizes this problem, and he sets out in rest of *On the Trinity* to respond to it. The solution he attempts to provide begins with the observation seen already in *On Faith and the Creed*: The Holy Spirit is known from Scripture to be the Spirit of both Father and Son (4.20). The Spirit is something the two have in common, therefore, and this leads Augustine to an important conclusion: Given the doctrine of trinitarian relations, the Spirit can be defined in terms of a relation common to both the Father and the Son. The Holy Spirit, Augustine then claims, is "a certain inexpressible communion or fellowship between the Father and the Son *(spiritus sanctus ineffabilis quaedam patris filioque communio)*" (5.11), a phrase that expands upon and clarifies the position outlined in Augustine's earlier work in 393. He then attempts to provide a clearer definition of the Holy Spirit in terms of this communion or relationship, beginning with the concept of the Spirit as gift (5.15-16). The Spirit is not, according to Augustine, merely the gift given to the church in time but rather is the eternal gift of the Father to the Son and of the Son to the Father; thus the Spirit constitutes a mutual relationship between the two.

Augustine's argument is a brilliant, if difficult, piece of constructive theological thought, relying on and developing the significance of the Christian ideal of *caritas*. For Augustine, *caritas* is fundamentally a pneumatological category, and, as has already been observed, he develops a whole theology — not just of the inner-trinitarian status of the Spirit but also of the doctrine of salvation — around it. In this way, the Holy Spirit is given a key place in his theological system, for insofar as love, *caritas*, is central to the Augustinian worldview, so is the Holy Spirit. In his wider theology, Augustine presses this theological insight in another important direction toward what would eventually be seen in the Reformation as an unacceptable conclusion. According to Augustine, the work of salvation brings about a real change in the human being who is saved, so that it is possible, and indeed essential to the matter, to say that we are justified by love.[21] In the inner life of the Trinity, this same centrality of love is given substance in the distinctive Augustinian doctrine of the Holy Spirit.

Much ink has been spilled regarding the question of the Augustinian doctrine of the images of the Trinity in the soul, and in particular over the role of the celebrated image of memory, understanding, and will. This question need not detain us, except to the extent that we note that the image of the Trinity in Augustine's thought is intended to help us understand the primary mystery of God, and not to replace the content of Christian creedal

21. See the account in McGrath, *Iustitia Dei,* vol. 1, pp. 23ff.

confession and Christian proclamation. The role of the so-called psychological analogy, therefore, is purely secondary in Augustine's theology. The whole account is introduced by a discussion of divine incomprehensibility and of the difficulties of an intelligent faith, which leads Augustine to pose the following question: "by what likeness or comparison with known things can we believe, so that we may also love the God who is yet unknown?" (8.5). This little question, buried in the midst of *On the Trinity,* is in many ways the key to understanding the role of all of Augustine's discussion of the images of the Trinity, the point of which is to illuminate the content of faith and not to replace it. This is confirmed in book 15 of the work, where Augustine makes the point that, in view of God's greatness, all attempts to uncover traces of the Trinity in the creation are hopelessly flawed.

What is of more immediate significance for us is the question of the procession of the Holy Spirit, and here Augustine's influence on the Western theological tradition has again been enormous. The basic pneumatological claim made in *On the Trinity* is that the Spirit is something common to both Father and Son — namely, the bond of love between them. This is closely related to the idea that the trinitarian persons are constituted by relationships. The relationship of the Spirit to Father and Son is constituted by the procession of the Spirit, so that the two, relation and procession, are identical. The Spirit, then, having a relation to the Son, being the love of the Son or the gift of the Son to the Father, must therefore proceed from the Son as well as from the Father, whose love for the Son the Spirit is also. The Spirit therefore necessarily proceeds from both. Augustine is still aware that the fountainhead of the trinitarian persons is the Father, a point made explicitly in *On Faith and the Creed,* and so he adds the following qualification: Since the Son is begotten by the Father, he receives from the Father the capacity to breathe forth the Spirit. Therefore the Spirit proceeds "principally" from the Father, and mediately (though this is understood in a different sense than is the Eastern *per filium*) from the Son (15.17).

Augustine claims no ultimate authority for his views, and although his position in the North African church at the time of the writing of *On the Trinity* was unassailable, he simply presents his conclusions, in the main, for consideration by the wider church. The subsequent pneumatological tradition of the West, however, took a harder line on these matters. Beginning in Spain and southern Gaul, the notion that the Spirit proceeds from the Father *and the Son* was given the status of doctrinal definition through its insertion in the liturgy. The so-called Athanasian Creed, which dates from the very early sixth century, incorporates the idea (though not the technical term *filioque*).[22] Through the next five hundred years, liturgical use of the *filioque* was sporadic, even though the doctrine was defended; by 1014, however, we find it inserted on papal authority into the Western version of the Nicene Creed. By 1054, the schism of Latin West and Greek East, which happened as a result of the *filioque* doctrine, had taken place. There followed a sorry history of polemic and counter-polemic that, when combined with the marked chauvinism of the Christian West over against the East, makes the *filioque* controversy a matter of real division and bitterness for Eastern Christians even today.

A Theological Assessment of the *Filioque* Doctrine

The history of the *filioque* controversy has been written many times and need not be treated in detail here.[23] On the theological side, however, important issues are at stake in the whole matter. The most basic is clearly the question of trinitarian theology, and in particular the question of the role of the Holy Spirit in the trinitarian life. Different views here have implications for the way in which the *work* of the Holy Spirit is understood in Western and Eastern theology respectively. A major question of theological authority as understood in the Christian West and East is also at stake. That the *filioque* clause came to be introduced in the Latin version of the

22. J. N. D. Kelly, *Early Christian Creeds,* 3rd ed. (London: Longman, 1972), pp. 86-90.

23. See, e.g., the contributions of Dietrich Ritschl, "The History of the Filioque Controversy," and Michael Fahey, "Son and Spirit: Divergent Theologies between Constantinople and the West," in *Conflicts About the Holy Spirit,* ed. Hans Küng and Jürgen Moltmann (New York: Seabury Press, 1979), pp. 3ff. and 15ff.

Nicene Creed after 1014, purely on papal authority, is, for the East, the prime illustration of what is wrong with the ideal of the papacy as it evolved in the West. For the Christian East, authority is collegial, so that, quite apart from the important differences in trinitarian thought that divide the two traditions, the authoritarian manner in which the West has attempted to lord it over the East in this matter is totally without justification. Thus, for the East, while the *filioque* doctrine itself does not strictly depend upon such agreement, the fact that the whole church has never agreed that the *filioque* is necessary, or even defensible, means that the *filioque* as a creedal insertion is by nature schismatic.

Among the reasons why the *filioque* doctrine was adopted in parts of the West so soon after Augustine's death is one relating to a late form of Arianism that appeared in fifth- and sixth-century Spain.[24] The argument used against the Arians then was that the Son must be the equal of the Father, because like the Father, the Son gives the Spirit, and like the Father, the Son breathes forth the Spirit. It is interesting to note against this background the language used much later on to defend the *filioque* in the otherwise oppressively anti-Eastern *Decree for the Greeks* of the Council of Florence (1439), when Eastern and Western representatives met (in the end, unsuccessfully) to discuss the prospect of reunion: "We define that the explanatory words '*Filioque*' have been added in the Symbol legitimately and with good reason for the sake of clarifying the truth and under the impact of a real need at that time."[25] The East never accepted this statement, but in any case does it represent a worthwhile argument? If the point was to demonstrate that the Son is one substance with the Father because the Spirit proceeds from both, then the full deity of the Son is indeed established, but only, it would seem, at the expense of the full deity of the Spirit, who has no analogous function in the inner-trinitarian life. The Son is begotten of the Father only and is of one substance with the Father, as is evidenced by the doctrine of double procession, but what of the Spirit? If the logic of the

24. Fahey, "Son and Spirit," pp. 16-17.
25. *Decree for the Greeks*, in *The Christian Faith*, ed. J. Neuner and J. Dupuis, rev. ed. (New York: Alba House, 1982), §324.

argument is that to be consubstantial with the Father a trinitarian person must be the eternal origin of another, then we cannot extend the argument to the question of the status of the Spirit, who is no such thing. The Spirit was certainly never conceived to be such by the defenders of the *filioque*. The argument is thus profoundly unhelpful to the cause of pneumatology, whatever it may or may not establish in christology.

This criticism of the *filioque,* however, still leaves the insights of Augustine intact, and so we turn to consider the relative merits of the Augustinian position, which is at least a more consistent attempt to deal with the question of the doctrine of the Spirit on its own terms. The particular strengths of his position are related to the fact that, on the one hand, Augustine is able to develop a whole pneumatology of love, both inner-trinitarian and economic, which is satisfying to the mind and to the heart, and, on the other, that he does this in part by taking up the biblical theme of the Spirit as common to both the Father and the Son and using this as the key to the doctrine of the Spirit as a whole. We need to consider both of these themes together, and that all the more because no adequate doctrine of the Spirit can be formulated that does not do justice to the theme of love and to the theme that the Spirit is the Spirit of both Father and Son. This is not to say that these two together exhaust all pneumatological possibilities, however — an important point to which implicit reference has already been made.

It would be best here to begin with Augustine's trinitarian conclusion. The Spirit, he argues, is the bond of love between the Father and the Son, the mutual gift of each to the other, proceeding principally from the Father, since the Father is the "principle" of the Son, but also from the Son, who receives from the Father all that he is, including the capacity to be the co-principle, in his turn, of the Spirit. Two things are especially striking about this conception. First, despite Augustine's tendency to appropriate a very great deal in the economy of salvation to the Holy Spirit, the ultimate basis of the work of the Spirit in his understanding of the person of the Spirit suggests a certain priority of the Father-Son relation over everything else; indeed, strictly speaking, the Spirit *is* this Father-Son relation. Seen in this way, there seems to be nothing to prevent a consistent Augustinian theologian from gathering the whole of what is understood under the heading of pneumatology into a theology of the first and second persons. In fact, this is what has sometimes happened in the history of theology in the Christian West; once one has said what needs to be said about the Father and the Son, in short, there is little else that remains, since the Spirit can theoretically be comprehended in terms of them.

Second, however, a larger difficulty looms. In the early work, *On Faith and the Creed,* we have seen that Augustine speaks of the Holy Spirit as if he were the common divinity of the Father and the Son.[26] The obvious question to ask here is what distinguishes the Holy Spirit from the divine substance. Augustine appears, in fact, to conflate the doctrine of the Holy Spirit proper with the Johannine statement, "God is Spirit." One might expect that his later clarification of the status of trinitarian relationality over against divine substance in book 5 of *On the Trinity* would make such confusion impossible in his mature treatment of the problem, but in fact the difficulty remains. On the one hand, what is common between the Father and Son is encapsulated, for Augustine, in the technical term *consubstantiality,* deriving from Nicea; on the other hand, the Holy Spirit serves precisely the same function in Augustine's trinitarian conceptuality.

Much has been made in discussions of Augustine's trinitarian thought of what is characterized as the priority of the one divine substance over the persons; Jürgen Moltmann, for example, condemns Augustine for his tendency to modalism, according to which the threefold relations of the Father, Son, and Spirit are swallowed up by an excessive emphasis on the *una substantia.*[27] There is, however, little to warrant such a wholesale dismissal of Augustine on these grounds, since so much is evidently made of the relations of the persons at the very center of what Augustine has to say. Nevertheless, the limitations of Augustinian trinitarian theology *do* reveal themselves in the detail of his doctrine of the Spirit, where the question of the underlying unity of substance is seen even in

26. Augustine, *On Faith and the Creed,* 19.
27. Jürgen Moltmann, *The Trinity and the Kingdom of God,* trans. Margaret Kohl (London: SCM Press, 1981), pp. 16-17.

the development of the supposed distinctiveness of the third person, not as a distinct third so much as the oneness of the first two, and in the overcoming of the perceived *threat* of plurality in God. The irony is that this problem in Augustine's theology derives from what began as one of the strengths of his position, namely, the seriousness with which he takes the biblical themes of the Spirit as the Spirit common to the Father and the Son, and the Spirit as the Spirit of love.

Moltmann's argument is more justified in the case of the psychological analogy, which is used by Augustine himself as an aid to understanding and then finally abandoned, but which subsequently becomes virtually a point of faith in medieval thought. Thomas Aquinas, for example, uses the psychological analogy as evidence in an attempt to explain why it is that there are three persons, and not four, in the triune God — why it is, in short, that the divine multiplicity ends with the third person.[28] The characteristic acts of a spiritual substance, he tells us, are those of knowing and loving, so that once we have exhausted these possibilities in the spiritual substance "God," arriving in this way at the persons of the Son and the Holy Spirit, the triune identity is complete.

Especially when used in this way, however, the psychological analogy appears to establish the unity of consciousness in God rather more effectively than might be prudent. Problems emerge at the points where real relationship between the persons of the Trinity come into view — in Jesus' obedience to the Father, or in his being led by the Spirit into the wilderness. Within the terms of the psychological analogy, where one consciousness is in view, can we conceive of understanding as praying to or obeying memory, in any sense? There can be tension between the different psychological faculties, or conflict within the one consciousness — we might know better, for example, but we still fall in love — but intersubjectivity of the sort we see in the Gethsemane narratives of the Gospels is not possible in the one consciousness, not even in the case of the split personality. There remains, of course, the question whether real intersubjectivity of this sort ought to be projected from the life of Christ into the life of the Trinity in itself — I shall

28. Thomas Aquinas, *Summa Theologiae*, 1a.27.5; 28.4.

argue in favor of this in detail later in this book — but there is little doubt that such intersubjectivity is not possible if there is in God the Father, Son, and Holy Spirit one consciousness that is simply present in three successive phases of some sort. It is the impossibility of this to which Moltmann's objection can legitimately be said to refer.

Some account of the role of the *filioque* doctrine in Protestant theology is also needed, for here the *filioque* doctrine has been used to tie the *work* of the Spirit to that of the Son in a more defensive way, with less reference to a developed trinitarian understanding. From the beginning, the classical Reformers wished to steer a middle course between Rome and the radicals of the Reformation movement. An important feature of their strategy was to tie the work of the Spirit to the Word, by which was meant chiefly the Word of Scripture in the first instance. The fact that the Spirit's work was to bear witness to the Word meant to the Reformers that there is no fellowship with God that can be detached from the Word of the gospel written and preached; thus the unbiblical claims of Rome and the spiritual "revelations" of the radicals were alike excluded from the sphere of legitimacy. Since the written Word derives from the eternal Word, however, the connection between Spirit and Word must also pertain to the Trinity itself. The *filioque* doctrine was taken to be the guarantor of this link, for it implies that the Spirit can never be without the Word, since the Spirit from all eternity is none other than the Word's, the Spirit proceeding from the Word and the Father together.

More will be said in the next chapter about the content of Reformation pneumatology, and specifically about the Word-Spirit connection in the theologies of the classical Reformers. For the present, we may simply say that there are alternatives to the *filioque* as proof of this Word-Spirit connection, and that one need not attempt to establish an explicitly trinitarian doctrine on such grounds. One could assert the connection of the Spirit to the Word just as easily by means of a strong doctrine of trinitarian *perichoresis*, the mutual indwelling of each of the persons in each of the others, for example, as by means of the *filioque*. The Protestant defenders of the *filioque* thus tried to build too much upon too slender a foundation. Moreover, it even has to be asked if such a defense of the *filioque* actually achieves something desirable in the first place. The degenerate forms of what might be called the spirituality of the Word are well known. Yet a theology of this sort does violence to the word of Scripture itself concerning the Spirit. The Word and the Spirit work together and can never be separated, but the Spirit cannot be comprehensively subordinated to the Word, as in much of the Protestant tradition, without damage to the Christian gospel itself. Therefore, while it is clear that there are pneumatological excesses to be avoided and that a doctrine of the Spirit is needed that does justice to the Spirit-Son relation, we may conclude that it is neither necessary nor obvious that this can be adequately achieved through the *filioque.*

The Eastern Position

The *filioque* controversy acquired fatal momentum in 1014 with the addition of the *filioque* clause to the creed, but the beginnings of the crisis can be dated more accurately to the time of the patriarch Photius of Constantinople, who engaged in the latter half of the ninth century in a prolonged political and theological struggle with Rome largely connected with the *filioque* doctrine.[29] In his theology, which has become a normative source for the Christian East, Photius argues that the Western understanding of the double procession of the Spirit from the Father and Son introduces into the Trinity the alien notion of a Father-Son dyad, which he nicknames *huiopatria* ("Son-Fatherhood"). Over against this, and in keeping with the theology of the Cappadocians and their successors in the East, Photius argues that there is one sole source of both Son and Spirit in the Trinity, the Father, whose distinctive property it is to be the unoriginate origin of the other two persons; these in their turn are distinct from one another and from the Father by virtue of their different "modes of origin" *(tropoi hyparxeos),* begetting and spiration. The formula coined by Photius to define the proces-

29. Cf. the contributions of Markos Orphanos and Dietrich Ritschl to *Spirit of God, Spirit of Christ,* ed. Lukas Vischer, Faith and Order Paper no. 103 (Geneva: World Council of Churches; London: SPCK, 1981), pp. 21ff. and 46ff.

sion of the Holy Spirit over against Western theology was accordingly that the Spirit proceeds "from the Father alone." Though never added to the creed in the East, the word "alone" as used here has ever since been taken to be authoritative by most Eastern theologians.

The key to understanding the Eastern position lies in its conception of God the Father. There is a much stronger sense in the Christian East than in the Christian West that the Father is himself the principle of unity in the Trinity; as the one source of the Son and Spirit, the Father, in effect, and not the Spirit, is the unifying bond between the three. Although Augustine, who knows that the Father has a certain rightful priority among the three, argues that the Spirit must proceed "principally" from the Father, both he and practically the whole of the Western tradition have a tendency to see the unity of the three as a function of the *una substantia*. The East does not deny the unity of the divine *ousia*, naturally, but in practice the East tends to place less emphasis on it than the West because of the role given the Father in Eastern trinitarian theology. Furthermore, the East tends to make the dynamic, relational unity of the Father with the Son and the Spirit as important a principle of unity as the one *ousia*. This relational unity derives ultimately from the Father's role as the eternal origin of the other persons.

Judged from the Augustinian standpoint that predominates in the Western tradition, such a theology seems to leave a very significant question unanswered. Presupposing that all trinitarian relations are identical with the processions of the persons (the Western view) implies that the procession of the Spirit from the Father alone leaves the Spirit with no relation to the Son. This clearly stands in tension with the biblical theme of the Spirit as the Spirit of the Son and of the Father, and leaves us, it is alleged, with the danger of a mysticism of the Spirit without any foundation in or relation to christology. In fact, of course, the Eastern tradition is perfectly able to speak of the eternal relation between Spirit and Son. This is one of the functions of the distinctive Eastern trinitarian doctrine of the divine "energies." The energies are in effect the livingness of God — Father, Son, and Spirit. The energies also crucially touch the creation by grace in a way in which the inaccessible divine *ousia* cannot and does not. The doctrine of the energies is foreign to Western theology, but it is of great importance in the East, providing a theoretical foundation both for communion with God and for much of what needs to be said about the Trinity itself.

Although the doctrine of the energies is not derived strictly from Scripture, neither is the theology of divine *ousia* or *hypostasis*. What we can say is that this third possibility for speaking about the persons provided by the category of energies allows a more differentiated approach to the question of the Trinity than is possible in Western theology. The persons have relations here that are not reducible to the processions; one obvious field of contemporary theological thought that this bears upon is the social doctrine of the Trinity, which depends precisely upon this possibility, and which inevitably tends to speak of *some* such thing as the energies, even when unaware of the possibilities the explicit Eastern conception affords. Over against the Western medieval view that there are merely four real relations in the Trinity, begetting, being begotten, breathing, and being breathed, any social doctrine of the Trinity positively requires that there be other available categories of relation.

One of the key factors in the development of Western understanding of Eastern thought on this point in the twentieth century was the Russian diaspora following the Bolshevik revolution; in France, above all, a succession of Russian Orthodox theologians, writing in French, made the Eastern position accessible in a way that it simply had not been before. Crucially, however, the Russian émigrés in question also often attempted to engage creatively with Western theology and, to a lesser extent, with the theological questions posed by modernity, with the result that their theology is more than simply a repetition of old formulae (still the weakness of much of the theology of the Christian East) but offers a genuine advance beyond the older tradition while still preserving its insights. Foremost among these have been such theologians as Nicolas Berdyaev and, more crucially for us, Paul Evdokimov.[30] The Romanian

---

30. The well-known critic of the West, Vladimir Lossky, also belongs here, although he himself is much more of a reactionary vis-à-vis the *filioque* than many. Nevertheless, Lossky's achievement — to have made certain themes from the East clear to a wide theological audience for the first time — is very real.

theologian Dumitru Staniloae should also be placed among this number as a figure of major importance for ecumenical dialogue in general and ecumenical pneumatology in particular, and perhaps also, more recently, the Greek theologian John Zizioulas.

Evdokimov will here serve as the representative of such creativity in Eastern pneumatology. In an important little book, *L'Esprit Saint dans la tradition orthodoxe,* he maintains that while the question of the procession of the Holy Spirit has dominated pneumatology for a thousand years, the reality must be judged to be more complex than the inflexible filioquism on the one hand and monopatrism on the other that have predominated in traditional polemics.[31] The alternative, he argues, is to recognize that the trinitarian relations are indeed fully *trinitarian* — that is, that in the divine life, there is a relation of interdependence and mutuality among the three persons, including between the Spirit and the Son. Building on the theology of the divine *energeia,* Evdokimov goes so far as to argue that the term *filioque* might be acceptable from the Eastern point of view if the technical term "procession" were abandoned when the *filioque* is affirmed, and also, significantly, if a reciprocity of the Spirit and Son were to be secured by the simultaneous affirmation of a parallel *spirituque* formula in speaking about the Son.[32] In the end the argument is that each trinitarian person must be understood in his simultaneous relations to the other two, and that at the level of the energies the relations are always *triple.* Evdokimov suggests that the Trinity might be represented pictorially as a triangle inscribed in a circle, with the Father at the top and the Son and Spirit at its base angles; while generation and procession are represented in the triangle, the reciprocal "energetic" relations of the persons are represented in the circle, in which movement occurs in both directions.[33]

While it is difficult to make any final judgment about this Eastern view, it is clear that the standard Western criticism that the distinction between essence and energies in this form threatens to

31. Paul Evdokimov, *L'Esprit Saint dans la tradition orthodoxe* (Paris: Cerf, 1969), p. 69.

32. Evdokimov, *L'Esprit Saint dans la tradition orthodoxe,* p. 71.

33. Evdokimov, *L'Esprit Saint dans la tradition orthodoxe,* p. 48.

reduce the Spirit-Son relationship to a second, inferior level of the trinitarian being cannot be sustained, since the divine energies are as irreducibly eternal as the divine essence. It would appear in any case that if such an obvious criticism could be made, the Eastern tradition itself would have seen the point long ago. The real question is rather one concerning the foreign conceptuality employed in the Eastern distinction, in the sense that this conceptuality, and, indeed, much of the trinitarian theology it presupposes, is alien to Western theology. In fact, the problem that we have in attempting to resolve the theological confrontation caused by the *filioque* resides not so much in the *filioque* itself as in the conflict between the more general trinitarian positions of the West and the East. Yves Congar, who has undertaken a lengthy study of this question, has argued that we simply cannot expect the two trinitarian traditions ever to agree, since the fundamental presuppositions underlying the way in which they deal with the question differ. Many of the greatest minds of the East and West have labored over this problem, without success, for well over a thousand years. All that can be hoped for, he argues, is mutual acceptance and toleration, grounded in the conviction that both traditions attempt in their own ways and with integrity to articulate the mystery of God the Father, Son, and Holy Spirit.[34]

Perhaps this judgment is unnecessarily pessimistic, although Congar is a theologian of the Holy Spirit to reckon with, a man whose conclusions ought to be taken with some seriousness. The fact is, however, that theologians like Evdokimov, who are clearly in the business of building bridges, have gone a great way toward a more fruitful dialogue between East and West than Congar, strangely, seems to think possible. Whether or not either tradition will see fit to explore such possibilities further on an institutional level, and whether over time our theological traditions will become more mutually transparent, is another matter, but that is something that we must leave to time and to the work of others.

34. Yves Congar, *I Believe in the Holy Spirit,* trans. David Smith, 3 vols. (London: Geoffrey Chapman; New York: Seabury Press, 1983), vol. 3, p. 201.

4. The Reformation Tradition

The Word and the Spirit

We begin here, as we must, with one of the great themes of sixteenth-century theology and of the whole of the tradition stemming from the Reformation — the relation between the Word and the Spirit. One cannot discuss either the spirituality of the Reformation or its doctrine of the Holy Spirit as such apart from this theme. If the doctrine of the *deity* of the Spirit is the central concern of the fathers of the fourth century, and if the *filioque* preoccupies medieval pneumatologists, then the intrinsic connection of the work of the Spirit in the church with the doctrine of the Word of God as written and preached constitutes the distinctive emphasis of the pneumatology of the Reformation.

A new emphasis on the Word of God characterized the whole of the Reformation era. There was, for example, a rise in literacy, which coincided with the invention of the printing press and made the latter a source of great commercial wealth as well as just a "new technology." Together with this, the rediscovery of the classics of Greek and Roman antiquity amid the culture of Renaissance humanism, and in particular the return to "sources" that was so characteristic of humanism, made the return to the *biblical* source that was so distinctive of the Reformation movement more than just a religious theme. Rather, the Reformation of the sixteenth century was a *modern* movement that drew inspiration from the general culture and learning of the time. It is no accident, therefore, that the earliest heroes of the Reformation were, when all is said and done, not visionaries or social revolutionaries or even religious mystics, but scholars and Bible translators.

This is not to say, of course, that the Reformation was not also a movement that involved real spiritual renewal and met a real religious need in the peoples it influenced. The church system of the late medieval era was notoriously corrupt, while its theology — rather like the academic theology of our own day — did nothing for religion either at the popular level or among the more educated of the time. The mass of distinctions and "insofars" that late scholastic theology had become, when allied with the philosophical disaster of nominalism, in which not even theological words were taken to convey a content beyond human convention, served only to heighten the sense that the old religious system had run out of vital energy and was in near-terminal decline. Against this, the vigorous, populist, realist approach of the Reformers in their essentially biblical theologies could only prevail, whatever the weight of tradition might have been.

A great deal is sometimes made in accounts of the Reformation of the development of the modern concept of the person, and of the freedom of the individual conscience, as central to its appeal and dynamic. One is asked to conceive of the sixteenth century as giving birth to a consciousness centered in the individual as arbiter of religious truth. This is, however, a misconception, for the individual was of far less importance to the culture and thought of the Reformation than was the return to the Bible as the fundamental "source." Protestantism today badly misrepresents the nature of its own project when it sees its original historical task as the enlightening of the individual. Although this later came to be a major theme in Protestant thought, and in particular in the theology of the Enlightenment, the theme of the individual conscience as all important is virtually impossible to find in the work of the theologians of the Reformation itself.

Thus if we were to present the Reformation systematically or schematically in terms of its view of experience of the Spirit, we would have to speak, not of freedom or of conscience, but quite simply and directly of a book, and of that book as containing the address of God to the world. The Christian's faith, as John Calvin would come to say, is not in God or in Christ directly, but in God as perceived through his scriptural promises, and in Christ as clothed in the gospel.[1] The spirituality of the Reformation, by which the divine presence is discovered and expressed and lived with, is above all else a spirituality of the Word, a spirituality that has the Bible at its center and in a very real sense at its heart. That one encounters God here, distinctively and authentically, in the simple reading or preaching or hearing of the text, constitutes the great burden of the Reformation approach to the claims of religion and to the substance of the religious life. One of the greatest of modern Catholic theologians, the Swiss-German Hans Urs von Balthasar, recognizes this when he writes of the vital sense of the "word-character of revelation" in Protestantism, and of its ideal spirituality as that of the "hearer of the Word."[2]

The centrality of the Word in Reformation theology is matched by the importance attached to the theme of the Spirit as the inner witness to the truth that God has revealed. John Calvin puts the matter as follows: Just as God alone is the only fit witness of himself in the written Word, so also that Word does not come to be accepted in the human heart without being "sealed by the inward testimony of the Spirit."[3] Luther expresses the intimacy of the Spirit-Word relation even more strongly, though always with reference also to the sacraments as well as the outward ordinances of God: The Reformation radicals, he complains, speak incessantly about the Spirit, and then proceed to do away with "the very bridge by which the Holy Spirit can come . . . namely, the outward ordinances of God like the bodily sign of baptism and the preached Word of

---

1. John Calvin, *Institutes of the Christian Religion,* ed. John T. McNeill, trans. Ford Lewis Battles, 2 vols. (Philadelphia: Westminster Press, 1960), 3.2.6.

2. Hans Urs von Balthasar, *Prayer,* trans. Graham Harrison (San Francisco: Ignatius Press, 1986), p. 28.

3. Calvin, *Institutes,* 1.7.4.

God."[4] This is not the only theme to be found in Reformation pneumatology, as we shall see, but this link between the work of the Spirit and the gift of faith, seen as a response to the Word of the gospel, is fundamental. The point is that faith, by which we appropriate the promises of God, is the gift of the Spirit. Because of the centrality of faith, however, the implication is that the main work of the Spirit must be to create faith in or to give faith to those who believe. Calvin makes this point quite explicitly at the beginning of his lengthy discussion of the Holy Spirit: "the principal work of the Holy Spirit," he argues, is faith.[5]

As is often the case in theology, the theological position thus presented, and which now seems so conventional, is one that in its time was carved out amid much controversy. The sources of this controversy, as has already been indicated, were the Reformation radicals on the one side and their Catholic opponents on the other. We will deal with each of these in turn.

In his study of the radical Reformation, George H. Williams has highlighted a series of issues that lay at the heart of the conflict between radicals ranging from Carlstadt to Müntzer and the magisterial Reformers. The basic thrust of the position of the radicals is to distinguish between the "outer Word," which can be anything from Scripture itself to the words of Jesus or even the historical Jesus himself, and the "inner Word," by which is meant the underlying principle of these, but that principle apprehended subjectively and inwardly, and thus by the power of the Spirit. The latter is held to be more basic than the former, so that it becomes the criterion by which the former is judged. Carlstadt's statement of his case is programmatic: "As far as I am concerned, I do not need the outward witness. I want to have the testimony of the Spirit within me, as it was promised by Christ."[6] For his part, the extremist Müntzer went so far as to propose that the written Scriptures have a merely preparatory role; they slay the believer so that he

---

4. *WA* 18:137, quoted by George Huntston Williams, *The Radical Reformation*, 3rd ed. (Kirksville, MO: Sixteenth Century Journal Publishers, 1992), p. 1249.

5. Calvin, *Institutes*, 3.1.4.

6. Carlstadt, *Vom greulichen Missbrauch des heiligen Abendmahls*, quoted by Williams, *The Radical Reformation*, p. 1249.

may finally come to respond truly to the Spirit and so to adhere to the inner Word.[7] Thus the outward Word must be left behind by the mature believer, who is the temple of the Holy Spirit, and who therefore no longer requires the outward helps on which Luther placed such emphasis.

The stress Luther placed on the working of the Spirit through the channels of the Word and the sacraments as "visible words" is best understood as a response to the exaggerated claims of the radicals, or the "spiritualists," as he called them at times. In fact, as Gordon Rupp has noted, such interest as there was in the Spirit in the early years of the Reformation was entirely derivative of the concern for a right doctrine of the Word. Pneumatology as such is not a primary motif either in Luther or in the theology of the Reformation radicals. "Despite Luther's complaint that with them all is 'Geist, Geist, Geist . . .' they are not obsessed with pneumatology, but more concerned with the contrast between the 'outer' and 'inner Word,' or between 'spirit' and 'letter,' or the 'inward' and 'outer man.' "[8] The importance of the theme of how one comes to "hear" the Word of God, and what it is that constitutes that Word, is hardly surprising, particularly given the political and religious excesses of the radicals; Müntzer himself became a notorious outlaw, inciting the peasants to revolt in order to usher in the end of the world, with all its suffering and sorrows. One can only note how sane the position of the classical Reformers appears by comparison: To say that Christianity is spiritual does not commit us to the absurd implication that everything outward is unspiritual.

On the other hand, Rupp contends that the polarization of the debate between the two camps also had a negative result. The "close alliance of Word and Spirit became pressed by controversy and misunderstanding into an antithesis, until on the one side the Word approaches equation with 'pure doctrine' and the Spirit becomes the cover for human subjectivism."[9] When pressed to

---

7. Quoted by Williams, *The Radical Reformation,* p. 1250.

8. Gordon Rupp, "Word and Spirit in the First Years of the Reformation," *Archiv für Reformationsgeschichte* 49 (1958): 13.

9. Rupp, "Word and Spirit," p. 13.

extremes, in other words, the ideal of holding the Word and the Spirit together resulted in a dichotomy between the two, so that subjectivity tended to be excluded in favor of the objective Word. George H. Williams, similarly, is left wondering how much has been lost as a result, the excesses of the radicals notwithstanding, since in his view we have here the reason for the Reformation tendency to identify the scriptural Word and the experienced Spirit in terms of doctrine (the Lutherans), or doctrine and polity (the Reformed), or a purified national church under the Word and the royal headship of the episcopate (the Anglicans).[10] Experiential religion, in short, is thus made peripheral to the theology of the various mainline Reformation traditions.

At best, however, this is a caricature, for there is far more to be said of Reformation pneumatology than this. Calvin, for example, has a rich doctrine of the Holy Spirit and attaches great systematic importance to "piety," which is indicative of his great interest in what we are calling religious experience. But perhaps the best illustration of this would be Luther's 1520 exposition of the Apostles' Creed, which is repeated later in the *Deutsch Catechism* and the *Kleiner Catechismus*. Here, Luther comments on the third article as follows:

> I believe, not only that the Holy Spirit is the only true God together with the Father and the Son; but also that, apart from the operation of the Holy Spirit, no one can come to God, nor receive any of the blessings effected through Christ, His life, cross, and death, and whatever else is ascribed to Him. Through Him, the Father and the Son move me and all others that are His. Through the Holy Spirit, the Father and the Son rouse, call, and draw us; and, through and in Christ, give us life and holiness, and make us spiritually-minded. Thus the Holy Spirit brings us to the Father, for He it is by whom the Father, through Christ and in Christ, does all things, and gives life to all.[11]

10. Williams, *The Radical Reformation*, pp. 1254-55.

11. Martin Luther, *A Short Exposition of the Decalogue, the Apostles' Creed and the Lord's Prayer*, in *Reformation Writings of Martin Luther*, trans. Bertram Lee Wolff (London: Lutterworth Press, 1952), vol. 1, p. 87.

We see here the characteristic move made in Reformation pneumatology: Emphasis is shifted explicitly away from the doctrine of the deity of the Spirit, though it is obviously acknowledged, to the real point of interest, the doctrine of the work of the Spirit in the subjective appropriation of the content of the gospel of grace by the believer. There is no pure reduction of Spirit to Word, whether outer or inner, but instead a fairly expansive view of the Spirit as mediating the incorporation of the believer into Christ, so that a theology of the Head and members of Christ's body emerges, in keeping with the strongly christocentric character of the theology of the Reformation.

The real situation is thus more complex than we might initially have been led to suppose, but we might summarize as follows. First, the challenge presented by the Reformation radicals in their doctrine of the inner Word, apprehended by the Spirit, to the mainstream Reformation doctrine of the Word of God as publicly revealed in the Bible leads to the assertion of the link between the work of the Spirit and public discourse about the Bible. A plausible case could even be made that this, as much as their humanist suspicion of medieval exegesis, underlies the general tendency of the magisterial Reformers to opt for the literal sense of the Bible in exegesis, for this makes the Word of God all the more public and all the less inward. Second, and conversely, this public discourse can only affect the heart, or rise to the level of faith, by the inward work of the Holy Spirit. Since faith is lodged in the divine promise as revealed in the Word of God, and since faith is a gift of grace, effected by the Spirit, faith has a certain primacy in all Reformation discussion of the Spirit. Third, the doctrine of the inspiration of the Bible is thus highlighted, so that its importance extends beyond a simple concern for the authority of the Bible as the foundation of faith and practice; it goes to the roots of the whole of the spiritual life, and to the event of faith itself. This helps to explain the special place of the doctrine in Protestantism, even at the popular level. Finally, however, despite the fact that this view of the Spirit has the potential to degenerate into a theology in which the Spirit might appear not merely to be understood in relation to the Word but to be straitjacketed by the Word, Reformation pneumatology is open in principle to the richer theme of mystical union with Christ. This theme will be developed further in the next section.

The other side of Reformation controversy that forms the background and context for its doctrine of the Holy Spirit is, of course, the protest against Rome. Here, however, the pneumatological question is primarily ecclesiological, and therefore "objective" rather than "subjective" in character. A series of questions relating to this arise. Does the church's authority underlie the authority of the Bible, which is such a central theme in Reformation theology, or is the Bible the immediate instrument of the Holy Spirit himself? Is the Holy Spirit as the gift of grace mediated through the church, or is the Spirit in a more fundamental sense the Lord of the church? Does the Spirit work in the church in such a way as to make a continuing revelation possible?

All of these are facets of the one question, or the one problem, of how Spirit and church are related, and how this relation affects Christian faith, self-understanding, and practice in the Reformation context. When Calvin, for example, argues that Scripture is "self-authenticating," in the sense that "the certainty it deserves with us, it attains by the testimony of the Spirit,"[12] his point is designed not just to exclude the notion that biblical authority rests on human argument or proof. It is also a response to the Catholic idea that biblical authority rests on the authority of Christ bestowed on the church itself, which initially produced the Bible, which continues to recognize it to be authoritative, and which thus speaks with the authority of Christ entrusted to it. The argument from canonicity is summarily dismissed: According to Calvin, since the church is "built on the foundation of the prophets and apostles" (Eph. 2:20), the authority of apostles and prophets cannot rest on that of the church. The church, Calvin argues, does indeed give its seal of approval to the voice of God speaking in the Scriptures, but it does not thereby validate or authenticate what God has said, as if it were in itself something questionable (1.7.2).

The issue here is again that of teaching authority, therefore, and with teaching authority we arrive once more at the central notion of the Word of God. Calvin's position, and the consistent position of all the classical Reformers, is that the claim that the

12. Calvin, *Institutes,* 1.8.5. Subsequent references will be given parenthetically in the text.

church is governed by the Holy Spirit through the bishops and councils, and that the teaching of the latter is authoritative and infallible, even when it conflicts with the teaching of Scripture, cannot be sustained religiously or rationally. The accusation is that this effectively locates the authority of the church outside God's Word and instead vests it in the frequently corrupt or misguided ecclesiastical powers that be — those very powers who, according to the Reformers, had utterly corrupted the true teaching of the Word of God.[13]

The "marks of the church," which for both the Lutheran and the Reformed traditions are constituted by the faithful preaching of the Word of God and the right administration of the sacraments, must also be considered in this context. If the Holy Spirit is in any sense at work uniquely in the church, as opposed to the world — a point that is axiomatic for the magisterial Reformers — then the question of where the true church is to be found must be central to their theology in general and to their pneumatology in particular. At this point, however, pneumatology is subordinate to the Word of God. One of the interesting and important things about the Reformation marks of the church is that nothing is made in them of religious experience, or even of the "new birth." The latter is no doubt assumed, but assumed in the precise sense that where the Word of God is rightly preached and the sacraments properly administered, everything else will follow — faith, religious conversion, justification, sanctification, the life of prayer, Christian discipleship in obedience, or whatever else might be mentioned in this context. This is one of the important features of the whole of the

---

13. It must be said, however, that although the Reformers wish to distance themselves from the idea that the Holy Spirit's authority is mediated through the leaders of the church, rather than through the Word of God as contained in Holy Scripture, they are not entirely successful in their claim. The fact is that, in some cases, it is necessary for them to assert a version of the Catholic position: that there have been certain people, namely, the prophets and apostles, who were "sure and genuine scribes of the Holy Spirit," and whose ministry was to write what would be considered by others to be the oracles of God. The most that can be said is that their ministry was unique, and that it does not continue. Since the canon and so the content of revelation is now closed, the ministry of others can only be "to teach what is provided and sealed in the Holy Scriptures." Calvin, *Institutes*, 4.8.9.

magisterial Reformation movement as distinct from the radical Reformation and from some of its heirs: The canons of authenticity, and the measure of God's presence, are objective and public, rather than subjective and experiential. Because of the Reformation controversies between the extremists in the Reformation camp itself, and because of the polemic against a doctrine of continuing inspiration and revelation on the Catholic side, all possible subjective or experiential criteria for the true presence of God and the true people of God seem to be deliberately excluded.

One of the interesting and important implications of this for the doctrine of the Holy Spirit in Reformation theology is that the Spirit can only be named or known, and his presence in some sense validated, by reference to other things. If experience of the Spirit comes through the written and preached Word, and through the visible words of the sacraments — if these are, in Luther's vivid terms, the "very bridge by which the Holy Spirit can come" — then it is pointless to attempt to speak of the Spirit in any other way. Or so it would seem, unless an alternative space in which pneumatology could have developed in the Reformation context can be identified. We turn to this question in the next two sections, but not without noting the tendency of much of Protestantism to remain at this first level, where the Spirit and the Word are so tied as to be virtually indistinguishable.

Justification and the Spirit

It is possible to understand the Reformation in a number of ways. It can, for example, be seen as the outworking of northern humanism's return to biblical sources, or as an assertion of political autonomy on the part of emerging northern European nation-states, or as a redefinition of the nature and structure of the church. Each of these factors is undoubtedly important, but for those most intimately involved the great issue at the center of the Reformation was the doctrine of justification by faith. It was for the sake of this doctrine that Luther risked everything in his break with Rome. Later, John Calvin, the great systematizer of Reformation theology, summarized its importance in his *Institutes of the Christian Religion;*

the doctrine of justification, he claims, is nothing less than "the main hinge on which religion turns" (3.11.2).

We saw in Chapter 3 that Latin theology, following Augustine, understands justification partly in christological and partly in pneumatological terms. In baptism, not only are original and actual sin remitted by the merits of Christ, but by the gift of the Holy Spirit sufficient grace to provide for holy living is granted to the faithful. Clearly, this gift must be nurtured so that there is development throughout life in obedience to God and in charity, but fundamentally the Western Catholic tradition understands justification as a process in which human beings are *made righteous* in a concrete way. While insisting that grace is given by God, in the sense that this concrete righteousness has its source in the free gift of the Spirit, Western theology before the Reformation consistently sees justification in these terms. One might say that in the end there is no clear distinction drawn in the Latin tradition between justification and sanctification; although different metaphors, there is an inner unity between them, in the sense that they are seen as referring to the same reality.

The Reformation preserved intact the patristic and medieval teaching on the *person* of the Spirit, but brought about a major shift in the theology of the *work* of the Holy Spirit in this respect. Much has been said already concerning the Reformers' opposition to the pneumatic movements known collectively as the radical Reformation and their resulting emphasis on the link between the Spirit and the Word. There was little that was genuinely new in this, however, for the subordination of the Spirit to the Word, particularly in the form of the teaching of the church, was standard in Western theology. The Reformation doctrine of justification, however, involving as it did a denial of the identity of justification and sanctification, actually constitutes something of much more far-reaching significance. Indeed, the Reformation-era debate concerning justification involved such important pneumatological issues that it is fair to say that, together with the *filioque*, the role of the Holy Spirit in justification constitutes the key pneumatological point of controversy in the whole of Western theology.

One of the goals of Reformation teaching was to overcome one of the most significant problems arising in late medieval piety, where too much attention was focused on the effects of grace in the moral life of the one justified, largely as a result of the nominalist emphasis on the finite individual, and too little on the fact that justifying grace is precisely *grace*, and therefore a free gift of God. It was this problem that lay at the root of Luther's allegation that Roman teaching had become Pelagian. Seen in these terms, the Reformation movement was an obvious response to a genuine theological difficulty. In detaching the doctrine of sanctification from the doctrine of justification, an attempt was made to focus attention away from the believer — and in particular from his or her "works" — and onto the grace of God; works, and therefore the doctrine of sanctification, were secondary. In adopting such a view, however, the Reformers initiated a profound change in the understanding of the work of the Spirit in the Christian life. Although there are certain definite strengths in the new conception, it also results in a certain displacement of the Spirit from the center of the scheme of salvation. Rather than being the agent of renewal by which we are made righteous, the Spirit becomes the means by which we come to Christ, who alone justifies, and only secondarily the agent of moral renewal — a moral renewal that is located only at the periphery of soteriological theory.

Luther's doctrine of justification is generally understood in terms of a Pauline reassertion of faith over works; justification by faith, or by faith *alone*, as Luther famously put it, became the key slogan of the Reformation movement. What does this involve? First, justification is here defined as a forensic declaration of righteousness, rather than as a process of being made righteous. The change is one of status rather than of nature. Second, as already noted, justification is deliberately distinguished from sanctification, even though the first leads necessarily to the second in experience. Third, that which justifies is the righteousness of Christ, a righteousness that is described as "alien" to the sinner, precisely because it is the righteousness of *Christ* rather than the intrinsic righteousness of the one being justified. The justified sinner is therefore at one and the same time both sinful in his or her own intrinsic being and yet righteous by virtue of inclusion in Christ.

The key concept used to explicate these aspects of the doctrine of justification in Reformation theology is that of "imputation," which is derived from the Pauline forensic term *logizomai* of Romans 4, and which is asserted by the Reformers, often without due explanation, over against the scholastic notion of "infused" righteousness. According to Luther, justification is freely promised to us by God and cannot be acquired by merit. The manner by which it is received is faith, which is laying hold of the promise of Christ's righteousness for salvation. Alister McGrath rightly argues that though the technical notion of imputation is not Luther's own preference — for he tended to use relational language of union with Christ rather than legal language at this point — it nevertheless derives directly from Luther's theology.[14]

Imputation became the keystone of the Lutheran doctrine of justification through Luther's colleague Philipp Melanchthon, who was the primary mover in systematizing Luther's theological insights. In his *Loci Communes* of 1555, Melanchthon speaks of justification and imputation in the following terms:

> Although in this mortal life believers have a spark [of righteousness in themselves], the gospel nevertheless preaches to us the justification of *Christ*, of the *Mediator* between God and us, and says that the Mediator's entire obedience, from his Incarnation until the Resurrection, is the true justification which is pleasing to God, and is the merit for us. God forgives our sins, and accepts us, in that he imputes righteousness to us for the sake of the Son, although we are still weak and sinful. We must, however, accept this imputed righteousness with faith.[15]

Along with the concept of imputation, one of the interesting things about this statement is the phrase "from his Incarnation until the Resurrection," which indicates that Melanchthon's theology involves something more than justification on the basis of the cross. The cross is obviously central to the whole soteriological scheme,

14. Alister McGrath, *Iustitia Dei* (Cambridge: Cambridge University Press, 1986), vol. 2, p. 14.

15. Philipp Melanchthon, *Loci Communes 1555*, ch. 13, in Clyde L. Manschrenck, ed. and trans., *Melanchthon on Christian Doctrine* (New York: Oxford University Press, 1965), p. 161.

but it would be better to say that Melanchthon's soteriology, like Luther's, is incarnational, and that the righteousness by which we are justified is found in Christ in his *whole* life of obedience.

With characteristic clarity, Calvin for his part defines justification as a two-sided event. It involves on the one hand the nonimputation of sin, or forgiveness, and on the other the positive imputation of the righteousness of Christ (3.11.2). This definition is not unique to Calvin, of course, for, as we have seen, there was already a tradition in which justification was defined as such before Calvin, and which he simply inherited. For two reasons, however, and for our purposes, Calvin is the most important exponent of this view. First, he provides a clearer definition of the substance of justification than do his predecessors. Second, Calvin's theology generally is strongly pneumatological, which means that it provides us with an ideal *locus* for discussing the relation between Reformation pneumatology and soteriology.

The point at issue with regard to the doctrine of justification in scholastic theology and in the theology of the Reformation is brought out well in Calvin's *Institutes:*

> on the beginning of justification there is no quarrel between us and the sounder Schoolmen: that a sinner freely liberated from condemnation may obtain righteousness, and that through forgiveness of sins; except that they include under the term "justification" a renewal, by which through the Spirit of God we are remade to obedience to the law. (3.14.11)

The basic problem Calvin sees in this is very simple. It is only if we are without sin that God can accept us, for wherever sin exists, there too can be found the wrath of God against it. To be justified in God's sight must therefore involve being righteous rather than a sinner (3.11.2). Thus, whatever justification is, it must be *total;* a total righteousness is required if we are ever to stand justified before God. It is largely, though not entirely, for this reason that the notion of a renewal by the Spirit as a function of justification is rejected. Because in this life, even under the Spirit's renewing power, the traces of sin always remain in the believer, because God must always be hostile to sin, and because justification is the basis of our whole relationship with God, it is essential to exclude the renewal of the Spirit from the doctrine of justification.

There is, however, another more positive reason in Calvin's theology for the claim that justification is total and excludes in itself the renewal of the Spirit, and this relates to Calvin's doctrine of union with Christ. Like Luther, in short, Calvin understands salvation in fundamentally christological terms. The whole question of the medieval doctrine of merit, therefore, is excluded not only because it leads to uncertainty concerning salvation, or because it conflicts with the anti-Pelagian doctrine of salvation by grace alone, but because it suggests that salvation resides outside of Christ. The logic of union with Christ *itself*, rather than more general considerations of sin and salvation, dictates the terms in which the doctrine of justification is to be understood, as well as the idea of imputation itself:

> that joining together of Head and members, that indwelling of Christ in our hearts — in short, that mystical union — are accorded by us the highest degree of importance, so that Christ, having been made ours, makes us sharers with him in the gifts with which he has been endowed. We do not, therefore, contemplate him outside ourselves from afar in order that his righteousness may be imputed to us but because we put on Christ and are engrafted into his body — in short, because he deigns to make us one with him. (3.11.10)

It is also clear from this quotation that the popular caricature of Calvin as having a merely forensic understanding of salvation based on a penal theory of atonement is mistaken. Calvin's soteriology is admittedly complex and does include a doctrine of penal substitution, but it also involves much more than a merely forensic soteriology based on penal, retributive concepts. At its center, in something of a competition with the penal theory, stands also the ancient doctrine of the "wonderful exchange," in which union with Christ is all-embracing, having a total, life-giving impact on the believer. Calvin speaks openly, in fact, in this context of a sharing through Christ in the life of God — which is self-evidently far more than the soteriological "legal fiction" of which he is often accused (cf., e.g., 4.17.2).

What, then, is the role of the Holy Spirit in salvation if salvation consists in union with Christ? Is the Spirit left with nothing to do? In fact, the Holy Spirit has a central place in Calvin's understanding of justification and union with Christ, for it is the Spirit who effects the union itself, and who is therefore the instrumental cause of justification. In one sense, the Spirit can be said to do this by giving faith to the believer (3.1.4), but the Spirit's role, rightly conceived, involves more than the bare fact of awakening faith, for Christ unites us with himself by means of his Spirit. Calvin has a developed doctrine of the Spirit as given by Christ for this purpose (3.1.1). Faith, in the end, is the *result* of the Spirit's work in uniting us with Christ rather than a prerequisite for this union; by faith we cling to Christ, it is true, but the union effected is something that consists in more than faith and that is the Spirit's doing. Calvin's doctrine of mystical union by the power of the Spirit involves a real sharing in Christ, just as the incarnation involves Christ in a real sharing of our life.[16]

In close connection with this idea of mystical union, Calvin even develops the outlines of a genuinely pneumatic christology. In a series of important statements, he makes clear that it is because Christ bears the Spirit as the Mediator that he is able to effect the union of believers with himself that is so important in Calvin's theology. For example, Calvin writes that "Christ came endowed with the Spirit in a special way . . . to separate us from the world and to gather us unto the hope of the eternal inheritance" (3.1.2). Or again, in the next paragraph, "God the Father gives us the Holy Spirit for his Son's sake, and yet he has bestowed the whole fullness of the Spirit upon the Son to be minister and steward of his liberality." Calvin even argues here that the Spirit is not called the Spirit of Christ only because of the eternal relation of the two, but

---

16. One of the interesting things about Calvin's theology at this point is that the incarnation and the death of Christ do not suffice for salvation. Although Christ identifies himself with us, the union of God with humanity in Christ is not sufficient to bring about our salvation. Rather, after his lengthy discussion of the incarnation and work of Christ in book 2 of the *Institutes of the Christian Religion*, Calvin feels compelled to speak of how all this is of no use to us so long as Christ remains "outside of us" — so long, in other words, as the mystical union with him effected by the Spirit is not realized in each believer.

because of what happens in the history of Jesus, where the Spirit is given to him for our sake.

One of the more interesting and important ways in which Calvin's conception of Christ as the anointed one is expressed appears in the celebrated discussion of the threefold office of Christ, the *triplex munus,* in the account of the work of Christ in book 2 of the *Institutes* (2.15). Christ can be known as Savior in his capacity as prophet, king, and priest, as the fulfillment of these three religious "types" of the Old Testament. The theme is well known and is frequently taken to be a prime characteristic of Calvinist soteriology. What goes largely unnoticed, however, about Calvin's own exposition is the pneumatological dimension of the threefold office. Underlying his thinking here is the idea that all of the three — prophets, kings, and priests — were anointed with the Spirit in the Old Testament, and that Christ, as the ideal fulfillment of each type, is likewise anointed with the Spirit in his messianic work. For example, Calvin argues with respect to the prophetic office that Christ was anointed with the Spirit to be "herald and witness of the Father's grace," both for himself and for the sake of his whole body, the church, so that in it, too, the power of the Spirit would be present in the preaching of the gospel (2.15.2). The idea is that those incorporated into Christ were anointed *in him* with the Spirit. Calvin relies here on an older insight found in the patristic theology of baptism, as we have seen, and further developed in scholastic theology, which Calvin knew well, in the notion of the *gratia capitis,* the grace of the Head, which flows to the members of his body. It is the idea of Christ as representative that is presupposed at this point. Not only is Christ righteous in our place, so that we are reckoned to be righteous by union with him, but he receives the Spirit in its fullness so that the Spirit can be given to us as well. Because we participate in Christ, the anointed one, we also have a share in his prophetic anointing and can therefore continue to speak his word with his authority.

The discussion of Christ as king is even more illuminating in this respect.[17] Christ's kingship, Calvin argues, is spiritual, having

---

17. Calvin, *Institutes,* 2.15.3-5. Cf. Jean Bosc, *The Kingly Office of the Lord Jesus Christ,* trans. A. K. S. Reid [*sic*] (Edinburgh: Oliver and Boyd, 1959).

to do with the great issues of the spiritual life and with Christ's lordship over sin and death. It is not, therefore, in any sense a worldly, political kingship. Calvin claims that the title "Christ" strictly refers to this office more than to the other two, for here Christ is the triumphant champion in the war against sin and death. It might be expected that in the context of this christological office, where we are concerned with the *Christus victor* theme, Calvin would especially emphasize the fact that the eternal Word who assumed human nature is doing battle with evil. Calvin does speak in this way in places. For example, in his account of the Mediator, Calvin argues that this task was to swallow up death and conquer sin, and asks the rhetorical questions, "Who but the Life could do this?" and "Who but very Righteousness?" (2.12.2). However, in his account of Christ as king, it is surprisingly Christ's anointing with the Spirit that has special significance. The doctrine of Christ's kingship in Calvin is concerned with how Christ never leaves us destitute but provides us with everything needed for the salvation of our souls and for standing against Satan's assaults, so that in the end we can enter the heavenly kingdom. It is only if we are so furnished that we can inherit eternal life. We receive what we need, however, through the Holy Spirit: By the Spirit we are made spiritually alive in this way, so that by union with Christ we become victorious over sin and death. At the center of Christ's office as king, therefore, is the Spirit:

> For the Spirit has chosen Christ as his seat, that from him might abundantly flow the heavenly riches of which we are in such need. The believers stand unconquered through the strength of their king, and his spiritual riches abound in them. (2.15.5)

Unfortunately, the pneumatological aspect of Christ's priestly office is undeveloped in the account of the *triplex munus,* but the central role of the Spirit for Calvin's christology and soteriology has already been established in what has gone before.

Thus, while the work of the Holy Spirit is made peripheral to the doctrine of justification in one sense in Calvin's theology, in that the whole question of the *works* inspired by the work of the Spirit are excluded from consideration, in another sense the Holy Spirit's role is pivotal, since without the Spirit we could not be united with Christ. The concept of the imputation of righteousness must also be considered in this context. Although it is alleged that the Reformation doctrine of imputation is novel, in that the previous tradition knows only of the nonimputation of sin, the christological ground for the Reformation doctrine of justification means, in fact, that there is basic common ground between Reformation theology and, among others, those patristic writers who understand salvation to consist in a union with Christ that, faith declares, fundamentally alters the human condition. Although use of the word *imputation* may be novel in this context, the underlying conceptuality is clearly not new.

The Reformation doctrine of justification represents a profound and coherent alternative to the Augustinian doctrine that had previously been normative in Latin theology. Though its pneumatological implications tended to shift the emphasis away from the Spirit as the direct *source* of justification to a more instrumental role, which effectively resulted in a basic move away from what was at the time the general doctrine of the Spirit's work, the Spirit nevertheless has an important place in the soteriological scheme, particularly in Calvin. What this involves, as has already been noted, is a separation of justification and sanctification, the former becoming a matter of status before God, one might say, and the latter remaining a matter of one's empirical being in the world. Although both are included in Christ, as Calvin puts it, the two are logically distinct and must be clearly differentiated.

Does theology require such a distinction? One argument against the Reformation approach is that it involves the loss of a sense of the organic wholeness of theology generally and of salvation in particular. The result is that the variety of images used to describe salvation in Scripture and tradition come to be seen as contradictory rather than as complementary. In his book *The Shape of Soteriology*, John McIntyre has indirectly addressed the problem this involves. All soteriological models, he argues, are best seen in their original setting, particularly in the case of the biblical models, as "imaginative constructs" that serve to interpret the meaning of salvation.[18]

18. John McIntyre, *The Shape of Soteriology* (Edinburgh: T. & T. Clark, 1992), pp. 67ff.

From these pretheoretical imaginative constructs the various full-blown theories of salvation have developed. Arguing from the original situation of the church, for which the death of Christ was an incomprehensible mystery on the one hand and yet the most intimately held *datum* of faith on the other, McIntyre concludes that the biblical models originally provided basic metaphorical schema by which Christians interpreted their faith. In the New Testament itself, the models have not yet become theories and are ranged side by side in a way that suggests that later differentiations were not yet in view. While on the one hand their diversity deepens Christian understanding of the event of salvation, on the other hand this diversity passes on to subsequent generations a series of confusions. These confusions derive from the tendency of the more imaginative constructions of the New Testament, when pressed to the point of systematic rigor, to become mutually exclusive systems of ideas. Although McIntyre does not draw this particular conclusion, a prime instance of this may well be the way in which the theory of justification comes in Reformation theology to exclude complementary ideas such as sanctification.

In fact, even Calvin's own doctrine of union with Christ, which includes both justification and sanctification, confirms this, for the concept of union with Christ transcends his clear-cut distinctions. There is no doubting that the semantic range in the two cases is different, for justification is a forensic and sanctification a cultic notion, but according to Calvin union with Christ involves both. Could we not therefore argue on this basis alone that each must be understood to complement, rather than to contradict, the other? This is not to say that the Calvinist position on justification as involving inclusion in Christ is necessarily mistaken, for there would still be a rationale for this view, but it is to say that the proper function of the biblical metaphors at stake here is not to provide primary and secondary concepts to describe salvation but rather to provide a range of ideas that, taken together, mutually enrich and deepen faith in Jesus Christ as Savior. To argue that one's legal status before God is primarily what is at issue in salvation rather than, for example, being a son or daughter of God, or a member of the people of God, or being made holy and thus set apart for God's service — which is the proper signification of the verb "to sanctify" — seems from this perspective to miss the point of the biblical language.

A second objection to the isolation of justification by faith from concrete obedience in Reformation theology is the charge that the theology of the Reformation is antinomian. The problem is this: If our status before God depends upon Christ's work on our behalf, and not at all on our own works, then can we in any sense be said to need to obey the law of God in order to be saved? This was the chief objection made at the Council of Trent (1545-1563) against justification in Reformation theology. Since it took the view that justifying grace involves not only faith but also works, the Council anathematized those holding the doctrine of justification by faith alone. The Council was able to amass an impressive catalog of scriptural citations that contradict the Reformation claim and that speak of the necessity of obedience for salvation.

Even within the Protestant tradition, however, the same perception is endemic. In Anglican theology, for example, a clear movement away from justification by faith alone can already be seen in the Reformation era between the theology of Cranmer, who was Lutheran on this point, and Hooker in the next generation, who sought to hold justification and sanctification together more closely.[19] Similarly, though somewhat more radically, in John Wesley there is a deliberate attempt to emphasize the importance of works on the grounds that Jesus instructs us to be perfect. Although Wesley distinguished between justification and sanctification (or the new birth), he saw the former as consisting in forgiveness, or the nonimputation of sin only, and the latter as the source of the positive righteousness by which we please God.[20] In one of his more polemical works on the subject, a 1762 pamphlet entitled "Thoughts on Christ's Imputed Righteousness," Wesley went so far as to reject the classical Reformation phrase "the imputation of the righteousness of Christ" as unbiblical and as something used to "justify the

---

19. Peter Toon, *Justification and Sanctification* (London: Marshall Morgan & Scott, 1983), pp. 89ff.

20. John Wesley, Sermon 5, in *The Works of John Wesley*, 3rd ed. (Grand Rapids: Baker, 1986), vol. 5, §2.5.

grossest abominations."[21] He concluded with a *reductio ad absurdum* of the classical Reformation position:

> doth not this way of speaking naturally tend to make Christ the minister of sin? For if the very personal obedience of Christ (as these expressions directly lead me to think) be mine the moment I believe, can anything be added thereto? Does my obeying God add any value to the perfect obedience of Christ? On this scheme, then, are not the holy and the unholy on the very same footing?

Wesley's views must have shocked many of his Protestant contemporaries, and might have pleased some Catholics, but he was not a lone voice. A critical estimate of the Reformation theology of justification could already be found in his native Anglicanism, while Wesley could also appeal to Continental Pietism, with which he had come into contact early in his career. The Pietists, too, attempted to move away from classical Reformation theology at this point in order to counteract a purely forensic understanding of our relationship with God, which in their view seemed to make the human response to God in obedience and love peripheral to salvation.

The view taken on the role of the Holy Spirit in justification in the Protestant tradition is therefore not all of a piece. It is not difficult to discern the point at which the classical Reformation distinction begins to break down: the ethical teaching of Jesus. A good example is the interpretation of the Sermon on the Mount. Some years ago, Joachim Jeremias pointed to the incoherence of the Lutheran idea that the teaching of the Sermon is incapable of being realized in any life and therefore represents an impossible ideal.[22] On the Lutheran reading, so lofty is the ideal Jesus teaches that it can only be intended to drive people to despair in order to prepare the way for faith. The interpretation of Jesus' teaching as representing an impossible ethical ideal, and especially as intended to induce guilt and a sense of failure, is condemned by Jeremias

21. John Wesley, "Thoughts on Christ's Imputed Righteousness," in *Works*, vol. 10, pp. 312-15.

22. Joachim Jeremias, *The Sermon on the Mount*, trans. Norman Perrin (London: Athlone Press, 1961), pp. 11ff.

on the grounds that it represents a "Paulinizing" of Jesus, in which unacceptable conclusions derived from quite another source are read into the teaching of the Gospels. In the light of more recent critiques of the classical Augustinian-Lutheran understanding of Paul,[23] it might be added here that this interpretation of the Sermon represents not just an example of Paulinizing exegesis but an example of how a faulty interpretation of Paul has distorted a whole tradition of understanding the teaching of the Gospels. Jeremias himself argues that the Sermon on the Mount presupposes that the reader has already heard the *kerygma,* which is here then followed by the *didache* — that is, that faith now issues in works. However, he also integrates these two sides, for his ultimate conclusion is that "these sayings of Jesus delineate the lived faith."[24] One might equally say that Jesus' teaching is at variance with the Reformation doctrine that works righteousness is alien to faith.

The strength of this alternative view is that it allows us to understand the words *justification* and *sanctification* as pointing to two sides of the same thing. Each enriches our understanding. Salvation involves *both* a new status that is not our doing *and* a human response of obedience that is, in some sense at least, precisely our doing. In addition, salvation involves being adopted, reconciled, and redeemed from hostile forces. The range of metaphors flesh out its presuppositions and implications, while their inner unity is less a matter of logical priority than of a person and a history: Jesus Christ himself, and the human reality he establishes by his grace.

The Liberals and Their Critics

There is, of course, much more to Protestant theology than the theology of the Reformation. In particular, liberal Protestantism has a long and venerable history that we need to explore. The liberal theological tradition, which emerged during the Enlightenment era, is associated classically with the name of the "father of liberal

23. E.g., E. P. Sanders, *Paul and Palestinian Judaism* (London: SCM Press, 1977).

24. Jeremias, *The Sermon on the Mount,* p. 32.

theology," Friedrich Schleiermacher (1768-1834), as well as with such direct and indirect influences as the achievements of modern science, the development of historical-critical biblical scholarship, and Enlightenment philosophy generally. For pneumatology, the claims of the liberal tradition are of great importance. We have seen that much of the doctrine of the Holy Spirit traditionally has been concerned with the doctrine of the person of the Spirit. The central question here concerns the Spirit's divinity. Broadly speaking, the doctrine of the Trinity has served as the framework within which this question has been addressed in Christian thought. The challenge of liberal Protestantism for pneumatology is its claim that the trinitarian doctrine of the Holy Spirit is both misleading and unnecessary. On the one hand, it does not actually match up with the religious facts, while on the other, it is not needed in order to explicate what is of importance in the doctrine of the work of the Spirit.

Much of both nineteenth- and twentieth-century theology has effectively been a running argument about the virtues and vices of such theology. One immediately thinks of the reactionary response of theological fundamentalism in its various guises, with its appeal to the teaching authority of church or Scripture over against the claims of mere human beings. In both its Roman Catholic and Protestant varieties, fundamentalism has openly set out to do nothing less than to exclude liberal ideas from the church. Of greater theological importance, however, is the equally hostile criticism of the liberal tradition that emerged in dialectical theology following the First World War. The leading figure in this movement was, of course, the great Swiss-German theologian Karl Barth (1886-1968).

Barth's contributions to twentieth-century theological thought are many, but they begin with his attempt to reassert the primacy of God in theological scholarship over against the liberal tradition's emphasis on human religious life. In effect, Barth's theological project was to reassert the claims of theological metaphysics, though he did so in a radically new way. As a result, though Barth set out in his theology expressly to counteract what he saw as the corrupting influence of nineteenth-century thought, his response was more than to erect another form of fundamentalism. Characterizing the liberal tradition of the nineteenth century as anthropocentric in a basically *antitheological* way, to the extent that it was concerned with the *act* of faith rather than with the *object* of faith, he engaged in a prolonged examination of the nature and methods of theology, and of its content, as grounded in God's action in Jesus Christ. In his late essay "The Humanity of God," Barth summarizes a lifelong obsession with the weaknesses of the liberal tradition in what has become a famous passage:

> To speak about God meant to speak about humanity, no doubt in elevated tone, but . . . about human faith and human works. Without doubt *human beings* were here magnified at the expense of *God* — the God who is sovereign Other standing over against humanity. . . . This God who is the free partner in a history which he himself inaugurated and in a dialogue ruled by him — this divine God was in danger of being reduced to a pious notion: the mythical expression and symbol of human excitation oscillating between its own psychic heights or depths, whose truth could only be that of a monologue and its own graspable content.[25]

Barth here sums up his view that liberal theology is effectively left without God, despite its intentions, because it is constructed on improper foundations. As Barth came to see things, the gospel itself provides us with the basis for a critique of such a theology, for the gospel is not about human religion or human ethics but about God's acts in history.

Barth's theology, particularly in its early phase, is in this way polemical and reactionary in the strictest possible sense. It is, in other words, constructed explicitly as an attack on the nineteenth-century tradition. Since he alleges that that tradition confuses God with humanity, he sets out to say the opposite, that God confronts humanity as the "totally other." This is what makes his early theology dialectical, for dialectical thought is thought that has two poles and, in Barth's case, stresses the opposition between them.

---

25. Karl Barth, "The Humanity of God," trans. James Strathearn McNab, in *Karl Barth: Theologian of Freedom,* ed. Clifford Green (London: Collins, 1979), p. 48.

Thus in the early *Epistle to the Romans,* which effectively began the tradition of dialectical theology, almost every page is concerned to stress the difference between God and humanity over against liberal theology. God stands against humanity and condemns it, Barth argues, so that human righteousness in its attempts to reach God, whether in pharisaic legalism or in the modern attempt to effect a philosophical accommodation of God to humanity, meets its condemnation in the judgment of God. For Barth, God wants to put an end to human self-righteousness in order to reveal his own proper and divine righteousness.

One of Barth's friends and critics, Hans Urs von Balthasar — whom Barth regarded as one of his best interpreters[26] — argues that almost the only concept Barth works with in his early phase is the concept of *diastasis* or opposition.[27] Balthasar criticizes Barth for not making more of analogy in his theology, but he also points out that neither does Barth in his dialectical phase make anything of the point at which God and humanity meet in the incarnation.[28] It is a notable fact that Barth's dialectical theology scarcely develops christology at all, whereas the later theology of the *Church Dogmatics* is concerned through and through to consider and to explicate the Christ-event as the sum and substance of Christian theology.

We will return to this development in Barth's more positive theology later. For the moment, we need to address the question of his assessment of the liberal tradition, and in particular of its pneumatology, and to ask whether he is in fact fair to it. Barth's view suggests that in their doctrine of the Holy Spirit, the liberals confused the Spirit of God with the human spirit, since their intention was to speak of God only from the standpoint of human religious sensibility. This frank assessment of liberal pneumatology is a view that has heavily influenced Barth's followers, who regularly describe the liberal tradition as erring by identifying the Holy Spirit with the religious and ethical aspects of the human mind, thus

26. Eberhard Busch, *Karl Barth,* trans. John Bowden (London: SCM Press, 1976), p. 371.

27. Hans Urs von Balthasar, *The Theology of Karl Barth,* trans. John Drury (New York: Holt, Rinehart and Winston, 1971), pp. 43ff.

28. Balthasar, *The Theology of Karl Barth,* pp. 73ff.

treating the Spirit as merely "a cipher for the realm of moral and spiritual values."[29]

The problem, of course, is that this judgment is not accurate. It must be said first of all that the doctrine of the Holy Spirit was not, properly speaking, the primary concern of the great liberals. Liberal theology did not set out to be a theology of the Holy Spirit, for example, since this would have run quite counter to its own expressed intentions. Indirectly, however, because of its concern for religious experience, it is possible to understand the tradition as intimately concerned with *aspects* of pneumatology, for its concern is with the experiential arena within which the doctrine of the Spirit is located in Christian theology. Questions of faith, obedience, and church are all pneumatological questions in essence, even though it was the *human* dimension that in many ways preoccupied the liberals in all of them.

Nevertheless, the doctrine of the Holy Spirit is an important theme in the theologies of the classical liberal theologians Schleiermacher and Ritschl; Harnack, for his part, though perhaps the greatest of the liberal scholars, is insignificant by comparison as a pneumatologist. For Schleiermacher, what is central in theology, since it is the fountainhead of all religion, is our experience of "God-consciousness" or the "feeling of absolute dependence," by which the relational dimension of the life of faith in the psychological — or better, the romantic — sense is brought to the fore.[30] This religious intuition, as we might call it, is what is really at the center of Schleiermacher's theology. Formally, in terms of its structure and contents, the doctrine of the Spirit is not obviously a major theme in Schleiermacher's system, but in another sense it can be seen to underlie the whole. This is because of the connections between the Spirit and religious experience; the Spirit for Schleiermacher is effectively the spiritual influence left behind by Jesus that gives coherence to the life of the church as a spiritual entity, and therefore to the life of Christian faith (§§121-25).

---

29. Alasdair Heron, *The Holy Spirit* (London: Marshall Morgan & Scott, 1983), p. 113.

30. Friedrich Schleiermacher, *The Christian Faith*, ed. H. R. Mackintosh, trans. James S. Stewart (Edinburgh: T. & T. Clark, 1928), §4. Subsequent references will be given parenthetically in the text.

The eighteenth-century background to Schleiermacher's theology is important here, and in particular the massive influence of the philosophy of Immanuel Kant, who brought to an end the earlier rationalist tendency toward understanding God as a component of the scientific worldview. In his *Critique of Pure Reason,* Kant not only demonstrates the impossibility of the classical proofs for God's existence but does away with the whole attendant system of natural theology that had earlier prevailed in European thought. The key point Kant makes is that scientific reasoning, by which we make sense of the world, can only operate on the basis of sense experience.[31] Since we have no sense experience, or intuition, to which to relate the concept of God, God simply does not come within the compass of scientific reasoning and so must be resolutely excluded from it.

Kant does, however, allow a limited scope for religious claims and for God in the realm of morality and moral discourse; according to Kant, the concept of God is a necessary postulate of moral reasoning, in the sense that God's existence as the ultimate guarantor and judge of moral goodness must be postulated in order to make sense of the absolute claim that the moral law makes upon us. Immortality and freedom, similarly, are the correlative postulates of moral reason by which we make sense of moral life as an integral whole.[32] Religion in Kant's philosophy is a rather barren affair, concerned only with moral duty as the true service of God; Kant has no interest in prayer or worship, and is in fact agnostic when it comes to such classical theological questions as the doctrine of God or of the Holy Spirit. What Schleiermacher sought to do was to react against this barrenness in order to make room for religious experience — to rehabilitate it, as it were — but to do so in a way that built upon Kant's positive achievement.

Schleiermacher actually claims in the preface to the second edition of his greatest work, *The Christian Faith,* that he says nothing at all new in his theology. He agrees with Kant, in short,

31. Immanuel Kant, *Critique of Pure Reason,* ed. and trans. Norman Kemp Smith (New York: St. Martin's Press, 1965), A50/B74.

32. The most complete discussions are found in Immanuel Kant, *Critique of Practical Reason,* trans. T. K. Abbott (London: Longmans, 1909), book II, chap. 2, §§4-5; and Kant, *Critique of Judgement,* trans. James Creed Meredith (Oxford: Clarendon, 1928), part II, §§26-30.

that religion has to be disentangled from questions of scientific fact and that religion is concerned with the realm of ethics, but behind the latter, and unlike Kant, he finds beckoning the religious consciousness, the whole realm of human piety, of prayer, joy, love, and so on. His opening argument in the work is that we cannot establish doctrine on grounds of rational objectivity of the sort seen in Newtonian physics but must rather look at doctrine as a function of the Christian church, which is a free association voluntarily entered "through the medium of ethics" (§2). One of the branches of the latter is what he calls the philosophy of religion, by which he means an account of the phenomenon of piety in human nature. This, as Schleiermacher sees things, not only leaves the Kantian system intact, though improving on it by escaping from its tendency to religious agnosticism, but crucially, it is also faithful to the intention of the Protestant tradition. Protestantism is not concerned with God in himself, according to Schleiermacher — this is expressly denied by both classical Lutheranism and Calvinism — but with questions of personal faith and piety, which is precisely what Schleiermacher speaks of under the heading of God-consciousness. What he attempts to do, therefore, is ultimately nothing less than to use Kant to escape from the straitjacket of Enlightenment rationalism in order to make room for piety in theology, and so to allow the latter to be true to its real roots in human religion.

The Holy Spirit in Schleiermacher's theology, as in all Christian thought, needs to be understood in relation to God, to Jesus Christ, and to the religious dimension of human being. One way of understanding the church, for example, is to see it as based on the religious impulse as an essential element in human nature, for every such essential element is the basis for some sort of fellowship or communion (§6). The church, or the churches, are associations of people whose religious intuition — what Schleiermacher calls the feeling of absolute dependence — is expressed in space and time in similar ways. The term *church*, from this point of view, is elastic, extending to extra-Christian religious bodies as well as to Christian bodies, for the feeling of absolute dependence is written into human nature as such and does not strictly or simply derive from any historical revelation.

Nevertheless, the existence of the Christian church is in

another and perhaps even a more basic sense entirely dependent on historical revelation, for the particular form that the feeling of absolute dependence assumes in Christianity is determined by the figure of Jesus Christ. This is so much so in Schleiermacher's theology, in fact, that it is possible to speak of Schleiermacher rather than Barth as initiating the tradition of christocentrism in modern Protestant theology![33] One of the theses of *The Christian Faith* brings this out well, in the context of an attempt to define Christianity in relation to the general account given of religion:

> Christianity is a monotheistic faith, belonging to the teleological [i.e., ethical] type of religion, and is essentially distinguished from other such faiths by the fact that in it everything is related to the redemption accomplished by Jesus of Nazareth. (§11)

Redemption for Schleiermacher involves the development of God-consciousness, the feeling of absolute dependence, and its pervading the whole of life, so that one's entire being is directed through the God-consciousness to the kingdom of God. (The influence of Pietism can be seen here.) But Schleiermacher insists that this can only be fully realized through the relation to Jesus, for the ideal fulfillment of God-consciousness is seen in him, and comes to be in us through our participation in his God-consciousness, in a relationship that can only adequately be understood as grace (§100). What is interesting about the thesis quoted above is that "everything" is related to this: All other doctrines, even the Christian doctrines of God and creation, are a function of the primordial doctrine concerning redemption through Jesus Christ, for they need to be developed as extensions of the God-consciousness, the feeling of absolute dependence, which the Redeemer imparts.

Schleiermacher attempts to preserve the doctrine of Christ's humanity and divinity by way of an ingenious reinterpretation destined to be repeated many times in subsequent theology:

---

33. A point emphasized by Keith Clements in his editorial introduction to *Friedrich Schleiermacher: Pioneer of Modern Theology* (Edinburgh: T. & T. Clark, 1987), p. 41.

The Redeemer, then, is like all men in virtue of the identity of human nature, but distinguished from them all by the constant potency of His God-consciousness, which was a veritable existence of God in Him. (§94)

We can see here something of the way in which what the older tradition saw in metaphysical terms is now expressed in terms of the religious consciousness — in Schleiermacher's view, without the loss of anything distinctive to Christian faith. The religious consciousness, however, is in both Christ and us the work of God, a function of the presence of God. This provides us with the clue needed to see how Schleiermacher understands the person and work of the Holy Spirit. First, the metaphysical definitions of older trinitarian theology are ruled out, for theological discourse is only meaningful if claims to metaphysical truth are excluded and only "ethical" claims are made in it. Concretely, this means that in Schleiermacher's pneumatology we are concerned again with the God-consciousness and its role in the whole of life, which is determined in *Christian* faith by Jesus of Nazareth. Schleiermacher thus argues that the Holy Spirit is the union of "the divine essence" with human nature in the form of the common Spirit that exists among believers, or among those who have been regenerated by Christ (§123). He repeatedly refuses to consider the question of the Spirit's metaphysical status apart from this relationship of human beings to God, for the latter alone is the concern of theology rightly conceived. What this means, however, is that the Holy Spirit is the presence of God in the Christian community in awakening and animating the life of faith, discipleship of Christ, and therefore devotion to the kingdom of God. The same God present in Christ is present in the church, in other words, the only difference being that in the one case his presence was particular, while in the other case it is general and corporate in the ecclesial sense.

Although the Holy Spirit is not, therefore, understood in an explicitly trinitarian way in Schleiermacher's theology (in fact, his view approaches modalism), neither is it merely a cipher for human religious-ethical feeling. It may be true that from the point of view of the God of dialectical theology, who is indeed the *totaliter aliter*, Schleiermacher's doctrine of the Holy Spirit seems to be merely humanistic. However, this is not Schleiermacher's own intention.

For him, the Spirit is truly God present here and now in the church, which is itself the product of God's presence in Jesus Christ in the past, and the result of the continuing influence of his mode of life. The Spirit cannot, in other words, be considered apart from the church, but it is nevertheless God's presence, mediated by Christ, with which we are concerned in the doctrine of the Spirit.

The same basic insight emerges from the theology of Albrecht Ritschl (1822-1889), although Ritschl is much more suspicious of mysticism and of "feeling" than Schleiermacher. In his little book *Instruction in the Christian Religion,* Ritschl lays out the basis for his doctrine of the Holy Spirit, which he treats under the heading of the Christian life.[34] The work of the Spirit is understood to consist in the development of the Christian community first and foremost, rather than in regenerating the individual. This involves the communal knowledge that we have of God as Father, the loving one of whom Jesus taught, who wills his kingdom to come about on earth — and the desire on our part to help bring that kingdom about. Throughout his theology, however, Ritschl refuses to be drawn any further than this. In his view, it is impossible to speak of the Holy Spirit, or in fact to speak of God at all, apart from his activity in history. Anything else, according to Ritschl, would amount to a spurious metaphysics rather than a theology based, as all real theology in his view must be, on the revelation of God in Christ. Ritschl thus tries to avoid using language about the Spirit as such; one can only properly speak of his *effects* in the Christian life. As a result, the doctrine of the work of the Spirit in and of itself constitutes the whole Ritschlian pneumatology.[35] Once this is understood, Ritschl's claim to have always maintained that the ground of Christian life is the Holy Spirit — whether in the consciousness of being children of God or in the realm of ethics — must be taken seriously.[36]

---

34. Albrecht Ritschl, *Instruction in the Christian Religion,* trans. A. M. Swing, in A. T. Swing, *The Theology of Albrecht Ritschl* (New York: Longmans, Green, 1901), §§46ff.

35. Ritschl's clash with the Tübingen scholar Hermann Weiss on the question of pneumatology in Albrecht Ritschl, *Theology and Metaphysics,* in Ritschl, *Three Essays,* trans. Philip Hefner (Philadelphia: Fortress Press, 1972), §5, brings this out well.

36. Ritschl, *Theology and Metaphysics,* §5.

Ritschl's doctrine of God is what it is, therefore, not because he sets out deliberately or *a priori* to accommodate God to the structures of the religious consciousness in a reductionist way, but rather because he does not admit that language about a God somehow known or accessible to us outside the religious life is legitimate. In short, the concept of "God" is a *religious* concept, which functions as it does just because there is such a thing as religious faith. God must be consistently thought of as such.

We can see, then, that Barth's claim that in liberal theology to speak about God really meant to speak of human faith and of human works amounts to a serious distortion of the real intention of liberal thought — at least as represented by Schleiermacher and Ritschl. Barth's almost overpowering desire to understand theology as reflection on the Word of Christ alone helps us to understand *why* he misrepresented the liberal tradition as he did, but it does not altogether excuse that misrepresentation. One can and must say this, even if the question of which of the two approaches is the more adequate remains an open one.

The contribution of the liberal tradition to a contemporary pneumatology, and the limitations of that tradition as well, can best be assessed through an examination of the continuing place of its "anti-metaphysical" claims in more recent theology. We can still find, for example, many of the prevailing concerns of classical liberal pneumatology resurfacing in the work of the Anglican scholar Geoffrey Lampe in his influential book *God as Spirit*.[37] The problem of history, for instance, is central to Lampe's argument, since in his view it is the category of Spirit that enables us to bridge the historical chasm between Jesus, God, and ourselves. Similarly Lampe, unlike Barth, assumes and makes use of the results of modern historical-critical biblical scholarship. Lampe further argues that a concept of the Spirit drawn from and faithful to the original, biblical understanding of Spirit will bypass the question of trinitarian theology in favor of how the Spirit is encountered in Christian existence. He summarizes his project in the following way:

37. Geoffrey Lampe, *God as Spirit* (Oxford: Clarendon Press, 1977). Subsequent references will be given parenthetically in the text.

We are speaking of God disclosed and experienced as Spirit: that is, in his personal outreach. The use of this concept allows us to say that God indwelt and motivated the human spirit of Jesus in such a way that in him, uniquely, the relationship for which man was intended by his Creator was fully realized; that through Jesus God acted decisively to cause men to share in his relationship to God, and that the same God, the Spirit who was in Jesus, brings believers into that relationship of "sonship" towards himself and forms them into a human community in which, albeit partially and imperfectly, the Christlike character which is the fruit of their relationship is re-presented. (11)

Lampe's affinity with the classical liberals is evident in his view, drawn from his analysis of the biblical witness, that the Spirit is a bridge-concept, a "power" that mediates between God in his transcendent glory and his creation (34-60). According to Lampe, "power" in this context does not refer to God himself, as if the Sprit *is* God in the literal sense, but rather is a concept denoting how we experience God in his outreach *to us:*

> Such terms as "Word," "Wisdom," and "Spirit" are quasi-poetical words, expressive of a profoundly mysterious inner awareness of confrontation with transcendent personal grace, love, demand, judgement, forgiveness, and calling. In their original usage they are not metaphysical terms, analytically descriptive of the structure of deity itself; nor do they denote hypostatically existent mediators between God and the world. They refer, rather, to the human experience of being, as it were, reached out to and mysteriously touched and acted upon by transcendent deity. (37)

God is known to his creatures as Spirit, therefore, whereas the trinitarian conception of the Spirit that Lampe rejects serves to deflect attention away from the properly *relational* context within which the concept is meaningful to the dubious realm of speculative theological ontology.

One implication of all of this, Lampe argues, is that there is no need for a metaphysical mediator, in the person of the incarnate Word, who stands between God and humanity in the order of being. This older christological idea is no longer relevant to twentieth-century humanity, and is, furthermore, *unnecessary* since the concept of Spirit is already presented in the Bible as God's concrete relatedness to men and women in their temporal humanity. The category of Spirit thus ultimately refers to God as he is experienced here and now, in the immediacy of existence and history. Given this, it makes no sense to indulge in the artificial speculations of traditional trinitarian theology in developing a doctrine of the Spirit. For Lampe, the question of how God, Jesus, and Christians are related can be resolved in the concept of Spirit, which is purely a religious concept oriented to the experience of faith, rather than a concept oriented to the being of God himself.

Lampe does not intend by this to make Jesus theologically irrelevant. Rather, according to Lampe, the real significance of Jesus in salvation history and in soteriology can now emerge: Jesus is the new Adam, whose life was lived for and with God in obedience and selfless love (23-25). This was possible for him because of the unqualified presence of the Spirit in his life. Jesus, in other words, shares with us the basic condition for the possibility of all fellowship with God: the presence of God as Spirit in his human life. In his teaching, in his practice, and in his obedience, which is seen supremely in his martyr death, Jesus shows himself to be the archetype of the human life lived under God, and thus also the archetype of life in the Spirit — or, in Lampe's words, the "pattern," "inspiration," and "power" that can create in us a response to God "analogous" to his own. In this sense, we become children of the Father, together with Jesus the Son, for the same Spirit that rested on him and that determined the shape of his life now rests on us and determines, though imperfectly, the shape of our lives also.

Although the philosophical differences between Lampe's view and those of Schleiermacher and Ritschl are clear enough, the theological similarities are also evident. In particular, all present a fundamental challenge to a trinitarian conception of the Spirit. The latter, it is argued, serves to distract from the real question of religious import, which concerns the human relationship with God, expressed in faith and practice. It is, in fact, difficult to disagree with the positive intention of this argument. "Trinity" is nowhere mentioned in Scripture, and we ought to judge the adequacy of our doctrines of the Spirit by reference to the biblical witness. Scripture speaks of the work of the Spirit but appears to be completely or almost completely disinterested in the question of the Spirit's "personhood." Can we therefore say, with the liberal tradition, that the trinitarian question is inappropriate?

No complete answer to this question can be given in the present context. It is, however, feasible to sketch the outlines of a possible response in the following way. First, it is not true that all trinitarian theology is by definition an abstraction from the life of faith. The Irenaean doctrine of Son and Spirit as the "two hands of the Father," for example, and the third-century patristic sense of the Father's outreach through the Son in the Holy Spirit, both of which serve to structure the church's response to God, can hardly be said to be irrelevant to the life of faith. On this view, where the Son is identified with Logos and is so asserted to be the principle of both divine and *human* reason, and where the Spirit is the source of sanctity, we are by virtue of the ordinary sense of the words *knowledge* and *love* alone ultimately in touch with God himself. In this way, a profound vision of the nature and structure of the spiritual life emerges in Christian theology. The doctrine of the Trinity therefore does not always serve to distract us from our relation to God; it can at times, at least, serve to structure the human response to God and deepen that response in very direct ways.

Furthermore, the continuing potential of this trinitarian model as a "source" for the spiritual life can be seen in, for example, such contemporary theologians as Karl Rahner (1904-1984). Rahner is himself also highly critical of the tendency in some theology to make the doctrine of the Trinity an abstract metaphysical one rather than something integral to ordinary faith and to the spiritual life.[38] Repeatedly, he poses the question whether it would actually make any difference to ordinary Christians if the doctrine of the Trinity were denied. As we have seen, the liberal tradition, on the whole,

---

38. Cf. Karl Rahner, *The Trinity*, trans. Joseph Donceel (London: Burns & Oates, 1970); and Rahner, *Foundations of Christian Faith*, trans. William V. Dych (London: Darton, Longman and Todd, 1978).

considers that it would not; Rahner, for his part, holds that it remains important to affirm, with the bulk of the Christian tradition, that we are indeed in touch with God himself rather than with some inferior mediation of divinity when we are in touch with God in Word and Spirit. Nevertheless, according to Rahner, there is a long tradition of exposition of the doctrine in Christian theology that is profoundly unhelpful in this respect, since it does not make clear that the Christian concept of God is that of the God who "communicates himself," as he puts it, by means of Word and Spirit, so that he gives himself in history in the incarnation, and makes himself the inmost constitutive principle of the human being in the gift of the Spirit. This, Rahner argues, is what is both most distinctive of and most important in the Christian doctrine of God.

Second, if it is true that the doctrine of the Trinity that emerges in fourth-century theology and becomes normative thereafter leans heavily toward the question of God's immanent trinitarian being, it needs also to be recognized, as we have seen, that a very specific difficulty necessitated this move. This was the Arian claim that the Son and Spirit are ontologically inferior and ultimately created levels of divinity that do not and by definition cannot convey the full presence and power of the "unoriginate" Father to the world. In fact, neither the classical liberals nor Lampe are committed to a return to the Arian cause as stated here; all alike wish to argue, though in a way that bypasses traditional orthodoxy, that it is truly God whom we encounter in life. The real question, we might say, that we have to face concerns the manner in which it is possible to speak of God. For the liberal tradition, the old "metaphysical" concepts employed by the church fathers and the early councils are philosophically dubious and a religious distraction. In this sense, the positive point made by the liberal tradition needs to be recognized. Its critique of metaphysical theism in the end applies to Arian and orthodox alike, insofar as *both* wish to make metaphysical claims about the Trinity in itself. I shall argue later that the metaphysical enterprise is actually justified, but we need at the same time to acknowledge the fact that liberalism, since it does not presuppose the kind of theological metaphysics that was common to *all* classical theologians, heretical and orthodox, cannot simply be judged according to whether or not it meets the demands of classical orthodoxy. In fact, as I have pointed out, liberalism's own exercise in theological reinterpretation is susceptible to a positive evaluation from the standpoint of someone who, like myself, is convinced of the continuing theological value of classical trinitarianism. This is not, however, to say that the claims of liberal theology can go unchallenged.

Perhaps the most obvious criticism that needs to be made of the liberal tradition is that it is itself the product of Enlightenment epistemology and metaphysics — most obviously in the case of Schleiermacher and Ritschl, whose dependence on Kant is clear, but also in the case of Lampe, who rather naively assumes a very modern and rather English philosophical bias against "Hellenistic" theological metaphysics of the old sort. The sheer fact that one rejects such metaphysical discourse about God, however, whether on the grounds that such knowledge does not come within the ambit of science or on the grounds that it is Hellenistic, does not mean that no claim concerning ultimate reality remains. One needs to be aware that even the claim that the only reality is a this-worldly one is as metaphysical in the strict sense as the Platonic philosophy of the Forms, for both claims are finally about the ultimate nature of things. Given the fact that theology is by definition concerned with the relation between God and the world, if not with the nature of God himself, it is difficult to see how a metaphysic of transcendence can ever be entirely purged from it. The real question, therefore, is how its claims are to be pursued.

The objection to this, of course, is that we should restrict our language about the Spirit to what is the proper concern of religion, which is an ethical matter in Schleiermacher's sense, or a subjective and relational one in Lampe's, rather than something descriptive of ultimate reality. It is, however, difficult to see how God can have a moral claim upon us unless God is real — unless, in short, God "exists" in a realist sense. In Lampe's own words, it is as transcendent deity, calling and challenging us, that we encounter God. A "metaphysical" doctrine of Spirit, therefore, to use the liberals' own expression again, seems to be necessary — unless, that is, one opts out of consistency for a more radical and ultimately *anti-theological* position.

5. Experience of the Spirit

The Holy Spirit and Theological Anthropology

Some years ago, Karl Rahner coined the expression "anonymous Christianity" to give a name to his conviction that each human being, whether saint or sinner, Catholic or Protestant, Christian, Hindu, or atheist, is a recipient of the grace of God and therefore, implicitly or explicitly, a member of the Christian church.[1] The anonymous Christian, of course, is the one who defines himself or herself differently, but who is nevertheless, despite all assertions to the contrary, a recipient of grace as conceived in the Christian religion. According to Rahner, what is distinctive about Christianity is that, unlike any other philosophy or faith, it speaks of an absolute self-communication of God to the world. It posits this at two points: in the person of Jesus Christ the God-man in a uniquely unsurpassable way, but also in an analogous way, though with diminished

---

1. Karl Rahner, "Anonymous Christians," in Rahner, *Theological Investigations,* vol. 6, trans. K. H. Kruger and B. Kruger (London: Darton, Longman and Todd, 1969), pp. 390-98; and Rahner, "Anonymous Christianity and the Missionary Task of the Church," in Rahner, *Theological Investigations,* vol. 12, trans. David Bourke (London: Darton, Longman and Todd, 1974), pp. 161-78.

124

intensity, in every human being. The self-communication of God to humanity is such, Rahner argues, that the category of *grace* is fundamental to all theological anthropology and all human life; God himself is present in us and to us in such a way as to be a "constitutive principle" of human existence.

Along with the concept of the self-communication of God goes another key concept in Rahner's theology: the self-transcendence of human beings. According to Rahner, human life is such that at the basis of everything there is a development from below to above, from matter to spirit, from fact to truth and value, from truth and value to absolute truth and value, and from absolute truth and value to God himself. The ground of such self-transcendence is the presence of God at the center of human existence. God is himself, according to Rahner, the principle of transcendence that works from within human being and from within history. The story of human self-transcendence, therefore, whether in the development of a child into adulthood, leaping over and beyond the goals and norms of youth, or in the continual recognition of the unconditional nature of the good in each particular moral act (as Rahner insists), or even in the evolution of the human species itself, is also the history of the divine self-communication to humanity and thus to the world. At the summit of this history stands the incarnation of the Word, where both divine self-communication and human self-transcendence are definitively expressed. The inner mystery of the incarnation is also, however, the inner mystery of all human life as predicated upon what Rahner calls the event of God's "free," "unmerited," and "absolute" self-communication.[2] There is continuity between the two, rather than a fundamental distinction. This also suggests a continuity between the decisive event on which the Christian religion is based and the general religious and secular experience of all humankind.

Rahner's theological approach, grounded as it is in a view of human life in which grace is a key conception, and in which the Spirit is accordingly at the center of everything, suggests an inclusive view of the role of the Holy Spirit at work in all of human life and

---

2. Rahner, *Foundations of Christian Faith,* trans. William V. Dych (London: Darton, Longman and Todd, 1978), pp. 116ff.

religion. Grace is, for Rahner, a pneumatological category; the self-communication of God that makes the act of human self-transcendence a possibility and a reality in all of its many modalities is something that can be summed up in the simple observation that the Spirit of God is present in and to each human person. We have seen this theme before, in the doctrine of the Creator Spirit in the Old Testament — only there the gift of the divine *ruach* is seen as the life-principle in the whole of creation, and not merely in human creatures. Rahner himself does not embrace the possibilities for a theology of nature implicit here but is content to develop the concept of Spirit anthropologically.

If nothing else, Rahner's theology shows us something of the importance of theological anthropology, in the sense that in his theological system it is the consideration of the human being as the locus of a divine self-communication that is at the center of everything. I have already argued that although theology can be legitimately constructed in other ways, any theology of the *Spirit* must be a theology of the spiritual life, or else the real point of pneumatology is lost. But here, too, we see the significance of theological anthropology, for it is in our theological anthropology that we conceive of ourselves as human precisely and supremely in relation to God.

Two statements from the Pauline corpus will serve to take the discussion further. The first is the benediction found at 1 Thessalonians 5:23: "May the God of peace himself sanctify you entirely; and may your spirit and soul and body be kept sound and blameless at the coming of our Lord Jesus Christ." This is a difficult enough text, but the second is even more cryptic: "If Christ is in you, then though the body is dead through sin, yet the spirit is alive through righteousness *(to de pneuma zoe dia dikaiosune)*" (Rom. 8:10, my trans.). The *New Revised Standard Version* misleadingly translates "the Spirit is life" at this point, but this is inexplicable except as an unnecessary paraphrase; Paul's thought is of the human spirit *made alive* by being made righteous in Christ, that is, by being within the sphere of the *Holy* Spirit's presence and power in mediating the risen Christ to the believer. To the Pauline texts the Johannine declaration can be added: "What is born of the flesh is flesh, and what is born of the Spirit is spirit" (John 3:6). For both

Paul and the author of the Fourth Gospel, therefore, the Christian is awakened to a new dimension or a new kind of life by virtue of the activity of the Spirit upon or within; the new life is defined accordingly as *spiritual.*

What is distinctive about this conception is that the spirit that is thus awakened to life by God is in some sense properly the possession of the one given spiritual life. The Pauline benediction cited from 1 Thessalonians conveys the sense that there is a *human* spirit, as well as a soul and body, which is to be preserved until the end and also, by the act of God, at the end. Historically, this has been the sponsoring text for what is called "tripartite anthropology," as opposed to the competing dichotomous anthropology of the body-soul, which is perhaps more common, and which sees "spirit" and "soul" as parallel terms. Origen is the greatest exponent of tripartite anthropology in the ancient church, but even in modern theology the tripartite view has its defenders. According to Emil Brunner, for example, "The one fact of decisive importance is this, that man is a whole consisting of body, soul and spirit."[3] Rather like Origen, in fact, Brunner regards the soul as the life-principle of the body, a life-principle that has two tendencies: one turned toward the spirit, and one turned toward the natural life of the body. Human life, conceived as a whole, comprises both elements, spiritual and natural, and Brunner's thesis is that the whole must be conceived as an inseparable body-soul-spirit, the functions of which are distinguishable, but which is in itself metaphysically indistinguishable. The "thing" in question is simply the human person, and not the person's body as opposed to his or her soul or spirit.

Origen, for his part, said much the same thing long ago, though with somewhat greater imaginative insight. Even if elements of his anthropological vision are mythological, they are nevertheless illuminating and seem somehow right, imaginatively or otherwise, in the sense that they give a name and a place to basic dimensions of human life. Henri Crouzel, who has produced the most brilliant modern synthesis of Origen's vast and complex

3. Emil Brunner, *Man in Revolt,* trans. Olive Wyon (London: Lutterworth Press, 1939), p. 362.

theology, will serve as our guide to his theology.[4] Crouzel notes that the dominant concept that informs the whole conception in Origen's theology is *pneuma*, or Spirit, for Spirit is the divine, the immaterial within us; Origen relies at this point on the Old Testament concept of the divine *ruach* in living creatures. In human life, the Spirit is the origin of moral consciousness, which is nothing less than a created participation in God the Holy Spirit — which also helps to explain Origen's preoccupation with morals and asceticism in his theology. Soul, on the other hand, is a pure creature. It contains two tendencies, as in Brunner: *nous*, or "intellect," which is the ruling part of the soul, and a lower element that Crouzel designates *sarx*, the biblical word for "flesh," which in Origen's theology is conceived of as having been added to *nous* after the fall. The *nous* is the seat of the will, which is meant to be guided by the *pneuma;* when so guided, it becomes spiritual also. The *nous* is the location of the image of God, which is a central concept in all patristic anthropology and even soteriology, as well as the location of the faculty of the five "spiritual senses," the concept of which derives from Origen. The body, *soma,* is the most problematic element in the threefold schema. *Nous* is, it seems, in itself incorporeal, yet because Origen asserts repeatedly that God alone is incorporeal in the strict sense, created *nous* always exists contingently, that is, in an embodied form. Spirit, too, in its anthropological form is always embodied, even though it has a strictly divine source, and even though continuity with this divine source is maintained.

Origen's theology was controversial because of his view that there are various kinds of body to which our spirits and souls have been attached: dazzling bodies in our "preexistent" state, before the creation of this world, and grosser bodies now. His views are allied with a general tendency in Platonism, which he represents as one of the greatest of all its distinctively Christian exponents, to a doctrine of reincarnation, or *metempsychosis.* There is, however, for Origen continuity between the previous body and the present, and between the present body and the resurrected body, in that there

4. Henri Crouzel, *Origen*, trans. A. S. Worrall (Edinburgh: T. & T. Clark, 1989), pp. 87ff.

is a kind of principle of corporeality, a *logos spermatikos,* which remains constant and which we carry with us throughout our existence.

Origen's speculations on the nature of corporeality and its causes need not detain us. What is important is his view of the nature of spirit and soul, and his conviction that the spirit is the point of direct contact between God and the human being. For Origen, the intellect is capable of being what it is in relation to God because of the presence of the divine Spirit enlivening the human spirit so as to make it its guide. Origen's strong sense of the necessity of a spiritual exegesis of the Scriptures confirms this connection between Spirit and intellect in his theology: According to Origen, a literal exegesis is inadequate because it corresponds only to the flesh and is not truly open upward to God. Ultimately, it is even disobedient, for it ignores the spiritual interpretation practiced already in the New Testament and effectively commanded by the risen Jesus (Luke 24:45). What this suggests is instructive, especially for the discipline of theology itself: that it is not only a one-sided preoccupation with the body that leads to a stunted human development, to half-men and half-women, but also a one-sided preoccupation with the intellect. Unless the spirit, too, is cultivated, neither body nor intellect can fulfill its intended function, and the person falls away from the true goal and the highest calling.

Brunner, though apparently independently of Origen, says precisely the same thing:

> The spirit of man is not to be understood from below but "from above," . . . [It] has a permanent relation with the divine Spirit; but it is not the divine Spirit. . . . Spirit, in contradistinction from that which is merely functional and psychical, can only be understood as something "transcending" the ordinary level, aspiring after something "beyond the self," an original actuality. . . . It is this reference to a Beyond, the process of "transcending," which distinguishes the spirit and the spiritual from the *psyche* and the *psychical.*[5]

5. Brunner, *Man in Revolt,* pp. 238-39.

The mind, the *psyche* in the modern sense — for this is what Brunner has in view — intends something beyond itself when it is aware of meaning, for it reaches upward to the immaterial, which is already potentially present to and with and in it. This is spirit, or the Spirit in the absolute sense. Brunner, however, characteristically argues that the spirit is constituted as such by the address of the Word of God, for he insists that human relatedness to God is essentially a Word-event.

This is not the place to repeat arguments found elsewhere, or to embark upon what would necessarily be a long and tortuous journey through modern psychological theory in search of an analogue for the tripartite schema in order to attempt to defend it. Suffice it to say for the present only this, that the notion of levels of human existence can be found in modern psychology (e.g., the Jungian tradition), and that those levels to which Origen and Brunner give a name in their respective ways are undoubtedly real enough, whether they are or are not clinically based. For much of modern psychology, the "science of the soul," what matters in any case is only behavior observed through the measurement of stimuli and responses, whereas from the standpoint of religious faith and life it is encounter with the living God, which in turn brings life to what it touches, that is the source of everything. All the important *theological* questions are located here.

Religious Experience

It might be thought that the fact that institutional religion in the contemporary Western world is in decline numerically, socially, and, we might add, conceptually suggests that the philosophical revolutionaries of the modern world are correct — that God is dead and that a new, nonreligious humanity has been born. There is, however, evidence to the contrary, suggesting that the religious quest is very much alive and well. This is especially true if we take the "quest" in its most general sense as the search for ultimate existential meaning. Popular newspaper editors, for example, find it economically essential to include a horoscope column in their pages; evidently substantial numbers of their readers, many of whom will not darken church doors on a regular basis, nevertheless do engage in what must be described as a search for a kind of religious guidance. There have recently been a number of highly successful films that have also featured such explicitly religious motifs as life after death. Likewise, the success in capturing the imagination of young people seen in new age thinking, with its associated moralities of ecology and self-discovery, allied with a quasireligious spiritual quest, should be remembered as well. Though not always tied explicitly to traditional forms of belief, such things are a reminder that the case for the end of religion has been grossly overstated.

Jürgen Moltmann has recently argued that there is theological significance in the fact that religious experience is largely found today *outside* of the church.[6] Since the Spirit is declared in Scripture to blow where he wills, and since the Spirit is encountered by people in what are, to the ecclesial powers-that-be, unexpected places, theology must adapt itself to the facts. According to Moltmann, "the continual assertion that God's Spirit is bound to the church, its word and sacraments, its authority, its institutions and ministry, impoverishes the congregations. It empties the churches, while the Spirit emigrates to . . . spontaneous groups and personal experience."[7] Moltmann therefore begins his most recent work on pneumatology by arguing on Hebraic grounds for a view of the Spirit as the principle of vitality in creation generally. Only when one has recognized this is it possible to move on to posit a continuity between this aspect of the Spirit's work and the Spirit's presence in the history of Israel, in the life and work of Jesus, in the birth of the church, and in the experience of the saints. Throughout his theology, Moltmann wishes to remain open to the wind of the Spirit, wherever it is found, and to the continuity between this and the more overtly "Christian" doctrines he elaborates.

Moltmann's position is neither surprising nor entirely original; it belongs in that long tradition in Christian thought that sees all human life, sacred and secular, as life lived "in God" rather than in a kind of created isolation ward. "We are not alone, we live in

---

6. Jürgen Moltmann, *The Spirit of Life*, trans. Margaret Kohl (London: SCM Press, 1992), pp. 1ff.

7. Moltmann, *The Spirit of Life*, p. 2.

God's world," runs the first clause of an affirmation of faith from the 1960s.[8] One might likewise quote from the apostle Paul as reported in Acts, who already makes use of this theme from Greek natural theology: "In him we live and move and have our being" (Acts 17:28). A great deal of Christian thought, particularly in the Christian Platonic tradition, follows this Pauline text and attempts to understand any human experience of meaning, whether of the true, the good, or the beautiful, as leading to God. Moltmann's position is very different, for he is no Platonist, as he would himself no doubt wish to insist, but it is interesting for us both because of its emphasis on religious experience and because of its focus on experience *of the Spirit* outside the boundaries, or the apparent boundaries, of religious practice as such. One of the questions we need to face in what follows is the extent to which this judgment is justified, and the extent to which it needs to be developed as a theme in our own pneumatology.

Let us take the argument further by quoting a series of propositions from a very different source. Philip Toynbee, in a little-known work entitled *Towards the Holy Spirit,* a philosophical tract intended to defend the possibility and reality of religious experience against the strongly reductionist tendency of recent British philosophy, has written as follows:

> there are certain facts which require to be re-established; and the first of them is that a very high proportion of the men and women who have laid claim to [a mystical] order of experience were renowned in their daily lives for probity, charity *and good sense.* There have also, of course, been lunatics and charlatans among them, but it is certain that the great body of mystical *writing* which has survived is the work of human beings of exceptional repute and credibility.

> What we have here, in fact, is a large body of reported experience from the best of all possible human sources — many of them saints, not only by canonisation but by any reputable criterion

8. Taken from the *Service Book* of the United Church of Canada (Toronto: United Church Publishing House, 1969), p. 310.

of human excellence. And what those persons are telling us is that this particular experience has been incomparably the most valuable and the most significant that they have ever known.[9]

Toynbee's defense of mystical experience also leads to an argument that the concept "Holy Spirit" will serve the cause of the discussion of religious experience, and of its rehabilitation in contemporary thought, more adequately than the Christian symbols of "Father" and "Son." Chiefly, in his view, it offers the possibility of an understanding of religious experience that is neither reductionist nor doctrinaire, in the sense that "Spirit" as a concept can be linked with the general mystery of "mind" and with the whole realm of the "spiritual" in human experience more easily than can any other available idea, and in the sense that it is an essentially open, inclusive concept that is flexible enough to serve as the basis for the extraordinary wealth and breadth of the matter in hand.[10]

The intellectual suspicion of religious experience to which Toynbee responds is, of course, familiar enough. What may not be transparently obvious, however, is that the significance he attaches to such experience, and to the role of the saint in giving shape to religious consciousness and to human life and faith generally, can be justified. If his point is to be taken, two things need to be established. First, we need to see whether or not there is still something called religious experience. And second, we need an account of how and why such experience must have a function in theology as such. Only then can we take such experience into account as evidence against the contemporary tendency toward an antireligious doctrine of humanity.

Let us turn to the first of these questions and observe at the outset what appears to be a plain fact, that one of the most important things to be observed about the role of religion in contemporary Western culture is the extent to which institutional Christian religion appears to have ceased to mediate the primordial mystery of which Toynbee speaks. If, for example, one asks those

9. Philip Toynbee, *Towards the Holy Spirit* (London: SCM Press, 1982), pp. 98-99, 108-9.
10. Toynbee, *Towards the Holy Spirit,* pp. 208ff.

who have rejected institutional religion and regular Christian worship why they have done so, one of the most frequent answers heard is that they "get nothing from it." There is, of course, a notorious problem in religious institutions: Though they are intended to be mediators or channels of something else, these institutions all too frequently end up acting as if they were themselves the end and goal of the exercise, as if the institution were the mystery, rather than merely the medium. It is to this destructive tendency that all the great reform movements have responded — only to become, once again and in time, the very sort of agents of spiritual inertia and decline against which the original protest was made. Doctrine, too, is infected by this sorry tendency; although at its best doctrine is intended to open up new possibilities for thought and life, the propensity is all too often to close them off, as if the doctrinal formulae provided a patented all-in-one solution to every question.

Against this, the response of the disaffected sounds a loud and clear warning. It is, in fact, a classic and perfectly defensible response to a decadent institutional religion. One of the interesting things about it, however, is that it seems to presuppose that at least some of those who respond in this way must have some inkling of what it is they want to get from their religion. This is an often ignored but important point, for it raises the question whether the mystery is perhaps being found in other ways. Is the Spirit, as Moltmann says, *already* present to those outside the church? Or, if more neutral terms are to be preferred, is it possible that genuinely religious experiences, experiences of the transcendent or of a mystical character, still continue to occur widely in society, despite the fact that conventional religious practice itself is in decline?

There is, in fact, a surprising amount of *empirical* evidence that this is actually the case. Some of the most illuminating research in this whole area has been carried out under the auspices of the Alister Hardy Research Centre at Manchester College, Oxford. The Centre's extensive collection of contemporary accounts of experiences characterized as mystical or religious show a number of things. First, religious experience is a great deal more common than many suppose; some studies suggest that up to sixty percent of the population of the United Kingdom claims to have had a mystical experience of some sort.[11] Furthermore, although many of those who claim to have had such an experience are churchgoers, not all are by any means; a high percentage of such experiences appears to occur among people who are relatively unchurched.[12] The statistics are not to be taken uncritically, but they are potentially very significant, especially when set against the prevailing secularity of contemporary Western culture. At the very least, we must conclude that one of the conspicuous things about the claim to religious experience is that it is frequently made, and made by people who often do not describe themselves as practicing members of any religious organization. Also of interest is the extent to which such experiences appear to occur in nonreligious settings.[13]

Of course, none of this immediately implies that any or all such experience is legitimate or real, or that any of it is an experience of the Holy Spirit. Some of it happens to agnostics, and of course there is plenty of mysticism in the non-Christian religions that can be characterized in broadly similar terms to the Christian variety — as an experience of a transcendent power, of an uplifting and pervasive spiritual presence, and so on. For the moment, however, this is not my real concern. I wish only to argue that religious experience, which can be broadly characterized in terms of an experience of the transcendent and experience that leads to a positive transformation of the self, is much more prevalent than many care to admit, and that at least one *plausible* explanation of what is experienced is that there has been an encounter with the Holy Spirit, who is, after all, according to Christian theology, ever living and ever present in the world.

Both theology and church need to learn from these things. For example, there is a very good case to be made for the idea that young people's experimentation with drugs is related to a desire for an "expansion of consciousness," and further, that the reason why people continue to use them is because the initial

11. Meg Maxwell and Verena Tschudin, *Seeing the Invisible* (London: Arkana, 1990), p. 7.

12. David Hay, *Exploring Inner Space* (Oxford: Mowbray, 1987).

13. See the accounts in Hay, *Exploring Inner Space*, pp. 45ff., and in Timothy Beardsworth, *A Sense of Presence* (Oxford: Religious Experience Research Unit, 1977).

flirtation was successful in achieving it. Something or other must be "gotten from it" — and fairly often, given the pervasive presence of drugs in our society. In the case of certain hallucinogenic drugs, it has been clinically proven that statistically significant elevations of standard indicators of "mystical consciousness" can be attained by their use: Oneness within oneself and with one's environment, a perceived insight into "the meaning of life," a sense of timelessness and sacredness, positive moods of joy and love, paradoxicality and ineffability, and even positive changes in character can all, it seems, be achieved.[14] We also know, of course, that these same drugs can destroy the minds and personalities of those who use them, but this, it seems, is characteristic of the end rather than of the beginning of drug use. Could it be that the possibilities for the expansion of consciousness through *religious* experience of a sort that is not destructive and that, according to all the available testimony, leads to a richer rather than to a poorer existence would likewise appeal to our contemporaries? If so, then the closing off of the very possibility of such religious experience in our theology may be responsible for much of the religious alienation of our generation.

The Charismatic Movement

In addition to the seeming pervasiveness of religious experience in the secular sphere, there is another major factor that we must consider: the influence of the charismatic movement. This is a widespread phenomenon in the contemporary church that asserts the specific nature of experience of the Spirit in the "charisms" of the New Testament. The movement is of special importance in this context because of its scope, for when the massive number of people of all classes and cultures involved in the related movements of Pentecostalism, the charismatic movement itself in the mainline churches, and the independent "Spirit" churches of Africa is considered, the movement must now be reckoned as one of the great

14. Wayne E. Oates, *The Holy Spirit and Contemporary Man* (Grand Rapids: Baker, 1968), pp. 17ff.

movements in the whole of church history, and not just a major force in *contemporary* Christianity. This worldwide movement has experienced explosive numerical growth in the twentieth century, and it presents a series of important challenges to traditional theology and church practice. In many ways, it is best understood as a living critique, mostly from the pews, both of the church's traditional thinking about the Spirit and of its general stance in relation to religious experience.

The challenge presented by the charismatic movement to contemporary theology is a direct one: The claim is to have returned to the primitive Christian outlook in which the kingdom of God is still anticipated, but is all the same breaking through into our midst in the present by the power of the Spirit in signs and wonders and in the fulfillment of religious expectation. In much of the developing world in particular, where the Christian church is currently growing at an enormous rate, such highly pneumatic expectations are frequently the norm rather than the exception, whereas the tendency of the Western institutional churches toward a more rationally definable ecclesial life ordered through ministerial office, the Word, and the sacraments tends to be regarded as culturally alien and religiously undesirable.

The most obvious theological question raised by the charismatic movement is also the most controversial: Are the gifts of the Spirit manifested in it really legitimate? This is ultimately a question concerning whether or not such gifts mediate grace and serve the Christian confession of Christ as Lord, or if they are actually highly subjective manifestations of the human psyche or imagination that provoke schism and detract from the human good. To this question we must reply both that the charisms can be empty noisemakers (1 Cor. 13:1) — or even pathological when detached from any deeper religious content — and that, in the case of most of those involved in the renewal, the thing of greatest importance is the deepening of faith and spiritual life that has been experienced. It is really this deepening of spiritual experience that has been the most marked feature of the charismatic movement, for at its center stands a new depth of prayer rather than the sensational experience of the gifts of the Spirit in and for themselves.

There are, naturally, questions that need to be raised. Yves Congar, who has undertaken one of the most careful analyses of the renewal movement, has pointed to a number of these.[15] First, he questions the emphasis on immediacy, the sense that God's presence is so near that older paths of spiritual discipline are apparently made redundant. Although the childlike dependence on God's immediate presence is not in and of itself a false ideal, he argues, there is a serious question of balance that needs to be addressed. Childlikeness and maturity need not be mutually contradictory. Second, Congar queries the use of Scripture in the charismatic movement, which again is characterized by an immediacy between the message and the present situation. Where experience takes precedence, the discipline of study and the difficulties of scholarship can find no place. In particular, the problem of our historical distance from the biblical writers is very real and not something that can easily be transcended. Given the words of Jesus in Luke 10:21 and the general theme that the Spirit is needed to understand the Scriptures aright, it is no doubt a good thing that scholars, the wise and learned, should be displaced from the center of biblical interpretation. Again, however, there is a question of maintaining a healthy perspective on all of this. Even spiritual interpretation can only take place within an intellectual framework and on the basis of a proper translation of the text. Third, Congar points to the superficiality of some charismatic spirituality — for example, the lack of the great mystics' sense that it is not *advisable* to seek great spiritual experiences, given that, if they are genuine, one's responsibilities are subsequently all the greater. Encounter with God is an awesome thing, and often a crucifying experience. Finally, Congar argues that there is a real problem of overemphasis on interiority in much of the movement, and frequently a corresponding loosening of commitment to social concerns, neither of which can be justified on biblical or theological grounds.

15. Yves Congar, *I Believe in the Holy Spirit*, trans. David Smith (London: Geoffrey Chapman; New York: Seabury Press, 1983), vol. 2, pp. 165ff.

The Source Experience

Paul, writing in 1 Corinthians, speaks in the following terms of the Spirit's role in the Christian life:

> No one comprehends what is God's except the Spirit of God. And we have received, not the spirit of the world, but the Spirit that is from God, so that we may understand the gifts bestowed on us by God *(ta hypo tou theou charisthenta hemin)*. . . . But the one who is unspiritual *(psychikos de anthropos)* does not receive the things of God's spirit, for they are foolishness to him, and he is unable to understand them, because they are spiritually discerned. (1 Cor. 2:11b-14, my trans.)

Much more is also said, of course, but the centrality of the experience of the Spirit for theological interpretation is here clearly and uncompromisingly stated. What might this mean, and what implications might it have for the activity of the theologian and for theology itself?

What should be absolutely clear is that such an approach could never lead to a Christianity defined purely by fidelity to ideas. For a theology of the Spirit, who is the "life-giver" as well as the Lord, what matters is the life embraced, and not simply the truth held, as if that were sufficient for itself, or as if it were its own goal. Here, we are approaching the requirements for a real pneumatology and leaving behind the abstract ideal of Logos as the self-sufficient, inclusive symbol of all theology. Or, to put the point another way, we are complementing the ideal of Logos with what it implies and that to which it leads — life in the Spirit.

It would be possible to draw on a number of sources to develop this theme, most obviously from the Pauline and Johannine documents of the New Testament, but also from the great Christian mystics. Let me begin, however, with a less well-known tradition, but one that is of increasing importance in worldwide Christianity: the African church. This is a relatively new field of study, but it is possible for Western theology to learn a great deal here. There is, for example, a basic vitalist outlook that characterizes both traditional African thought and contemporary African Christianity, according to which the world and human life are governed, not only by physical laws, but also by a vital principle that needs to be brought to fulfillment.[16] In keeping with this, salvation is understood in terms of the idea of *wholeness,* which involves the bringing of the life-principle to its proper goal. Wholeness, however, is not something that can ever be achieved by an individual, someone isolated from the rest of society or from the rest of the natural world. Rather, it is with others, both the living and the dead, and in playing one's part in the whole great stream of nature, tradition, and life that one comes oneself to perfection. The role of the Holy Spirit in African Christianity is closely related to this theme of wholeness, in terms of the perception and realization of the vitalist principle that ultimately binds the whole of society and world together, in the normal expectation of healing and visions, in the simple celebration of life, and now in the emerging liberation theologies that are geared to the ideal of wholeness and that are increasingly growing on African soil.

The limitations of so much of Western individualism and consumerism when set against this are only too clear, and while it may be false to suggest that there is a coherent metaphysics underlying this comprehensive vision of things — although one prominent student of African culture has suggested that there is[17] — folk cultures have their own wisdom. Certainly, they are frequently more perceptive of what is of real value in the human sense than the modern culture of our capitalist, technological world. Given the problems that the latter has brought into being — stress-related illness, Third-World debt, the ecological crisis, and the pervasive spiritual vacuum that is so much a part of modern society — it would not hurt us at all to ask again where wisdom can be found.

Closer to home, the seminal twentieth-century Catholic theologian Bernard Lonergan once raised the question of what the foundation for theology in our own era can be or can become in order for theology itself to survive. He concluded that theology

16. T. Tshibangu, "The Task and Method of Theology in Africa," in *A Reader in African Theology,* ed. John Parratt (London: SPCK, 1987), p. 42.

17. Placide Tempels, *La philosophie bantoue* (Paris: Éditions Africaines, 1949). Cf. also John V. Taylor, *The Primal Vision* (London: SCM Press, 1963).

can no longer be based on the logical-deductive methods of scholasticism, as if its first principles really were any longer self-evident or universally received, but must be constructed on analogy with the empirical sciences, so that theology becomes empirical theology.[18] It must, in short, be grounded in living religion, in the living processes by which human beings come to God and experience what Lonergan calls conversion: the lifelong change in relationship, in the self, and in the love for God that constitutes the life of faith. The "objectification of conversion provides theology with its foundations," he writes,[19] which means that the whole of theology must ultimately be traced to the dynamic of the spiritual life. Lonergan's position is not, of course, unique; in the Catholic theological world, Rahner must be understood in a similar way, while the *nouvelle théologie* of such scholars as Jean Daniélou is cast similarly.[20]

I wish to focus in particular, however, on the work of the Irish theologian and Carmelite mystic Noel Dermot O'Donoghue, whose concept of the "source experience" has already been mentioned. In many ways, his theology is not so far removed from that of many contemporary African Christians, for O'Donoghue locates himself squarely in the Celtic tradition, in which there is an elemental sense of the unity of all things in God, and of God in all things. His vision is a transforming one of wholeness, which builds bridges in the world of the spirit where others have burnt them, and which attempts a synthesis of the act of prayer and theology with life itself.

It is O'Donoghue's concept of the source experience that has particular relevance in the present context, however, for there would seem to be a strong case for regarding such a concept as amenable to the themes of pneumatology — though the pneumatological connection is not explicitly made by O'Donoghue. Nevertheless, he makes a number of perceptive points that are central to our own

18. Bernard Lonergan, "Theology in Its New Context," in Lonergan, *A Second Collection* (Philadelphia: Westminster, 1974), pp. 55-67.

19. Bernard Lonergan, *Method in Theology* (New York: Herder and Herder, 1972), p. 130.

20. For a survey of these trends in twentieth-century Catholic theology, an excellent source is Avery Dulles, *The Assurance of Things Hoped For* (New York and Oxford: Oxford University Press, 1994), pp. 130ff.

task. The source experience is introduced, for example, in the context of a discussion of the total commitment of the visionary (whether mystical, artistic, or moral) to what he or she claims to discover:

> For the mystic as such the commitment is, first and last, finalised and energised by an experience of the source of all man's words and works, an experience of the source of man's being and of all goodness. All truth and beauty as well. It is from this experience that all mystical imagination flows. I call it "the source-experience."[21]

The totality of the commitment that this source experience requires is something due to the nature of the source experienced: "As long as there is any attachment to something other than the source, then full attachment to the source is impossible, impossible by a kind of mathematical impossibility."[22] But this does not mean that the experience is barren or that it closes off the sources of the springs of life, for the "source" in the absolute sense *is* the source of all life and truth and goodness, "than which none greater can be conceived," to quote St. Anselm. And it is the authenticity of the source, rather than any external criteria, that lends authenticity and value to the source experience, and to the visionary-worlds of the mystical writers and poets that flow from it.

It is to a theology geared to such experience, an experience that we might describe in biblical terms as what occurs when seeking becomes finding, that the doctrine of the Holy Spirit itself calls us. It may even be that an openness to such experience is the one thing that might sustain theology itself, while also preserving it from becoming a moral or intellectual straitjacket. At times, in short, theological formulation must be secondary to spiritual experience, the "system" to the "vision," for it is only where the religious vision is kept alive that justice can be done to the object of the system itself, who is not *so much* the God of the philosophers as he

---

21. Noel Dermot O'Donoghue, "Mystical Imagination," in *Religious Imagination,* ed. James P. Mackey (Edinburgh: T. & T. Clark, 1986), p. 191.
22. O'Donoghue, "Mystical Imagination," p. 196.

is the living God of the human heart. For O'Donoghue, the one thing that enables theology to be developed in this way is prayer. It is in prayer that the source experience is both discovered and kept alive, and it is through prayer that it exists as something more than a secondhand object of detached theological reflection. This is not to say that the latter is unnecessary in its place, but only that it is secondary and derivative of the former. We are not far here from the Pauline text with which we began this section, or from the world of the New Testament generally.

Theology is an intellectual discipline — and perhaps even *the* discipline par excellence — in which the mode of human knowledge must be adapted to its object and to the media of knowledge. This is fundamental to O'Donoghue's approach to theology. To understand what prayer is, what it might mean to open up to God and to the experience of God in prayer, we must follow a route that leads us to that very goal. For whether in the soaring heights of the Magnificat or the searing depths of Jesus' words in Gethsemane, prayer is not something concerned with the philosophical problem of divine action or with the objective description and cataloging of prayer experiences culled from whatever source. It is, rather, at its heart, the opening up of a human being to the infinite, to transcendent Love itself. Only by entering into such experience can one understand what it is all about; "inside knowledge" is required, for prayer is more a craft or a "discipline" in the moral sense than it is anything else. Therefore, just as to understand the love poetry of John Donne one has first to be a lover oneself (and it is because one is a lover that one reads Donne), so also the only way to understand prayer is to pray — and then to look at our own experience in the light of another's, in order to help us to identify and to understand what corresponds to the word *prayer* in us. This may be contemplation, revelation, faith, hope, charity, suffering, joy, or all of them in some measure at various times. This is why the Psalms can be so profound and speak to us so powerfully, but it is also why to those who know nothing of, for example, the *de profundis* they can seem so mute.

In the same way, a theology that is really a theology of the Holy Spirit will be, in addition to all else, something capable of opening up new dimensions of the spiritual life and a theology of the experience of God. It will be, from this point of view, concerned more with life than with truth, the life lived "in God." As a result, it will be not so much a technical as a practical and even a popular theology. Spirit and spirituality go hand in hand. O'Donoghue at one point goes so far as to say, "A certain ponderous dullness and flatness of style is an infallible sign that a writer is not a true guide to the sacred places."[23] I would prefer to say that there is a place for technical vocabulary in theology, but it is not at this point, where everything is light and love and where the encounter with God is the theme.

One further point remains — a point that is strangely neglected across a range of recent theology. To speak of an experience of the Holy Spirit is to imply that there has been an experience of the holiness of the source of that experience. In fact, it is axiomatic for the writers of the New Testament and for the theologians of the early church that it is impossible to know God without holiness. Ethics, therefore, is crucially significant, not as the tail end toward which theology moves, but here at the point of entry, which I have argued is the experience of God. "Blessed are the pure in heart, for they will see God" (Matt. 5:8); we have it on good authority, but this is a precept that applies to the present as much as to the eschatological future, to the beginnings of the spiritual life as well as to its end. The early patristic approach to pneumatology, for all its weaknesses, firmly grasped this point, that the beginning of the knowledge of God implies a renunciation of sin and self, a process of repentance and renewal. There is, in the final analysis, no other starting place, no other point of entry, than this.

---

23. Noel Dermot O'Donoghue, *The Holy Mountain* (Dublin: Dominican Publications, 1983), p. 17.

6. The Spirit of Jesus Christ

Jesus the "Anointed One": The Theology of Heribert Mühlen

Some years ago, Hendrikus Berkhof, in a now-classic work entitled *The Doctrine of the Holy Spirit,* noted the fact that some of the earliest christologies of the church, even as late as the middle of the second century, were broadly pneumatic in character.[1] From the standpoint of later theology, of course, the understanding of Christ's Sonship and of the Holy Spirit involved in these early theologies came to be seen as problematic, and they were subsequently abandoned by the church. In this, however, Christian theology lost something important and distinctive, for the New Testament clearly understands Jesus as the goal of God's life-giving presence as Spirit in Israel's history, and as the focus and starting point of a new work of the Spirit in the world. The loss of Spirit as a christological category in the early tradition meant that this christological perspective went undeveloped, resulting in negative

---

1. Hendrikus Berkhof, *The Doctrine of the Holy Spirit* (London: Epworth Press, 1965), p. 20, with reference to Ignatius, *Epistle to the Ephesians,* 7.2; *2 Clement,* 9.5; and Hermas, *Similitudes,* 5.6.5.

145

implications that are still with us. According to Berkhof, the result is that, in our efforts to reconstruct a more inclusive concept of Christ and of the Spirit, we lack a developed conceptuality, and thus a clear starting point and basis for discussion.

Berkhof's pneumatology, and his plea for new development in the christology of anointing, anticipated developments that were to follow. These occurred, however, not so much in Berkhof's own (Protestant) theological tradition, but rather in Catholic theology, through a reappraisal of a doctrine that Berkhof himself overlooked: the scholastic doctrine of the "habitual" or "accidental" sanctification of Jesus. Scholastic theology differentiates between Jesus' "habitual" or "accidental" sanctity, which describes the relation of the Spirit and the Logos to the human nature of Christ, and his "essential" or "substantial" sanctification. (The same point can be expressed in terms of the "grace of union" on the one hand, over against "created grace" on the other.) The distinction was developed in the medieval schools, but it has its real roots in the development of christology in the patristic era, and particularly in the doctrine of the hypostatic union, according to which the human nature of Jesus has no independent "hypostasis" or personal existence, but exists hypostatically only in the Logos. According to the doctrine of the hypostatic union, in the concrete historical person of Jesus we are strictly concerned with the Logos who assumed human nature. In keeping with this, the "accidental" sanctification of Jesus, his anointing with the Spirit, is seen as a function of the hypostatic union, which constitutes his "substantial" sanctification.

In developing the doctrine of the hypostatic union in this way, scholastic theology actually went so far as to assert that the "unction" of Christ — the anointing that makes Jesus the "Christ," in short — is the anointing of human nature with the divine in the incarnation. Over against this, the accidental or habitual graces of Christ were taken to be logically distinct from the grace of union in the sense that they did not involve a hypostatic union, and to be logically secondary and derivative in the sense that they flowed from it. Jesus' habitual grace and infused virtues, together with the gifts of the Holy Spirit by which he healed the sick, and so on, were thus appropriated to the Holy Spirit's work in his human nature.[2] According to Thomas Aquinas, for example, one must acknowledge the fact that Christ possessed such habitual grace for the simple reason that Scripture teaches that the Spirit of God rested upon him; since the distinctive mission of the Holy Spirit is to bestow habitual grace, he argues, Christ must have possessed it.[3] Thomas also tries to construct a case for the necessity of habitual grace in Jesus through the doctrine of Christ's true human nature.[4] As a man, and because his human nature is not confused with the divine even after the hypostatic union, Jesus had to participate in the divine nature in the same way as do all men and women under grace. Jesus must therefore have received habitual graces like all other human beings — graces that enabled him to live a life of godliness by the characteristically human acts of knowledge and will. Thomas's thought is broadly representative of the scholastic tradition, with the exception of Duns Scotus, who apparently identified substantial holiness with the uncreated sanctity of God and therefore refused to attribute substantial holiness to Christ on the grounds that such an attribution might be taken to imply a denial of his true human nature.[5]

The reassessment of this scholastic doctrine in recent Catholic thought is largely due to the seminal work of Heribert Mühlen, a theologian who is unfortunately little known in English-language theology.[6] Mühlen, interestingly, provides an answer to Berkhof's question about the uniqueness of the union of the Spirit with Christ. He does so by means of his reexamination of the doctrine of accidental sanctification, so setting a theological agenda for subse-

---

2. A. Michel, "Jésus-Christ," in *Dictionnaire de théologie catholique,* vol. 8, ed. A. Vacant et al. (Paris: Librairie Letouzey et Ané, 1924), col. 1277-81.

3. Thomas Aquinas, *Summa Theologiae,* 3a. 7, 1; 1a. 43, 3.

4. Aquinas, *Summa Theologiae,* 3a. 7, 1, ad 1.

5. Michel, "Jésus-Christ," cols. 1275-76.

6. Mühlen has pursued this theme through a variety of works; Yves Congar, *I Believe in the Holy Spirit,* trans. David Smith (London: Geoffrey Chapman; New York: Seabury Press, 1983), vol. 1, pp. 22-25, provides a summary of his position from this point of view. In what follows, reference has been made to Heribert Mühlen, *Der Heilige Geist als Person,* 5th ed. (Münster: Aschendorff, 1988); and to his "Das Christusereignis als Tat des Heiligen Geistes," in *Mysterium Salutis,* ed. Johannes Feiner and Magnus Löhrer (Einsiedeln: Benziger Verlag, 1969), III/2, pp. 513-45.

quent theologies of the anointing of Jesus. Mühlen begins by accepting the scholastic idea that the role of the Holy Spirit in the life of Christ was a secondary implication of the hypostatic union. According to Mühlen, because the Spirit proceeds from the Father and the Son, and because the Son assumes human nature in the incarnation, the Spirit must rest upon that nature.[7] He thus attributes the anointing of Jesus ultimately to the Logos rather than to the Spirit, in the sense that the anointing of the humanity with the Spirit to make Jesus the "Christ" derives from the *assumptio carnis* in the incarnation.

Mühlen recognizes the limitations of the scholastic version of this doctrine, however, and attempts to overcome them. They derive, in his view, from an inability to conceive of the humanity of Christ in a fully historical way, and so to think of the relation of the Spirit to Christ in terms adequate to the historicity of human nature. According to Thomas Aquinas, for example, there was and could have been no increase in the habitual grace of Christ throughout his life. Since he had already reached the goal of creaturely union with God from his conception, through his substantial sanctification in the grace of union, the accidental graces of the Holy Spirit must also have been present in their fullness from the beginning.[8] Thus he possessed the fullness of faith, hope, and charity — not to mention the vision of God itself — from his mother's womb. This is implied, for Thomas, by the very concept of the hypostatic union; the humanity of Christ must have received perfect and complete habitual grace from the very beginning of its existence, since the union of divine and human natures in the *hypostasis* of the Son means that the Holy Spirit who proceeds eternally from the Son can never be separated from the human nature he assumed, but is necessarily communicated to it continually in its fullness.[9]

It is true that, within such a conception, the work of the Holy Spirit or habitual grace is still necessary for Jesus as man; Chalcedonian christological orthodoxy proclaims that the hypostatic union

7. Mühlen, *Der Heilige Geist als Person*, pp. 206-7.
8. Aquinas, *Summa Theologiae*, 3a. 7, 12.
9. Aquinas, *Summa Theologiae*, 3a. 7, 5 *ad* 2; 7, 13.

does not obliterate the distinction of natures, as Thomas was well aware. However, over against the incarnation as such, the work of the Spirit in the humanity of Christ appears to be of small and merely incidental significance; in many ways, it is simply a logical implication of other considerations. Above all, it cannot be seen as the ground of the divine Sonship of Christ. It is rather the result or "crown" of a divine Sonship that is already presupposed on totally independent grounds — that is, as the result of the hypostatic union. Jesus' Sonship is here strictly a function of the action of the Logos, whereas the work of the Spirit is secondary and derivative — to endow the humanity assumed with those created sanctifying graces and charisms by means of which the man Jesus could live in a holy manner.[10]

The intention in all of this was to acknowledge the true humanity of Christ and to provide a distinctive role in christology for the Holy Spirit in its relation to that humanity. However, the concept of human nature it involved was defective. It allowed no growth or movement in Jesus' human relation to God, whereas development is essential to human existence; without it, one cannot be a human being in a physical, psychological, social, or, we might add, spiritual sense. For this very reason, the role of the Spirit was also minimal in the medieval conception. The problem was that, in the end, the doctrine of the hypostatic union was interpreted in a timeless and static rather than a dynamic and temporal way. It was a conception that did not permit the humanity of Christ to be considered apart from its once-for-all assumption by the Logos. In the medieval conception, therefore, even the accidental sanctification of the humanity of Jesus by the Holy Spirit became a function of the incarnation, in the sense that the graces given to the human nature by the Spirit were seen to flow ultimately from the hypostatic union, and thus all at once.

This is a weakness that shows up perhaps most critically in less subtle versions of the scholastic position, in which the hypostatic union is of such importance that the Holy Spirit in effect has no place in christology at all. In the later medieval period, for example,

10. Yves Congar, *The Word and the Spirit*, trans. David Smith (London: Geoffrey Chapman, 1986), p. 86.

the tendency was to ascribe everything of positive importance to the hypostatic union as a result of an anti-Scotist concern to reassert the importance of Christ's substantial sanctification. The result, however, was that Jesus' habitual grace, deriving from the work of the Spirit, appeared to be superfluous.[11] This is a tendency that is not only found in the medieval period; it can be seen also, for example, in nineteenth-century scholasticism in the theology of M. Scheeben, who maintains that biblical and patristic references to the anointing of Jesus by the Spirit are to be straightforwardly understood in the sense that Jesus is anointed by the Word, who is the principle of the Spirit.[12] Any real christological role for the Holy Spirit is in this way effectively eliminated from theology.

Mühlen himself attempts to overcome the defects of this christology by developing a salvation-historical role for the work of the Holy Spirit in the life of Christ. In a contribution to *Mysterium Salutis,* for example, he distinguishes between the salvation-historical framework of the christology of anointing and the ontological christology of the theological tradition, arguing that the particular significance of the christology of anointing lies in its historical reference. This provides Mühlen with a theological horizon in which to discuss the place of the Holy Spirit in christology. He is aware that the biblical christology of anointing — as later developed in early heterodoxy by the Ebionites, for example — was inadequate and that it required substantial ontological elaboration, something achieved through the development of Logos christology.[13] Nevertheless, the salvation-historical aspect of christology, grounded as it is in biblical revelation and related as it is to the historical humanity of Jesus, needs to be reaffirmed in our theology.

Though Logos christology as ontological and pneumatic christology as salvation-historical are to be distinguished, Mühlen argues that it is nevertheless possible to draw an analogy between the

---

11. Cf. Liam G. Walsh, in St. Thomas Aquinas, *Summa Theologiae,* trans., with introduction and notes, by Liam G. Walsh (London: Eyre & Spottiswoode; New York: McGraw-Hill, 1974), vol. 49, pp. 46-47, note a.

12. So David Coffey, *Grace: The Gift of the Holy Spirit* (Sydney: Catholic Institute of Sydney, 1979), pp. 93-95.

13. Mühlen, "Das Christusereignis," pp. 519-24. Subsequent references will be given parenthetically in the text.

sending of the Son and the sending of the Spirit, so that just as the former is designated the incarnation *(Menschwerdung)* of the Son of God, so the latter can be spoken of as the *Zeitwerdung* of the Holy Spirit (530). The German word is virtually untranslatable, but the point is that in anointing Jesus, and in continuing to mediate between the risen Christ and the church, the Spirit becomes bound up in and with the temporal existence and mission of Jesus Christ. In this way, the Spirit assumes a role *in time* and thus in the outworking of God's work of salvation that, according to Mühlen, he did not have before (531-32). Mühlen does not limit the term *Zeitwerdung* to the Holy Spirit, for the *Menschwerdung* of the Logos can also be called a *Zeitwerdung* (531). In the incarnation, the Logos "became" something in time that he had not been from "the beginning." The crucial point, however, is that the Holy Spirit, in his activity in the life of Jesus, also becomes what he was not before. Mühlen develops this idea in two ways. In the first place, while presupposing the doctrine of the accidental sanctification of Jesus, Mühlen is able to argue that the Spirit created in Jesus such graces as were required for his messianic office and that, through time, these graces increased and developed in his personal history. This grace, for Mühlen as for the scholastics, derived ultimately from the hypostatic union but more immediately from the "unction" of the Holy Spirit — according to the infancy narratives, from the beginning of his existence. The total history of grace in Jesus' life, according to Mühlen, from his conception to his death, resurrection, and exaltation, must be understood as a history also of the Spirit who bestowed the grace.

Second, Mühlen takes up the Johannine theology of the Spirit, as expressed in particular in John 7:39; 16:7; and 20:22-23, and as developed, again, in the scholastic doctrine of the *gratia capitis* of Christ (which refers to the grace given to him as head of the church and for the sake of the church as his body), whereby the accidental sanctification of Christ is oriented *a priori* to the plurality of persons he represents as the incarnate one.[14] In his own development of the doctrine of the *gratia capitis,* Mühlen again emphasizes the stages of the work of the Spirit in the historical humanity

---

14. Mühlen, *Der Heilige Geist als Person,* pp. 229-30.

of Christ; in particular, he argues that it was only through the earthly obedience of Jesus unto death that the Spirit became in time the gift given also to the church, and not only to Jesus, forever (532). In this way, the *Zeitwerdung* of the Spirit continues beyond the Christ-event itself into the time of the church.

One of the strengths of Mühlen's wider pneumatology is that in this way it comes to be oriented as much to ecclesiology as it is to christology. It is, in fact, an attempt to relate the two together in a single systematic, pneumatological conception. Therefore, while the basis of the whole development lies in the activity of the Holy Spirit in the Christ-event, Mühlen refers to the characteristic work of the Holy Spirit in the economy of salvation as the Spirit's "corporeality" *(Leibhaftigkeit)* in the church (518). The connection between the two is that the continuing work of the Spirit in the church is the continuation of the salvation-historical anointing of Jesus with the Spirit. This reflects Mühlen's description of the Spirit as "One Person in many persons" — that is, in Christ and in the plurality of persons constituting the church. The point is that the Spirit must be understood in his presence and activity in the church as the same Spirit who anointed Jesus, the incarnate Son of God, and as the Spirit through whom this same Jesus now makes himself present to us (533). Two points follow from this. First of all, for Mühlen, the key difference as far as the church is concerned between the Christ-event and the Spirit-event that has its origin in the Christ-event is the "then" of temporal completion that attaches to Jesus' earthly saving work and the "now" of his present activity through his Spirit, though in the concrete economy of salvation these are aspects of a single divine work. Second, the Spirit does not mediate to us a heavenly Christ, someone abstracted from his history and ours, but rather makes possible a contemporary salvific participation in the historical Christ-event. Or rather, to be more precise, Christ himself allows such participation in himself through his Spirit (540-43).

One further theme remains to be mentioned: Mühlen's doctrine of the Trinity, where the emphasis falls on the personal character of the Father, Son, and Spirit, in clear contrast to a more ontological conception of the Trinity. Mühlen holds that a doctrine of the Trinity that is purely ontologically conceived is inadequate, in that it needs to be supplemented by a trinitarian language and conceptuality that can express more fully the mysterious personal life of God and can show how the divine life is the ground of the saving acts of God in history. His own understanding of the Spirit's role in the Trinity is built on the older Western model of the Trinity, in which the Spirit proceeds from the Father and the Son as from one principle. But Mühlen gives this an interesting new twist by defining the Spirit as "the subsistent We-act" between the Father and the Son, that is, as their We-relation or mutual love. Mühlen's theology here is a radicalized version of the Augustinian trinitarian theory of relational predication, and thus of the traditional Western relational understanding of the Persons, by means of what he understands to be a synthesis of the trinitarian theologies of Augustine and Richard of St. Victor.[15] In the immanent trinitarian life, the Father appears in Mühlen as the "I relation," the Son as the "Thou relation," and the Spirit as the "We in person." According to Mühlen, the Holy Spirit is thus eternally oriented to a plurality of persons and can be seen in his salvation-historical function as related both to the *person* of the incarnate Son (rather than to the human nature assumed) and to the whole of the mass of humanity whom the Son came to redeem. As the "We in person," the Spirit is thus in his salvation-historical function the personal bond between Christ and all those baptized into him.[16]

The Theology of Walter Kasper

We can see how Mühlen's theology has been taken further in recent christology by exploring the theology of Walter Kasper. Though Kasper begins with Mühlen's understanding of the salvation-historical significance of the anointing of Jesus, he goes on to develop

15. Mühlen, *Der Heilige Geist als Person*, pp. 81-82, 167. The new "personological" vocabulary also enables Mühlen to make an advance upon the older Augustinian theory of trinitarian relations. He characterizes the relation between the Father and the Son on the one hand and with the Holy Spirit on the other as a "We-You" relation, from the point of view, as it were, of the Father and the Son, and as an "I-You (plural)" relation, from the point of view of the Spirit.

16. Mühlen, *Der Heilige Geist als Person*, pp. 195-97.

a more radical and thoroughgoing Spirit christology. Unlike Mühlen, Kasper's approach challenges the older trinitarian and christological ideas to which Mühlen is ultimately committed. In particular, he argues that the *filioque* doctrine requires fundamental
revision and that the hypostatic union is not the presupposition of
Jesus' anointing with the Spirit but is instead its consequence.[17]
Kasper's claim, in fact, is nothing less than that Logos christology
derives from Spirit christology.

Let us take the christological point first. According to Kasper,
just as our sonship by adoption is the work of the Spirit, so Jesus'
Sonship can also be regarded from a pneumatological point of view
— without, however, thereby excluding the idea of the assumption
of flesh by the Logos. The basic issue is the sense in which Jesus
receives grace by the work of the Spirit as the Son of God in his
historical humanity. For Mühlen, the anointing of Jesus is an implication of the hypostatic union. For Kasper, on the other hand,
Jesus can only be the Son of God in his concrete history of obedience by virtue of the anointing of the Holy Spirit. The Spirit not
only created and sanctified Jesus' human nature at his conception
but also provided the temporal, creaturely humanity assumed with
continuing and increasing graces of love for and obedience to the
Father, thus *enabling* Jesus to be the Son of God in his concrete
human history. On this view, the "accidental sanctification" of the
humanity actually becomes the presupposition of the hypostatic
union, in the sense that the temporal work of the Holy Spirit in
the humanity of Christ is taken to mediate in a dynamic and
temporal manner the union of the human with the divine nature
of Christ. The Holy Spirit, in other words, constantly mediates the
incarnation.

Kasper's understanding of the role of the Holy Spirit in christology is a response to what he takes to be the central problem of
christology: how Jesus Christ can be the Word made flesh, or, in
Kasper's terms, the "self-communication of God in history." To
account for this, the Nicene-Chalcedonian christological axis affirms

---

17. Walter Kasper, *Jesus the Christ*, trans. V. Green (London: Burns & Oates,
1977), pp. 230-74. Subsequent references will be given parenthetically in the
text.

the doctrines of the consubstantiality of the Father and the Son, a true incarnation of God in a complete human nature without any confusion, change, or division of the two natures, and (by implication) the interpretative doctrine of the hypostatic union. Kasper's view is not so much that the traditional view is mistaken as that the doctrines in question are overly static and metaphysical in character, and too little concerned with Jesus' historical, human relation, not to his divine nature as the Son, but to the Father.[18] According to Kasper, the traditional account of Jesus as the incarnate Son separates his status as the divine self-communication from his history of obedience and love to the Father. But this, Kasper argues, threatens the total witness of biblical revelation that the God of history is revealed in Jesus Christ in such a way that this historical human being, Jesus of Nazareth, is the Word made flesh.

Kasper thus accepts Nicene orthodoxy in his christology but at the same time argues that under the conditions of the incarnation, and in view of the true human nature of Christ, it is necessary to reappropriate its meaning in a new way in order to understand it in "relational" or "personal" terms. The goal is to take up into christology the existential dynamic of human historical existence (238). For Kasper, the whole character of God's revelation and of the incarnation above all demands that Jesus' history of obedience to the Father be of fundamental importance (1-39, 240-52). His claim is that, like all men and women, Jesus Christ *is* his history, in the sense that his identity is constituted by his life, by the decisions and actions taken in it, and so on, and therefore that it must be in this history that Jesus is the Logos or self-communication of God.

The starting point of Kasper's whole conception is thus the humanity of Jesus, since it is in his humanity, according to Kasper, that he is the Son of God (245-48). For Kasper, Jesus as man is to be understood as a historical human being like other human beings, and to be defined like other human beings: Jesus is a person, a subjective ego constituted by a network of relationships; as such, he is to be understood in terms of his openness to others and

18. Kasper, *Jesus the Christ*, pp. 236-38. Cf. also David Coffey, "The 'Incarnation' of the Holy Spirit in Christ," *Theological Studies* 45 (1984): 473.

ultimately to God. From the New Testament, we know that Jesus' openness to God takes the form of obedience to and love of the Father. Kasper builds his christology on these anthropological presuppositions. On the one hand, Jesus' obedience to the Father, which in his case is absolute, presupposes that he relates to the Father as one from whom he is distinct. His being as a human ego is defined relationally in these terms, being wholly determined by his relation to the Father — and, of course, to his neighbor. On the other hand, his very obedience in love can only be the direct result of God's turning to him in love, for it is only God who can bridge the chasm between himself and humanity to fulfill the transcendent potentiality of his creature. The obedience of Jesus is thus, for Kasper, the result of the Father's perfect self-communication to him, the complete human response to the complete divine turning of the Father to him in love. It is therefore just because Jesus is nothing other than the Father's self-communication that he is also defined by his historical obedience to the Father in love. The two do not merely imply one another; they are intensified proportionate to one another, so that in Jesus they are completely identical: Jesus Christ is true God, the Father's Word, and true man, the perfect human response to God.

Kasper's approach presupposes the transcendental christology of Karl Rahner, who is an inescapable presence in much modern Catholic thought. In Rahner's reconstruction of christology, the basic strategy is to ask what the conditions are for the possibility of the incarnation of the Word in Jesus. Rahner himself does not develop a christology from the point of view of pneumatology; on the contrary, for Rahner the humanity of Jesus is related primarily to the Word who assumed it rather than to the Spirit or, indeed, to the Father.[19] However, as we shall see, his position lends itself to pneumatological development, and even requires such development.[20]

19. Karl Rahner, "Current Problems in Christology," in Rahner, *Theological Investigations,* vol. 1, trans. Cornelius Ernst, 2nd ed. (London: Darton, Longman & Todd, 1965), pp. 149-200.

20. This is suggested by Wilhelm Thüsing in conjunction with Rahner himself in Karl Rahner and Wilhelm Thüsing, *A New Christology,* trans. David Smith and Verdant Green (London: Burns & Oates, 1980), pp. 60 and 108ff. Thüsing argues that Rahner's transcendental christology must be interpreted in

Rahner's theology at this point is grounded in modern existential and phenomenological philosophy. It is, as Rahner himself says, an attempt to restate, in relational or "ontological" terms, the truth expressed in the "ontic" categories of classical christology.[21] In particular, his christology is a reinterpretation, in these relational terms, of the older idea of the *capax Dei*.[22] He understands the hypostatic union in terms of the human potentiality for obedience to God that Jesus, as man, shares with the rest of humanity:

> Human being is . . . a reality absolutely open upwards; a reality which reaches its highest . . . perfection, the realization of the highest possibility of man's being, when in it the Logos himself becomes existent in the world.[23]

Christology for Rahner thus largely becomes a function of theological anthropology. Insofar as the potentiality for obedience to God that is present in human nature can only be actualized by a divine self-communication, and insofar as the divine self-communication with which we are here concerned is to be understood as the Word of God, human being as such is to be seen as the potentiality for the hypostatic union. The claim is not that there have been many hypostatic unions, for there has only ever been one complete self-communication of God to humanity, Jesus Christ. Nevertheless, for Rahner, human nature as such is oriented to God's self-communication, and open infinitely upward, so that at the summit of its potentiality it is entirely appropriate to find that it has its *hypostasis* in the *hypostasis* of the Word, as the older christological tradition maintains.

Following Rahner, the basic christological problem posed by

---

the light of the biblical understanding of *pneuma* as that power by which the human openness to God is possible; he appeals in particular to the Pauline *pneuma* christology of 2 Cor. 3:17 and 1 Cor. 15:45 (cf. also Gal. 4:6 and Rom. 8:15).

21. Karl Rahner, "On the Theology of the Incarnation," in Rahner, *Theological Investigations,* vol. 4, trans. Kevin Smyth (London: Darton, Longman and Todd, 1966), pp. 105-20.

22. On what follows, see Rahner, "Current Problems in Christology."

23. Rahner, "Current Problems in Christology," p. 183.

Kasper is how the divine Son can be man in such a way that the Father's self-communication can literally *be* the history of Jesus Christ. The problem is one of mediation, of how it is possible for the divinity and the humanity, though distinct, to be one in Jesus (240ff.). It is here that Kasper goes beyond Rahner, and here that his theology is of particular pneumatological interest, for his argument is that only the Holy Spirit and a pneumatologically oriented christology can provide the answer. Kasper formulates his christological position as follows:

> By wholly filling Jesus' humanity, the Spirit endows it with the openness by which it can freely and wholly constitute a mould for God's self-communication. . . . The Spirit is thus in person God's love as freedom, and the creative principle which sanctifies the man Jesus in such a way as to enable him, by free obedience and dedication, to be the incarnate response to God's self-communication. (251)

Kasper's basic argument leads to the conclusion that if sacred history is not to be emptied of its content, and theological metaphysics made meaningless, then the doctrine of the Trinity must be understood as the "transcendental condition" for the possibility of the self-communication of God the Father to Jesus (251). The question is basically who God must be in order to make this historical self-communication possible. Kasper concludes that only a model of the Trinity in which the Spirit has a central role to play in God's outreach to the world can meet this requirement. He develops a theology in which the Spirit is not only the love between the Father and the Son, according to the Augustinian paradigm, but also the "surplus and effusion of freedom in the love between the Father and the Son."[24] The point is that, as this "surplus" of love, the Spirit is the personal agent within the Trinity itself in whom the Father, through the Son, reaches outward, in love, to the world. It is the Spirit who is the transcendental possibility of the divine self-communication to the creation: "The Spirit as mediator be-

---

24. Kasper, *Jesus the Christ*, p. 250. Like Mühlen, Kasper's theology draws heavily on the trinitarian pneumatology of Richard of St. Victor at this point.

tween Father and Son is at the same time the mediation of God into history" (250).

Once again, therefore, the basis of the Christ-event is seen to be pneumatological, in the sense that the love by which God in himself loves the world, so much so that he gave his only begotten Son, is somehow identical with the Holy Spirit. The Spirit thus serves a mediating role between God the Father and his self-communication in history in Jesus Christ. More than this, however, in Kasper's pneumatic christology it is *in the Spirit* that Jesus is the self-communication of the Father: Jesus is the Logos in his history of obedience and love precisely because the Spirit dwells fully within him. It is therefore the activity of the Spirit in the humanity of Jesus that makes him the perfect response of obedience and love to God and love of neighbor which constitutes him the Father's self-communication and thus the Son of God.

In Kasper's theology, therefore, the Spirit is the love by which the Trinity is impelled outward and not simply, as in the Augustinian model, the bond of love between the Father and the Son. Thus, for Kasper, the Trinity is eternally oriented *ad extra* through the Holy Spirit. As it is therefore in the Holy Spirit that the self-communication in love of the Father through the Son to the world takes place, so in the immanent Trinity the Holy Spirit is to be understood as the overflowing love of God in person, in whom God is eternally the gift of himself. Kasper argues that this is the irreducible minimum that both Eastern and Western pneumatology, divided as they are by the *filioque,* must be able to affirm.[25] This leads him to a critique of both East and West, who are equally unable to affirm the presence of the Holy Spirit in the economy as the gift of God himself as uncreated grace: the East because of its doctrine of the divine *energeia,* and the West because of its doctrine of created grace. For Kasper, by contrast, the Holy Spirit in the economy of salvation is the temporal realization of the eternal "Giftness" of the triune God.

25. Walter Kasper, *The God of Jesus Christ,* trans. Matthew O'Connell (London: SCM Press, 1984), pp. 214-29.

The Christlike Spirit

It is customary in much of Christian theology to understand the phrase "the Spirit of Christ," for which there is clear biblical warrant, as denoting the Spirit who is under the authority of Christ. It is as such that the Spirit mediates Christ to the church. Without such a christological restriction, it might be argued, the work of the Spirit could be detached from the concrete center of Christian faith, Jesus Christ, and could ultimately become a cipher for a vague mysticism. Karl Barth, in his early theology, openly used this argument against Eastern Orthodoxy, in order to buttress the Western doctrine of the *filioque* and to safeguard the connection between the work of the Spirit and revelation.[26]

If the line of thought explored in the previous section is justified, however, then it is possible to speak of the Spirit as the Spirit of Christ in another sense. The Spirit, seen from the standpoint of the christology of anointing, is not only the Spirit given by Christ, or the Spirit under his control, but is also the Spirit who rested on Jesus in such a way as to make him what he was. According to this view, the character of Jesus does indeed define the nature of the Spirit's work, so that we can speak of the "Christlike" Spirit, but only because the Spirit has *already* defined the character of Jesus as the one who loves God and neighbor to the end. In short, Christ is as like the Spirit as the Spirit is like Christ. In both cases, the Spirit can be understood to be "Christlike": The Spirit comes from Christ and takes from what is his, adding nothing of his own (John 16:14); alternatively, the Spirit is the one anointing Jesus so that he brings the gospel to the poor and proclaims release to the captives, recovery of sight to the blind, and freedom for the oppressed, for the Spirit is the kind of Spirit who, on such soil, produces such fruits (Luke 4:18, citing Isa. 61). Both of these are deeply embedded in the strata of the New Testament, but can the two ideas be brought together into a single conception, and if so, do both have something important to say to us?

26. Karl Barth, *Church Dogmatics*, ed. T. F. Torrance and trans. G. W. Bromiley et al. (Edinburgh: T. & T. Clark, 1936-75), I/1 (2nd ed., 1975), pp. 473ff.

The concept of Jesus as one anointed by the Spirit to become the righteous one, the one who does the will of God and the one who in so doing expresses parabolically the very being of God, is, of course, the primary theme of and point of departure for adoptionism in all ages. Adoptionism is what it is, however, not so much because of what it says about the Spirit and Jesus as because of what it says about Jesus' *Sonship:* For the adoptionists, his Sonship is essentially like ours, a *moral Sonship.* In this way, Jesus becomes the paradigm for the life lived in fellowship with God, the guide on life's way, and the true prophet who reveals both the Word of God addressed to the world from above and the true response of obedience and devotion from below. In the early centuries of the Christian church, adoptionism was characteristically concerned to stress that God's involvement in the world of time and space, of suffering and sin in Jesus, was only indirect and tangential. God himself does not incarnate, for he is one, impassible, infinite, and so on, rather than multiple, passible, and finite as the world is. Rather than messing his hands directly, therefore, which in any case might well lead to the world's dissolution, God reaches out through a created intermediary, who shows his way to men and women, a way that is revealed as the way of a Father with his children and, correlatively, utilizing one of the primary metaphors of the New Testament, as a glorious way of adoption and sonship.

The link with adoptionism past and present, however, is actually a distraction for Spirit christology. First of all, no adoptionist theology will ever be embraced by the church; since theology is either a servant of the church's faith or nothing, there is really no point in developing such an approach, for it is ruled out as something useless in advance. But more important than this is the fact that adoptionist christology is strictly unnecessary, for Spirit christology and Logos christology are surely no more incompatible than Spirit and Logos themselves. According to strict trinitarian orthodoxy, after all, the two are one as much as they are distinct.

Furthermore, as I argued in Chapter 1, there is already in the New Testament something of a "coincidence of opposites" of Spirit and Logos christology, not merely in the sense that the synoptic Gospels are characteristically on the "Spirit" side and the Fourth

Gospel on the "Logos" side of the divide, both together being within the one canon, but in the sense that the two can be found within the one tradition, in the Fourth Gospel itself. Right in the heart of the Johannine Logos christology, as we have seen, Jesus is anointed with the Spirit and receives the Spirit "without measure." Far from representing an alien theological principle within Johannine theology, this is in fact entirely in keeping with the christology of the Gospel, in which all the divine activities of Christ are activities committed to him by the Father, given over to him to exercise with the Father's own authority. The receiving and then the giving of the Spirit are no different in principle. Furthermore, just as all eschatological, messianic activities such as judgment are seen by the fourth evangelist as somehow concentrated already in the cross, so also the gift of the Spirit is seen to be defined in and through Jesus' cross — by his "glorification," as the evangelist puts it. It is for just this reason that the work of the Spirit is to cause the disciples to love one another, to serve in a lowly way, and to call to mind the words and acts of the one who loved his own to the end.

The Gospel of John is not, of course, the sole source for either sort of christology, and it is not in any case our *primary* source for Spirit christology, but it does illustrate that the two can be brought together, and that there is good theological precedent for so doing. Nevertheless, in contemporary theology, christologies "from above" and "from below" are still sometimes presented as if they starkly represented incommensurate alternatives that we must choose between. No doubt there is a real distinction to be drawn at the level of the basic orientations of different christologies. If the fundamental concern is to elaborate on the theme of Jesus as the divine address to the world, as the Word of God coming down from heaven as Lord and Savior, then it will be a christology "from above" and will almost certainly appear as a fairly traditional form of Logos christology. If, however, the fundamental orientation of a christology is in the direction of Jesus' own movement toward God, his life of obedience and self-giving in which love for God and love for the neighbor are of primary importance, then such a christology will be "from below" and will correspond to the concerns of Spirit christology. The source of tension between the two seems clear, for in the one Jesus is identifiably God, the eternal entering time, whereas in the other he is a man among human beings, a man in time in quest of eternity. If Logos christology and Spirit christology are ever to be drawn together into a coherent whole, therefore, a way beyond this apparent dichotomy has to be found.

There is a sense, perhaps, in which the basic choice between the two approaches defines whole theologies, but it is also true that there is no christology at all that is "from below" in a complete sense. Unless "God was in Christ," in short, there is no christology at all, so that all christology is in this sense "christology from above." By the same token, however, all christology is done "from below," by human beings reaching up to God by faith and reason, and by love as well, much as did Jesus himself. In this light, the contrast between the two seems a little less stark than is often supposed.

One way beyond the dichotomy might be to see the work of the Son as oriented toward the giving of the Spirit, and that of the Spirit as oriented toward the goal of Sonship. On this view, the gift of the Spirit is both the goal of the descending movement of the gift of the Son to the world and the beginning of the ascending movement of the world to God, which takes place "through the Son." In one place, Walter Kasper makes the point that the mission and even the very being of Jesus can be summed up in the phrase "from God and for God."[27] Jesus' uniqueness, the specific form of his existence that makes him who he is, is that he unites in himself both a "katabatic" and an "anabatic" movement, that is, from God to the world, and from the world to God. In Christ, the two are one.

It is helpful to note that Kasper's argument appears in an account of the eucharist, which is Jesus' personal testament, representing and summarizing his whole self. In the eucharist, according to Kasper, the two movements highlighted are represented in the unity-in-difference of "memorial" and "sacrifice." Kasper criticizes the Reformers for seeing the eucharist only as memorial, but his point is fundamentally positive. The church does not simply adopt

27. Walter Kasper, *Theology and Church,* trans. Margaret Kohl (London: SCM Press, 1989), pp. 177ff.

a stance of pure receptivity in the eucharist, any more than it does in its existence generally (an existence that is nevertheless always "in Christ"). The position of the Reformers was understandable and even justifiable given the decadent theology of the late medieval period, in which, Kasper concedes, the notion of sacrifice was distorted; but to deny the element of sacrifice altogether is to deny something essential: the idea of being bound up with Christ in his oblation to the Father, in his act of total self-giving. Kasper goes on to argue that the eucharist as *epiclesis*, as an event that is pneumatological through and through, is an event in which two movements naturally meet. Here the self-offering of God takes nothing less than the form of the offering of the human self to God; as it was in Christ, so it is in those who share in his testament. The Spirit who makes Christ present is also the Spirit who prays in us the prayer that God may perfect his act of salvation, the salvation that becomes present in the eucharistic memorial.

Kasper's emphasis on the two movements, "from above" and "from below," that together constitute the Christ-event and the eucharist helps to confirm what we have been arguing, and also, crucially, helps to ground it concretely in the worship of the Christian community. No theology can survive that is unable to find a home within the church as something that can sustain devotion, and no theological insight is likely to be of use if it cannot be contained within our traditions of worship and prayer, as well as in the structures of Christian thought generally.

There are people who find it impossible, whether because of misrepresentation of the faith or through some personal difficulty, to engage personally with the idea of the Holy Spirit as "proceeding from the Word" in the sense of being either the personal gift of Jesus or something entailed by preaching or reading the Bible. One encounters such people frequently; but are they not each in their own way in search of the Word of life? Their quest arises from the depths of their being, and it is a quest for God. Christian theology needs to be able to affirm this, and to give it its proper name: It is the work of the Spirit in them, and can even be understood to be something that they share with Christ himself in his human growth and struggle, in his faith and love. Only if their searching can be affirmed as such and in this way, in fact, are they ever likely to be able to identify with Christ or with the Christian community. But this is a possibility that is lost so long as the whole emphasis in our theology is placed on the descending movement by which God speaks his Word and establishes the church, to the neglect of the very thing for the sake of which all of this takes place: the gift of the Spirit in the human heart, and the movement toward God that it entails.

The Community of the Spirit

All of this points to a wider issue in pneumatology that must also be considered. This is the question of the church as the community of the Spirit — and the general tension this carries with it between charism and institution. This is sometimes taken to be a question of limited interest, something related to disputes about the charismatic movement. But it is a more central theme in theology than might appear at first sight, for the experience of the Spirit at the individual level, or in smaller ecclesial movements, where what is at stake is faith and life and the upsurge of Spirit in the church "from below," has perennially been set over against the claim that the Spirit is present in the church as such as a divinely ordered society. These two represent archetypal views of the Spirit's presence and work that frequently come into conflict — a conflict that is deeply felt on both sides of the divide.

Theologically, pneumatology and the doctrine of the church are closely related. The classical Christian creeds, both Eastern and Western, treat the two in the closest proximity, for example, so that creedal statements concerning the Holy Spirit lead in virtually the same breath to statements concerning the church. There is a logic in this movement, in that the gift of the Spirit exists for the sake of the people of God and is even constitutive of the people of God. Because of the promise that the Spirit, the "ladder of salvation" (Irenaeus), is given to the church, we also have confidence in what can be found in and through the church: according to the Apostles' Creed, the communion of saints, the forgiveness of sins, the resurrection of the flesh, and the life everlasting.

Debates concerning the nature of the church and where a true church can be found are important for just this reason. If the church were simply a social institution, or a "financial racket," as one long-suffering financial steward once complained to me, then the seriousness with which such theological questions concerning the church have been taken historically would be hard to understand. It is true that ecclesial and sociological or political identities have often been confused, but this means that the Protestant-Catholic or the Catholic-Orthodox struggles of past and present are, thank God, more than theological. Were theology to blame for all of this, it would be difficult to pursue it with any integrity. There is, however, a legitimate question concerning the church that is asked, a question that presupposes issues of fidelity and that has in view in an honest way the great commandments to love God and neighbor: Where is the church? One can ask this in a number of ways — for example, as a question that demands a general answer such as that the church exists "where the Word of God is purely preached and the sacraments rightly administered," according to Reformation teaching, or as a question demanding a more personal response, such as that the church for *me* is a place where *my* needs in worship or proclamation or service are met, whether this involves form or freedom, clear teaching or openness to the truth in its various forms. One only asks such a question, however, because of the expectation that the church *ought* in some sense to be the place where the Spirit is found, a place in which spiritual nurture is obtained and where the promises of God are embraced.

The relation between Spirit and church is thus an important theological question. A proper answer, however, seems frequently to be more a matter of finding a right balance than something involving a straightforward either/or decision. One of the sayings of Irenaeus relates to this issue: "Where the Church is, there also is the Spirit of God; and where the Spirit of God is, there also is the Church and all grace."[28] Each side of this is surely needed in a complete doctrine of the church. Without the second clause, the first might suggest that the church in its organized life is the gift of God to believers, and that the Spirit is given to it, almost as if the church were the container and the Spirit its contents. On this view, the church is a divine

---

28. Irenaeus, *Against Heresies*, 3.24.1, my trans.; Irénée de Lyon, *Contra les hérésies,* ed. Adelin Rousseau et al., 10 vols. (Paris: Cerf, 1965-82).

institution, the "mother of believers," in which alone salvation is found, because the Spirit is entrusted to it. This may be true in its way, but it is at best a half-truth, for many people are unable to find the Spirit amid the ecclesiological status quo, and for that very reason resort to anti-institutional religious worlds such as the house churches, or new age thought, or else abandon religion in favor of social activism or, for that matter, outright consumerism. On the other hand, without the first clause it is possible to read the second as saying something quite different, that the very existence of the church is dependent on the Lordship of the Holy Spirit, and ultimately on the sheer event in which the Spirit who blows where he wills comes to us to awaken faith and to give his gifts. On such a view, the church is not an institution at all. The problem with this is that spiritual life is thus left without structure; instead of the new wine in new wineskins, there appear as often as not to be no wineskins at all — which helps to explain, no doubt, why the membership of the house churches and in much of the charismatic movement is so transient. The issue this raises is clear: Is the Spirit found in the church as a divinely established institution, or is the Spirit free, and found only where he manifests himself?

This is really one of the most important questions in theology, given the fact that the life of faith, seen from the side of human experience, begins with the people of God. However, the fact that new wine requires new wineskins suggests that it is necessary to steer a middle course between the two extremes outlined, so that neither the physical and historical character of the church nor the sovereign freedom of the Spirit is marginalized. The goal of attaining a balanced view in one's ecclesiology therefore requires a recognition that form without freedom is stale, and that freedom without form is empty. On the one hand, the church is the mother of believers, a historical institution under God. On the other hand, the church is a community of saints and a family of believers, where the people whom God loves and not the institution itself have moral and theological priority. Both sides of this need to be held together, whatever the ambiguities. To use an analogy, just as vision, to be three-dimensional or to make depth perception possible, requires two eyes, each of which sees things slightly differently, so also a three-dimensional picture of the church requires these two points of view, rather than just one.

A christological analogy, based on the distinction between christology "from above" and christology "from below," may also be helpful at this point. On the one side, the divine outreach to the world comes to the fore, the divine incursion into flesh that is the thrust of revelation and the basis of human reconciliation with God; on the other hand, the human response to God in Christ, who pioneers the renewed creation's obedience, and finally its resurrection, is the predominant concern. In a similar way (though not, of course, in a way corresponding to any "incarnation" of the Holy Spirit) one can speak of pneumatology "from above" and "from below," and even of an ecclesiology of these two types. On the one hand, the sense that the church is divinely established and sustained comes to the fore, the notion that the church is the place where God condescends to meet us; on the other hand, we see that the church is something that happens when people encounter God and that comes into being at the point where human beings, in the power of the Spirit, respond to that encounter and go out to serve human needs. In this way the church follows Christ, who was obedient to his Father and went about preaching to the poor and setting the captives free. One might even suggest that just as classical christology sought to hold together the two sides of the christological definition, "without confusion" and "without separation," so ecclesiology, following the christological analogy, needs to hold together its two moments of divine outreach and human response.

Such a three-dimensional, "two-natures" doctrine of the church can shed light on the problem and promise of the charismatic movement and, indeed, on mystical and pneumatic movements generally. Both institution and charism are necessary in an ecclesiology uniting the descending and ascending movements of the Spirit in the world. The word *charism* itself, which in Greek is *charisma* and derives from *charis*, "grace," is used exclusively by Paul and can be found sixteen times in the New Testament. The plural is *charismata* (e.g., 1 Cor. 12:4), which is also paralleled by the Pauline *pneumatika* (e.g., 1 Cor. 12:1; 14:1), though the latter seems to have a more restricted sense. The charisms are many and are given to each for the benefit of all; they derive, however, from the one grace given by God in Jesus Christ. First Corinthians 1:4-7 is very clear on this point:

> I give thanks to my God always for you because of the grace [*charis*] of God that has been given you in Christ Jesus . . . so that you are not lacking in any spiritual gift [*charisma*] as you wait for the revealing of our Lord Jesus Christ.

The descending movement of God's grace in Christ, fulfilled in the gift of the Holy Spirit, is paralleled by the response that the Spirit inspires, expressed in the variety of charisms that work for the common good — ideally, at least, for the Corinthian correspondence reveals that the *charismata* were and are susceptible to misuse.

In summary, we may say that the church itself exists for the sake of the experience of grace among its members and for the sake of the world that its members serve, following in the way of Jesus himself. It exists as an institution in order that there might be a community of saints who love and serve God. Its location in theology, as it were, is at this point, the point where the divine outreach is fulfilled in the response of the creation. Without the institution, however, the community thus established would be anarchic and its energies dissipated; ultimately it would splinter into countless thousands of sects.

The two sides or "natures" of the church, therefore, are to be seen in the following terms. The descending movement of God in the world, which comes through the Son and in the Spirit, to adopt the ancient trinitarian formula, and which comes to us "from above," is fulfilled in the existence of the church. Though this descending movement is prior, however, it does not exist for its own sake. Rather, it exists for the sake of the movement of love and obedience "from below," in the Spirit, through the Son, to the Father. While the former has logical priority, its whole point is the latter. The movement from below cannot take place without the prior movement from above, but equally, the movement from above exists only for the sake of the corresponding movement from below. It is in such a way that each side of the church actually needs the other in order to be what it is itself, for the church can only thrive when the two can be brought together theologically and practically in such a way that each leaves room for and supports the other.

7. The Holy Spirit in Contemporary Trinitarian Theology

The Contemporary Trinity

In the older trinitarian positions of East and West, three related concepts govern the understanding of the Holy Spirit: (1) the *homoousion*, (2) the procession of the Spirit, and (3), in the West and East respectively, either support for or opposition to the *filioque* doctrine. In summary, we might say that the *homoousion*, the doctrine of the consubstantiality of the Spirit with the Father and the Son, which came to be affirmed by the theologians though not in the creeds, makes the Trinity a genuine problem for pneumatology: The Spirit is genuinely one of the three, and not a lesser emanation. The idea of the procession of the Spirit, for its part, and its elaboration in the *filioque* doctrine, is simply a correlative attempt to account for the trinitarian structure implicit in this affirmation. Such concepts serve a variety of theological functions, but prominent among them is an intention to ground the mission of the Holy Spirit *in the world* in the understanding of the divinity of the Spirit *within the Godhead*, the underlying principle being that the Spirit who is Savior and Lord in the working out of salvation is also, for that reason, one God with the Father and the Son.

It would be wrong, therefore, to suggest that Christian theology has actually intended any disengagement with the ordinary sphere of faith and practice in its concern for the doctrine of the Trinity. On the contrary, its point has been that since God truly gives himself in the saving activity of the Son and Spirit, there is, as a result, real access to him, in his own proper divinity. Whatever the eternal definitions and distinctions posited, there have always been temporal repercussions for the doctrine of salvation. To this extent, the economic implications of the doctrine have provided both the motivation and the criteria for the development of trinitarian theology. At the same time, however, for historical and theological reasons that we have already explored, the traditional content of trinitarian theology has had as its distinctive focus none other than the triune God as he is in himself, *sub specie aeternitatis,* for only thus has theology ensured that its proper object is truly God.

The new development of the doctrine of the Trinity in recent years, for its part, working as it does on the basis of the well-known Rahnerian axiom that "the 'economic' Trinity is the 'immanent' Trinity and the 'immanent' Trinity is the 'economic' Trinity,"[1] involves a rather radical and overt reorientation of the doctrine of the Trinity *in its own proper content* to the economy of salvation. Its preoccupations, in other words, are not those of the tradition — the eternal Logos, the eternal processions, or questions of *ousia* and *hypostasis;* instead, contemporary trinitarian theology is preoccupied with the involvement of God in the world and, correlatively, of the world in God. The question that we have to explore in what follows is the extent to which this offers the potential for the development of a new approach to the problem of a trinitarian doctrine of the Holy Spirit. Such an exploration is needed for the simple reason that, to date, most of the developments in contemporary trinitarian theology have been christological in character; the pneumatological implications of contemporary trinitarian theology are far too frequently overlooked. Here again, christology has tended to predominate over pneumatology. The attempt made to understand the immanent Trinity explicitly in its unity with the

1. Rahner, *The Trinity,* trans. Joseph Donceel (London: Burns & Oates, 1970), p. 22, italics omitted.

economic Trinity, however, has relevance to the problems of pneumatology as well as christology. In this chapter, we shall explore the implications of this principle, as it has been developed in recent trinitarian theology, for the doctrine of the Holy Spirit. This will then serve as our point of departure in Chapter 8, where we will ask what can be gained positively from such an approach.

The revolution in trinitarian theology today is due in large measure to the influence of Karl Barth. We have already seen something of the contribution made by Barth to theology in the twentieth century. His theology was, of course, partly a response to some of the anti-theological challenges presented by modern thought. Instead of beginning with humanity, he argues, theology begins with *God*. In Barth's mature theology, however, this principle is combined with an enormous emphasis on Jesus Christ as the ground and content of all thought about God. God becomes in this way not so much the *totaliter aliter* of Barth's early dialectical phase as the Immanuel, the God who is with us, of the Bible. This conception, allied with a theological and philosophical critique of traditional concepts of deity, has led to a series of new developments in trinitarian theology in the post-Barthian tradition.

Two signposts mark the way to Barth's mature christological emphasis. The first is Barth's study of Anselm, *Fides quaerens intellectum,* which dates from 1931 and is a book about theological method.[2] Liberalism, according to Barth, spoke about God by speaking about human religious experience; in his dialectical phase, Barth spoke about God by opposing God to human religious experience as the *totaliter aliter* who condemns human religiosity. In the book on Anselm, Barth makes a new departure, which is to speak about God on the basis of revelation. The order of theological method involves revelation, faith, and only then knowledge. To do theology, one must presuppose revelation and faith; there is no neutral, presuppositionless approach that can do justice to the subject, since the subject itself demands something different. In effect, from 1931 onward, theology becomes for Barth the task of reflecting on the content of the

---

2. Karl Barth, *Fides quaerens intellectum* (München: Christian Kaiser Verlag, 1931); *Anselm: Fides Quaerens Intellectum,* trans. Ian W. Robertson (London: SCM Press, 1960).

Christian confession, which basically means the content of Scripture and the creeds, the truth of which is presupposed in faith. That means, however, that what comes to be of central importance is not the infinite qualitative difference between God and humanity but the confession of faith in Jesus Christ the God-man.

This is the first signpost in Barth's movement beyond dialectical theology, but there is also a second, which comes some ten years after the project of the *Church Dogmatics* began: the doctrine of election developed in volume II/2 of this work. The doctrine of election in Barth is the fruition of his doctrines of revelation, Trinity, and God in earlier volumes of this work, and it represents what is perhaps Barth's most original and profound contribution to Christian theology. All that Barth would later say of the twin doctrines of Christ and salvation in *Church Dogmatics* volume IV would simply be an elaboration of the earlier treatment of election; indeed, Barth saw fit to preface his whole christology with a fresh reminder of the importance of the theme of election at the beginning of volume IV/1.

In his dialectical theology, Barth distinguishes sharply between God and humanity, and he sees God's action toward us as a divine confrontation of our creatureliness. He does this with the intention of asserting the "Godness of God" over against the perceived assimilation of God to humanity in the liberal tradition. On the basis of the doctrine of election, however, Barth himself came to assimilate God and humanity in his own way, for Barth was eventually led to conclude that his dialectical theology actually failed to understand God, in that the true Godness of God does not consist in his being totally other but rather in his being for humanity. "The *divinity* of the *living* God," as Barth later puts it, "has its meaning and power only in the context of his history and of his dialogue with *humanity,* and therefore in his *togetherness* with humanity." According to Barth's doctrine of election, God shows who he is precisely by *not* being the totally other who is utterly self-sufficient, by speaking and acting from all eternity as the partner of humanity. The freedom that God has to do this, to be God in this way, is precisely his divinity. Therefore, as Barth puts it, "God's *divinity* rightly understood includes his *humanity*."[3]

---

3. Barth, "The Humanity of God," in Barth, *The Humanity of God,* trans. John Newton Thomas and Thomas Wieser (London: Collins, 1961), p. 52.

What does this mean? First and foremost, Barth is making a christological claim. It is based ultimately on the simple — some might say simplistic — conviction that God has indeed revealed himself in Jesus Christ. To know who God is, one must begin and end with Christ, for he is the revelation or Word of God. Or alternatively, as patristic theology teaches, he is true God. But if the God-man is true God, then, according to Barth, he reveals to us that the true God is not without humanity. Barth's position here is also based on the principle that he had already developed in *Church Dogmatics* I/1: that there is no God hiding behind revelation, for if there were, then he would not have revealed himself. Our whole salvation would thus be placed in doubt. Because theology presupposes faith — the point of *Fides quaerens intellectum* — such a thing cannot even be *thought* in Christian theology, rightly understood. The very existence of theology depends upon the confession that God is truly revealed in Christ. Since in Christ God has chosen humanity for fellowship with himself and has chosen to be God *for us,* we have to understand who God is in the most direct and explicit sense possible in relation to that decision for fellowship with humanity that is revealed in Christ.

Another central theme in Barth's view of God, Christ, and election relates to this category of *choice,* namely, the doctrine of divine freedom. It is, in fact, possible to understand the whole of Barth's theology from about 1919 down to 1942 — that is, from the first edition of the *Römerbrief* down to *Kirkliche Dogmatik* II/2 — as an extended exploration of the concept of divine freedom. His dialectical theology is concerned to assert God's freedom from human manipulation, from accommodation to the human religious consciousness. God is not to be domesticated to finite human existence, for he is free. This, however, does not rightly express the full Barthian doctrine of the freedom of God, even though it is a fundamental insight that Barth carried with him from his dialectical theology to the end. It is rather constructed simply as an assertion of God's deity over against human religiosity. By the time we get to the *Church Dogmatics* I/1, Barth is dealing explicitly with the question of deity as in and of itself a question of freedom: "Godhead in the Bible," he says, "means freedom, ontic and noetic autonomy."[4] In volume II, the idea of freedom becomes the central concept in his doctrine of God. Here, according to Barth, what God is in the ontological sense is literally his free decision. Since he has freely chosen to be God in no other way than in fellowship with humanity in Jesus Christ, that is what he is: God is God in Jesus Christ. Or, to say the same thing in other words, God's divinity includes his (chosen) humanity.

While acknowledging the contribution of Barth, however, one has to look also beyond Barth's theology in order to understand the contemporary development of trinitarian theology. Wolfhart Pannenberg, for example, has pointed out that since the work of Rahner, the doctrine of the Trinity has increasingly been linked to philosophical critiques of the traditional metaphysical doctrine of God. The critique of traditional metaphysics and of older metaphysical presuppositions in Christian theology is already implicit in Barth's theology, of course, but in post-Barthian doctrines of the Trinity the philosophical problem comes to be of direct importance for the substance of trinitarian thought. Pannenberg writes, "A considerable number of contemporary theologians . . . converge in looking at the doctrine of the Trinity as an inexhaustible resource which allows Christian theology to make constructive use of antimetaphysical and atheistic criticisms of the concept of God."[5] The doctrine of the Trinity thus becomes the locus of a critique (often ostensibly relying on the philosophy of Hegel) of the older metaphysical contrast between an eternal and in himself immutable God and the changes of time and history — or, to use trinitarian terms, between the immanent and the economic Trinity. Elsewhere, I have challenged the contention that Hegel's support can be enlisted in this task as easily as is commonly assumed.[6] Nevertheless, this is a development that has been of central importance in recent theologies of the Trinity. Pannenberg believes, for example, that there has been "a deeper appropriation of the

4. Barth, *Church Dogmatics,* I/1–IV/4, ed. G. W. Bromiley and T. F. Torrance, trans. G. W. Bromiley et al. (Edinburgh: T. & T. Clark, 1936-69), I/1 (2nd ed., 1975), p. 307.

5. Wolfhart Pannenberg, "Problems of a Trinitarian Doctrine of God," trans. Philip Clayton, *Dialog* 26 (1987): 250.

6. Gary D. Badcock, "Divine Freedom in Hegel," *Irish Theological Quarterly* 60 (1995): 265-71.

specifically Christian concept of God contained in the revelation of Christ" as a result of these trends.[7]

Through such developments, the doctrine of the Trinity is today more central to developments in Christian theology than it has been for several centuries. Beginning with the basically Barthian insight that God is none other than who he is in his outreach to us and that he is free to be who he is in doing so, contemporary trinitarian theology has launched out into a wide-ranging discussion of the very being of God as open to history through Christ and the Spirit. A major attempt is presently under way to redefine divine being in such terms, apparently grounded in the content of the gospel itself, by way of an evangelical critique of older forms of Christian theism. God in contemporary theology is no longer seen as isolated from creation, nor regarded as absolute and eternal in the heavens, precisely because God is revealed through his Word and Spirit *not* to be such. Only through a trinitarian doctrine of God and a denial of the old notions of divine transcendence, it is argued, can we continue to maintain belief in God, on the one hand, and actually be faithful to the basic content of the Christian gospel, on the other.

None of this is straightforwardly unproblematic, and in fact I shall argue that there are frequently serious flaws inherent in the new approaches that have emerged. Nevertheless, even if a careful assessment of the new trinitarianism is required, there are genuine gains to be made through it. One of the things that needs to happen in Christian theology, for example, is for it to escape from the confines of a purely Western conceptuality. It may be that the search for a new trinitarian doctrine of God will open Christian thought up to non-Western sources — though it must be said that there is as yet little evidence of such openness among the major practitioners of the new trinitarian thinking. Furthermore, it is possible that the reaction against traditional metaphysical theism may lead at some point to a deepened understanding of what that theism truly involved, and what its strengths and weaknesses were. Again, there is no denying that any theology that is to address the concerns of the modern world must be a radical theology, a theology that gets to the root of things. But without an exploration of the doctrines of God and Trinity, the roots

7. Pannenberg, "Problems of a Trinitarian Doctrine of God," p. 250.

will be left uncovered. Therefore, though the eventual outcome of the contemporary debate is somewhat uncertain, it seems that theology has set itself a worthwhile task. Indeed, as we shall see, there is the prospect of real progress from the new trinitarianism on a number of fronts for a renewed doctrine of the Holy Spirit.

According to Rahner's axiom, the economic Trinity is the immanent Trinity, and the immanent Trinity is the economic Trinity. The most general implication of the axiom for the development of a trinitarian theology is clear: The immanent and the economic Trinity cannot be considered in abstract isolation; rather, each is to be understood in unity with the other. This marks an important departure from the older form of trinitarian theology, in which two levels of discourse are to be clearly differentiated, the one "theology" proper, referring to the immanent Trinity, and the other "economy." In the one case we are concerned in principle with the eternal Trinity in its self-relatedness, and in the other we are concerned with the historical condescension and manifestation of the Trinity in the incarnation and in grace. Formally, and indeed materially, we are concerned in the one case with the Trinity *sub specie aeternitatis* and in the other with the Trinity *sub specie temporis*.

In the contemporary trinitarian tradition, however, the idea of the Trinity *sub specie aeternitatis* has become problematic, along with the older metaphysical theism that underlies it, whereas the idea of the immanent Trinity survives and is reasserted. The survival of the idea of the immanent Trinity in contemporary theology, in other words, depends upon a considerable qualification of its form and content. What emerges from contemporary theology is that a doctrine of the immanent Trinity is possible to the extent that it is itself explicitly constructed *sub specie temporis,* an idea that is clearly based on the presupposition that a doctrine of the Trinity *sub specie temporis* can and does yield a doctrine of the immanent Trinity. In short, the Trinity in itself *is* the revealed Trinity, and vice versa, so that God in his own self-relatedness is in some sense to be identified also with his condescension in creation and redemption.

What this might mean in principle, and what the implications are for concrete trinitarian theologies of the Holy Spirit, is the primary subject matter to be explored further in this chapter. By way of anticipation, however, it is possible to say that when the doctrines of the immanent and the economic Trinity are conceived in this way, clear implications for pneumatology follow. Certainly the resulting theology is very different from the traditional pneumatological position defined by the ideas of the *homoousion,* eternal procession, and the *filioque.* While there are certain gains to be made from the contemporary approach, as we shall see, we will also discover certain weaknesses that issue in questionable implications, both for the doctrine of the Trinity and for the theology of the Holy Spirit. The result is that a certain theological discernment is needed in approaching the new trinitarianism, so that we neither reject the positive things that it has to offer nor accept uncritically those theological and philosophical themes found in it that ought to be evaluated more carefully.

The doctrine of the Holy Spirit has in fact been treated in a variety of ways in this theology. We have already examined certain of the trinitarian implications of such an approach in the last chapter, in connection with the theologies of Heribert Mühlen and Walter Kasper. In what follows, three further general approaches will be surveyed in order to provide a more comprehensive overview of recent scholarship. This will then lead on to the next chapter, in which a way forward will be proposed.

The first of these approaches represents the pneumatology of Barth himself, among others. It begins with the Pauline and Johannine understanding of the Spirit as the Spirit of Christ, who brings people to faith and who in some sense mediates the saving significance of Christ to the believer. In Barth's pneumatology, the Spirit accordingly appears as the "Revealedness" of "Revelation," that is, the Spirit of the subjective realization of the objective revelation that has occurred in the Christ-event.

A second approach focuses rather more narrowly on the role of the Holy Spirit in the cross. The theology of the cross has come to the fore in a great deal of recent theology in relation to the question of the suffering of God. One of the key issues here has been the nature of the divine unity in face of the suffering of the crucified Son of God. Here the Augustinian doctrine of the Holy Spirit as the trinitarian "bond of love" has been reappropriated as the "atoning" principle both in the Trinity itself and, by implication, also in the salvation of men and women.

The third and final approach takes up the problem of the Trinity and salvation history as such in a more general way. This theology begins with the fact that the economy of salvation, and thus the work of the Trinity *ad extra,* is not yet complete, but is oriented to the future consummation of the kingdom of God. The eschatological aspect of the economy of salvation can be associated particularly with the doctrine of the Holy Spirit. In the New Testament, and in particular in the Pauline literature, the Spirit appears as the seal *(arrabon)* that guarantees the future glorification of the children of God (2 Cor. 1:22; Eph. 1:13-14). In the theological tradition, the present and future work of salvation is correspondingly appropriated to the Holy Spirit; in the classical creeds, for example, the confession of faith in the Holy Spirit involves also the church, the resurrection, and the life of the world to come. If, however, the economic basis of the doctrine of the Trinity, thus conceived, is in essence incomplete, and if the economic and the immanent Trinity to be identified are one and the same, then the question arises whether or not the immanent Trinity is in itself oriented to the *eschaton,* and is thus itself in some sense incomplete.

Spirit, Trinity, and Revelation

Karl Barth's trinitarian analogy of the Revealer, Revelation, and Revealedness has already been mentioned. Barth is, of course, predominantly a theologian of the Word, whose main contribution to theology, and specifically to the doctrine of the Trinity, undoubtedly stems from his christology. At the same time, however, Barth's theology is not "christomonistic" in a narrow sense. Though Barth is not known for the strength of his pneumatology, he is profoundly aware of the importance of the doctrine of the Holy Spirit and devotes long sections of the *Church Dogmatics* to its characteristic themes.[8]

8. Philip J. Rosato, *The Spirit as Lord* (Edinburgh: T. & T. Clark, 1981), pp. 3-43, shows the extent to which Barth was concerned throughout his theological career with the problem of the doctrine of the Holy Spirit.

What is involved in the idea of the Spirit as Revealedness can be seen from an early representative subsection on pneumatology from *Church Dogmatics* I/2.[9] Entitled "The Holy Spirit the Subjective Reality of Revelation," this subsection presents the basic pneumatological problem as concerning how men and women can be the object of God's revelation, how God can be revealed to us, and how we can be free for God. The discussion therefore centers around this question: How can the revelation that is *objectively* given in Jesus Christ be *subjectively* realized by men and women? Barth's answer is that the subjective reality of revelation is the work of the Holy Spirit. Because salvation is wholly the work of God, he argues, it can only be by an act of God that we become open to receive God's Word. The revelation cannot be complete until it has been so received, and thus its reception is properly to be conceived as a moment within revelation itself rather than as an external response to it. According to Barth, therefore, "Not God alone, but God and man together constitute the content of the Word of God attested in Scripture."[10]

For Barth, then, the work of the Spirit can never be divorced from the "objective reality and possibility of revelation," Jesus Christ the Word. It is only in this event that God and humankind meet. In Barth's treatment of the church as the place where revelation has reached us to become subjective reality, for example, the life of the church is characterized entirely in terms of Christ, the Word.[11] It can be no other way for Barth: He has defined the work of the Spirit teleologically as geared to making the objective event of revelation in Christ a subjective reality in the awakening, confirming, and establishing of Christian faith in the life of the church. "Subjective revelation can only be the repetition, the impress, the sealing of objective revelation upon us; or, from our point of view, our discovery, acknowledgement and affirmation of it."[12]

A number of criticisms can be made of the idea of Revealedness in Barth's pneumatology: that it involves too limited a role for the

---

9. Barth, *Church Dogmatics,* I/2, pp. 203-42.
10. Barth, *Church Dogmatics,* I/2, p. 207.
11. Barth, *Church Dogmatics,* I/2, pp. 214-32.
12. Barth, *Church Dogmatics,* I/2, p. 239.

Spirit in soteriology and even in ecclesiology;[13] that it ignores the sustaining activity of the Spirit in creation, the movement from God to the world that takes place whether the world accepts it or not and, on its anthropological side, whether people know or believe it or not;[14] that it reflects the fundamental flaw in Barth of an unbiblical concern with the modern problem of knowledge rather than with the authentically biblical problem of sin and righteousness.[15] All such criticisms, however, derive from the fact that Barth's doctrine of the Trinity is structured around the problem of revelation.

A more serious problem for Barth, however, is that while the idea of Revealedness is perfectly intelligible, if somewhat restrictive, when considered in relation to the work of the Spirit, Barth is forced to move away from it when he comes to discuss the immanent Trinity and the person of the Spirit. The emphasis then perceptibly shifts from the idea of Revealedness to that of the communion of the Spirit, which is derived from the Augustinian-Western view of the Spirit as *vinculum caritatis,* the bond of love. That God is the Father and the Son is simply established for Barth in that, in order for revelation to be revelation, God must be what he shows himself to be, and must be capable of such self-showing. But problems begin to appear when the idea that God is in himself what he is *ad extra* is applied to the work and person of the Holy Spirit, since it seems to imply that the Spirit's role in the immanent Trinity should in some sense be understood as the Revealedness of Revelation. As Rowan Williams has argued, the linear understanding of the Trinity that is based on God's revelation to men and women begins to break down at this point in Barth's theology, while in its place there appears a view of the Trinity in which plurality, relationality, and fellowship feature prominently.[16] Here the Spirit's role is one of love, and not a form of inner-divine self-clarification or self-completion.

13. Rosato, *The Spirit as Lord,* pp. 157-66.

14. George S. Hendry, *The Holy Spirit in Christian Theology* (Philadelphia: Westminster Press, 1956), pp. 42-52.

15. Gustaf Wingren, *Theology in Conflict,* trans. Eric H. Wahlstrom (Edinburgh and London: Oliver and Boyd, 1958), pp. 28-29.

16. Rowan Williams, "Barth on the Triune God," in *Karl Barth — Studies of His Theological Method,* ed. S. W. Sykes (Oxford: Clarendon Press, 1979), p. 171.

Barth himself, of course, would not wish to admit this criticism. According to Barth, what brings him to affirm the *filioque* doctrine is nothing less than the fundamental thrust of his entire trinitarian theology, involving the principle basic to all his pneumatological thought. Barth's argument is straightforward: The Holy Spirit is the Spirit of the Son, the Spirit of Christ, who mediates Christ to the church. If this is so *ad extra,* however, then *ad intra* also the Spirit must be eternally the Spirit of the Son, who *ex patre filioque procedit.*[17] Barth's fear is that abandoning the *filioque* would open the door to the idea of an immediate relation between the human spirit and the divine Spirit, bypassing Jesus Christ as the mediator of that relation. As we have seen, he actually suspects that Eastern theology, particularly at its less restrained fringes, veers toward such a view, thereby surrendering the primary content of the Christian gospel.

At the same time, however, it is clear that the linear understanding of the Trinity at stake in the paradigm of Revealer, Revelation, and Revealedness is not easily reconciled with the *filioque* doctrine that Barth actually develops. What appears here is the idea of the Holy Spirit as "the fellowship, the act of communion, of the Father and the Son"; he is "the act in which the Father is the Father of the Son or the Speaker of the Word and the Son is the Son of the Father or the Word of the Speaker."[18] As a result, while Barth is consistently critical of Augustine's psychological analogy for the Trinity, he actually preserves the substance of the Augustinian-Western theology of the Holy Spirit intact:

> As God is in Himself Father from all eternity, He begets Himself as the Son from all eternity. As He is the Son from all eternity, He is begotten of Himself as the Father from all eternity. In this eternal begetting of Himself and being begotten of Himself, He posits Himself a third time as the Holy Spirit, i.e., as the love which unites Him in Himself.[19]

17. Barth, *Church Dogmatics,* I/1, pp. 480-81.
18. Barth, *Church Dogmatics,* I/1, p. 470.
19. Barth, *Church Dogmatics,* I/1, p. 483.

The problem here is that the Holy Spirit is presented as a middle term between the Father and the Son, rather than as the third term in a divine self-communication, bringing the process to fulfillment. The earlier Revealedness paradigm, therefore, is in conflict with the pneumatology enshrined in the *filioque*. The Revealedness idea, in short, ought to issue in an inner-trinitarian version of the pre-Nicene trinitarian *taxis* "from the Father, through the Son, in the Holy Spirit," which from the beginning connoted more than the order of transmission in the saving approach of God to the world. Here, too, the Spirit appears truly as the Spirit of the Son, but as the final moment of the divine outreach in the economic sense, and as the third moment of the divine overflow from the Father in the inner-trinitarian sense. Barth, however, explicitly rejects this view in his account of the *filioque,* arguing that it makes the Son merely a mediating principle and that it falls short of the pneumatological idea he wishes to defend: "the thought of the full consubstantial fellowship between Father and Son as the essence of the Spirit."[20] The limitation of the Revealedness idea, therefore, appears at the very point where Barth's most fundamental theological principle comes into play: that we deal in revelation with God as he is in himself, that the economic and the immanent Trinities are one.

Barth's position represents a common outlook in pneumatology and reflects biblical and patristic themes that have to be taken up in any doctrine of the Trinity. The pneumatological restriction introduced through the paradigm of the Revealer, Revelation, and Revealedness, however, comes into question, while the specific difficulty involved in reconciling this conception with the *filioque* doctrine renders Barth's version of it deeply problematic. The Revealedness idea might, therefore, be sustained, but only in the context of a more comprehensive trinitarian pneumatology, based on the total work of the Spirit in the economy and developed in a theology of the immanent Trinity in a more self-critical way. It may be, indeed, that this is what Barth's own call at the end of his life for a new theology of the third article actually requires.

Broadly speaking, however, subsequent trinitarian theologies

20. Barth, *Church Dogmatics,* I/1, p. 482.

of the Holy Spirit that take up the problem of pneumatology where Barth left off have concentrated less on the present moment of the realization of historical revelation and more on the primary event of the economy as such, the Christ-event. In this way, the role of the Spirit in the latter becomes the measure of the Spirit's present role in salvation, and, in a development of the formal trinitarian principles of Barth and Rahner, the primary analogy from which a doctrine of the Spirit in the immanent Trinity can be developed.[21] A strong criticism of the Revealedness paradigm in pneumatology is implicit in this. Instead of beginning with the problem of the knowledge of revelation in the church, the relation between Jesus and the Holy Spirit is regarded as the basic starting point. The noetic problem of faith is therefore purely secondary. The problem in Barth's pneumatology, from this point of view, is not that it is christomonistic, but rather that it is actually insufficiently christo-logical in character.

Whether or not subsequent trinitarian theologies of the Spirit can be said to be more adequately grounded in the economy remains to be seen. By way of anticipation, however, we may say that the general development of trinitarian theology following Barth has unfortunately been characterized by an even greater narrowing of vision with respect to the economy of salvation. Equally, because, as for Barth, the freedom of the immanent Trinity is its freedom to be the economic Trinity, and, as for Rahner, the economic Trinity is the immanent Trinity, and vice versa, there has frequently been a corresponding narrowing of perspective in the doctrine of the immanent Trinity.

Spirit, Trinity, and the Cross

In many respects, the theology of the cross is the embodiment of the new perspective in trinitarian theology par excellence, for the

---

21. Barth takes the opposite approach: His understanding of the role of the Spirit in the Christ-event is developed in terms of his view of the present role of the Spirit. See his discussion of "the miracle of Christmas" in *Church Dogmatics*, I/2, pp. 172-202.

cross brings the problem of the relation between God in himself and his presence in the world to a single, decisive focus.[22] Along with this, in broad traditions of Christian doctrine, the cross is understood to be the focal point of the New Testament message and the central content of Christian faith. Jürgen Moltmann, for example, states not only that the cross is "the *centre* of all Christian theology" but that the "content of the doctrine of the Trinity is the real cross of Christ."[23]

The basic question posed in the contemporary trinitarian theology of the cross is how it is possible to conceive of Jesus' death, the death of God's Son, as belonging within the being of God.[24] At this point the Holy Spirit is frequently a key theme. Although one might expect the theology of the cross to be primarily christological rather than pneumatological in character, the question of the personal relation between the Father and the Son in fact introduces a strong pneumatological element. Building on the traditional Western view, which understands the Holy Spirit's personal character in terms of the relation of love bonding the Father and the Son together, the theology of the cross is thus able to assume a pneumatological form.

The theology of the German Lutheran Eberhard Jüngel provides us with the most uncompromising example of this kind of theology. Jüngel attempts, in other words, to conceive of the Holy Spirit in his intrinsic trinitarian being as the unity in love of the Father with the crucified Jesus.[25] His pneumatology derives from the basic view that God has "defined his deity" in the event of the cross (219). The cross thus becomes in the strictest possible sense the hermeneutical basis for the whole concept of God, in the sense that the being of God must be conceived as the "event" of his

22. Jürgen Moltmann, *The Crucified God,* trans. R. A. Wilson and John Bowden (London: SCM Press, 1974); Eberhard Jüngel, *God as the Mystery of the World,* trans. Darrell L. Guder (Edinburgh: T. & T. Clark, 1983), pp. 141ff.; and Paul Fiddes, *The Creative Suffering of God* (Oxford: Clarendon Press, 1988).

23. Moltmann, *The Crucified God,* pp. 204, 246.

24. Jürgen Moltmann, *The Future of Creation,* trans. Margaret Kohl (London: SCM Press, 1979), pp. 63-64.

25. Jüngel, *God as the Mystery of the World,* pp. 368-76. Subsequent references will be given parenthetically in the text.

identification with the crucified one. God in his very trinitarian being, Jüngel repeats again and again, *is* his unity with perishability in Jesus Christ:

> The God who is in heaven *because* he cannot be on earth is replaced by the Father who is in heaven in such a way that his heavenly kingdom has come *into the world,* that is, a God who is in heaven in *such a way* that he can *identify himself* with the poverty of the man Jesus, with the existence of a man brought from life to death on the cross. (219)

In developing his position, Jüngel argues that the traditional distinction between the economic and the immanent Trinity must be transcended. The doctrine of the Trinity is to be formulated explicitly as an attempt to think the passion history of God, since God simply *is* his relatedness to himself in the crucified Jesus (370-71). According to Jüngel, the doctrine of the economic Trinity "speaks of God's *history* with man," whereas the doctrine of the immanent Trinity "must speak of God's *historicity.* God's history is his coming to man. God's historicity is God's being as it comes," God's "being in coming" (346-47). By this, Jüngel does not mean that God's being "becomes" in the sense current in process theology. Rather, the point seems to be that, as the immanent Trinity, God is intrinsically a loving self-movement toward his creation; since this self-movement requires a history in order to fulfill what it is, it can be spoken of abstractly as a historicity. It is, however, only made concrete in God's actual history with humankind, for which God makes space within himself.[26]

Jüngel's theology as a whole is complex and confusing, but it amounts to an extreme version of the Barthian attempt to think of God exclusively on the basis of revelation. What is required, for Jüngel as for Barth, is a movement away from the God of Christian theism toward what he describes as a consistently "evangelical" position. Jüngel constructs a dual case for this shift, arguing specifically for an approach consistent with the theology of the cross

26. Eberhard Jüngel, *The Doctrine of the Trinity,* trans. Horton Harris (Edinburgh: Scottish Academic Press, 1976), p. 96.

(185-99). In the first place, there is the theological necessity for this shift, deriving from the message of the gospel itself, which is at its heart the message of the cross. This leads to a rejection of the classical idea of God as the highest essence, incapable of suffering and death, which Jüngel understands to be fundamentally anti-evangelical (154). The case for a theology of the cross is complemented, secondly, by the possibility of a shift in thought provided by the philosophical collapse of the metaphysical positions allied with traditional Christian theism. The central expression of this collapse, and the real event that makes it inescapable for the Christian theologian, is the death of God in the context of modern thought (201-2).

Jüngel's approach is an attempt to reformulate the doctrine of the Trinity in this light, based both on the perceived necessity for a truly "Christian" trinitarian metaphysics and on the opening within theology itself for such a metaphysics provided by the collapse of the older position. This leads to Jüngel's central trinitarian conception: love. He writes, "To think God as love is the task of theology" (315), and he defines this task in relation to the cross: "We are to read the statement 'God is love' as an exposition of the self-identification of God with the crucified man Jesus" (326). The concept of divine love can be understood, however, in two ways: the first ontologically, in the context of the doctrine of the divine being, and the second relationally, in the context of the doctrine of the Trinity. Both are present in Jüngel.

In the first case, God is love in a sense akin to the old idea of God as overflowing being (222-25). According to Jüngel, God's very being is redemptive being, his overflow into the finite. God's grace is therefore not something secondary to his intrinsic being; rather, his intrinsic being is his grace. "We draw these theological considerations together into their ontological *concept*," Jüngel writes, "when we grasp the being of God as a Going-Out-Of-Himself into nothingness" (223). God is in himself a turning toward what is outside of himself. "Because God is love, this is then God's *being*: to be related to nothingness" (222). This helps to explain how God's union with the crucified Jesus is possible: It is because God is love in his immanent being that he thus goes out of himself into otherness, and yet in so doing remains one with himself.

In the case of the doctrine of the Holy Spirit, the concept of love is again paramount, but in a more specific sense. Love as the overflow of divine being is a conceptual abstraction used to comprehend the being of the God who identifies himself with nothingness in the cross. The concept of the Holy Spirit as love, however, is located more concretely within the trinitarian dynamic itself as a function of the relation between the Father and the Son. Jüngel uses the traditional language of the Spirit as the bond of love (or even "bond of peace," *vinculum pacis*) in this context (388). However, his treatment of the relation between the Father and the Son is developed solely in terms of the relation between the Father and the crucified Jesus. From this point of view, the doctrine of the Holy Spirit can be seen both to be hidden within the discussion of this relation and, as such, to be vital to Jüngel's theological program. In fact, it is his pneumatology that allows Jüngel to maintain the unity between the Father and the crucified Jesus, and therefore to develop his theology of the cross in a trinitarian way.

The role of the Holy Spirit in Jüngel's doctrine of the Trinity is thus to overcome the threat of the dissolution of the unity of the Father with the crucified Jesus, that is, to serve as the bond of love between the Father and the Son who is delivered over to death (346). To this extent, it is the doctrine of the Holy Spirit that underlies and emerges from the whole discussion, for the Spirit maintains the unity of the Father and the Son in the event of the cross. It is as such that God is Spirit:

> In that God differentiates himself, and *thus*, in unity with the crucified Jesus, suffers as God the Son being forsaken by God the Father, he is God the Reconciler. God reconciles the world with himself in that in the death of Jesus he encounters himself as *God the Father* and *God the Son* without becoming disunited in himself. On the contrary, in the encounter of God and God, of Father and Son, God reveals himself as the one who he is. He is God the Spirit, who lets the Father and Son be one in the death of Jesus, in true distinction, in this encounter. The "chain of love" *(vinculum caritatis)* emphasizes God's eternal being in the death of Jesus. Thus God is differentiated in a threefold way in his unity: in the encounter of Father and Son, related to each

other as Spirit. But in the fatal encounter, God remains *one* God. For he remains as Father and Son in the Spirit the one "event God." (368)

Thus the doctrine of the Holy Spirit enables Jüngel to articulate the truth that "God is love" in the context of the Christian gospel of the cross. It allows him, in his development of the doctrine of the Trinity, to understand the relation between the Father and the Son to be given in the cross by preventing this relation from issuing in a contradiction within God.[27] The unity of God thus survives, and God himself survives with it, but precisely *as Spirit*. In Jüngel's terminology, God is love, "the event of the unity of life and death for the sake of life" (317), but he is this as the Holy Spirit who unites in love the Father and the crucified Jesus.

At the beginning of this chapter, I argued that the general approach to the immanent Trinity that emerges from the contemporary development in trinitarian theology can be characterized as the attempt to construct a doctrine of the immanent Trinity *sub specie temporis*. This is clearly true of Jüngel's doctrine of the immanent Trinity, which is constructed from the standpoint of the crucified Jesus. With reference to the traditional position and to his own reformulation of trinitarian theology, he writes:

> The immanent trinitarian doctrine understands God himself with no regard for his relationship to man; the economic trinitarian doctrine, by contrast, understands God's being in its relationship to man and his world. . . . But [this distinction] is legitimate only when the economic doctrine of the Trinity deals with God's history with man, and the immanent doctrine of the Trinity is *its* summarizing concept. Here careful corrections to the traditional form of trinitarian doctrine are absolutely called for. (346)

The point is not that the concept of the immanent Trinity itself is to be altogether abandoned, but rather that the doctrine of the immanent Trinity must not be allowed to be structured by the dictates

27. John B. Webster, *Eberhard Jüngel: An Introduction to His Theology* (Cambridge: Cambridge University Press, 1986), p. 72.

of classical theism. The claim is simply that the triune God is in himself "for" humanity, that God has eternally chosen men and women for fellowship with himself, and therefore that the work of salvation is properly to be conceived as interior to God himself.[28] In this context, however, the doctrine of the immanent Trinity does not survive as traditionally understood; it is rather conceived in the closest possible connection with the economic, so that the two appear no longer as separable, but rather as aspects of a single immanent-economic reality.

In a key passage, Jüngel states: "Where the economic doctrine of the Trinity speaks of God's *history* with man, the immanent doctrine of the Trinity must speak of God's *historicity*. God's history is his coming to man. God's historicity is God's being as it comes (being in coming)" (346-47). These are deep waters, without doubt, but the language of God's being in "coming" (*Kommen*) seems to be intended to express the idea that God is in himself a movement of himself to himself in his trinitarian being,[29] a divine self-relation of the Father to himself, through the crucified Son and in the Holy Spirit (380-89). God's being is not something that exists apart from this self-relation or that can be isolated from it, even conceptually; rather, it *is* this self-relation in the sense that God's being is love, a passing beyond himself to the other, so as not to be himself without the other. The divine self-relation for this reason cannot be taken to be self-absorbed but is instead inclusive of the finite and sinful creation.

For Jüngel, then, the Holy Spirit can be said to be the "at-one-ment" of the Father and the crucified Jesus, and so also of the Father and the perishing creation. This view, however, presupposes that the cross is the single point at which the being of God is defined. This supposition is both the strength and the weakness of the position: the strength, because it enables a systematic understanding of the Trinity as the event of the self-identification of the Father with Jesus, in the Holy Spirit; the weakness, because, like

28. See Jüngel's treatment of Barth's doctrine of election in *The Doctrine of the Trinity*, pp. 68-83.

29. "The statement *God's being is in coming* implies . . . that God's being is the event of his coming to himself." Jüngel, *God as the Mystery of the World*, p. 380.

so many systematic principles, it prematurely restricts the subsequent content of the position. To the extent that the whole of the systematic conception is concentrated into this single point, the result is a relative loss of, for example, the idea of God as Creator, or again, of God as Sanctifier. In fact, the typically Western christological restriction in pneumatology appears here as something more than a simple christological restriction; the theological position as a whole is best described as "staurocentric" rather than as christocentric. Even the wider content of christology is seen as a function of the cross, so that christology suffers as well. It can, of course, be said in defense of the position that the phrase "the word of the cross" is meant to encompass more than simply the bare event of the crucifixion, but at the same time this does nothing to move the theology toward a more nuanced approach. It rather reaffirms the fact that the more comprehensive theological content of the gospel is forced into focus at this one, albeit decisive, point.

This criticism could be illustrated in a number of ways, but it would be best in this context to refer specifically to Jüngel's doctrine of the Holy Spirit. It is surely a telling sign of the limitations of Jüngel's position that, despite all the emphasis that is placed on the unity of the immanent with the economic Trinity, so little is made of Pentecost or of the church in his trinitarian theology. Jüngel does argue, certainly, that God's unity with himself in the Holy Spirit is an inclusive unity, and so something redemptive. This is clear from the fact that the point of the divine unity that is appropriated to the Holy Spirit as *vinculum caritatis* is the self-identification of God with the perishing creature, in such a way as to draw the creature into the life of God. Jüngel is also able, in his wider theology, to develop certain ecclesiological implications of this thesis. Divine love is therefore clearly not divine egoism; in a manner openly reminiscent of Barth, Jüngel does not allow that God should will to be God without humankind.[30] But such pneumatological conclusions are drawn from the cross rather than from properly pneumatological aspects of the gospel.

Closely related to this problem is the general difficulty involved in making the personal character of the Holy Spirit dependent on

30. Eberhard Jüngel, ". . . keine Menschenlosigkeit Gottes . . . ," *Evangelische Theologie* 31 (1971): 376-90.

the relation between the Father and the Son. The difficulty here is common in the Western-Augustinian pneumatological tradition: It is the problem of the personal character of the Holy Spirit. When the Holy Spirit is conceived as the bond of love between the Father and the Son, the role of the Spirit in the doctrine of the Trinity appears to be confused with the role of the one divine essence, which is likewise to preserve the divine unity by reconciling the plurality of trinitarian relations with the unity of God. Jüngel's common characterization of both the divine essence and the Holy Spirit as love is ultimately a product of this basic confusion. The idea tends to lead also, as ever, to a deficient view of the personal agency of the Holy Spirit. In Jüngel's theology, there is no doubt that both the Father and the Son are personal agents of some sort, having a genuinely interpersonal relationship; in the case of the Spirit, by contrast, it is difficult to resist the conclusion that here again the Spirit is reduced to a quality linking two agents.

This problem is made worse, in the end, by what I have called the attempt to think of the immanent Holy Spirit *sub specie temporis,* and by the rather restricted understanding of the scope of the latter as centered in the cross *exclusively.* In concentrating the temporal economy into the single *datum* of the cross, in other words, Jüngel in effect excludes the possibility of an understanding of the role of the Holy Spirit in creation, for example, and in the eternal generation of the Son from the Father. Instead, the Spirit is necessarily cast in the singular role of the bond of unity, overcoming the disjunction of Father and Son in the cross. There is unquestionably something extremely profound about the role the Spirit is given in such a dereliction theology, but at the same time it is a role that is very much pared down, and that can even be said to be simplistic, over against the wider possibilities for pneumatological development present in the biblical witness and in the wider theological tradition.

Spirit, Trinity, and Eschatology

The third and last approach to the Trinity in contemporary theology with which we shall be concerned involves the notion that the Trinity is in itself oriented, like the economy of salvation, to the future consummation of the kingdom of God. The category of time is generally taken up into contemporary trinitarian theology by virtue of the idea of the unity of the economic and immanent Trinity. Temporal aspects of the economy thus assume trinitarian significance. In the question of eschatology, however, the temporal aspect that comes to the fore is the anticipation of the coming kingdom of God, and thus the essential element of futurity in the Christian gospel — the element of hope that is so central to the gospel message. To the extent that the unity of the economic and the immanent Trinity has been presupposed in recent theologies of the Trinity, this has been an obvious development, since this presupposed unity is bound to raise the question of the significance for the immanent Trinity of the fact that the economy of salvation is not yet complete.

The origins of this position ultimately extend back to the "rediscovery" by such biblical scholars as Weiss and Schweitzer at the end of the nineteenth century of the central significance of eschatology in the message of Jesus and in the thinking of the primitive church.[31] As a result, eschatology became one of the crucial issues of early twentieth-century theology. This issue can, in fact, be traced back to the foundations of the tradition of trinitarian theology that we have in view, to the theology of Barth, as the attempt to recognize the importance of eschatology was one of the factors marking the shift from the early Barth of *Romans* to the theology of the *Church Dogmatics*.[32] The earlier, characteristically dialectical opposition of eternity and time, transcendence and immanence, thus gives way to the idea of the God whose very eternal transcendence is his freedom to be temporal and immanent, and in whom, through the concrete realization of this freedom in the incarnation, there exists for us the eschatological "new time" of reconciliation through Christ, over against the "old time" of sin.

In his *Theology of Hope*, Moltmann rejects Barth's assumption of eschatology into the being of God, essentially on the grounds

---

31. Jürgen Moltmann, *Theology of Hope*, trans. James W. Leitch (London: SCM Press, 1967), pp. 37-94.

32. T. F. Torrance, *Karl Barth: An Introduction to His Early Theology, 1910-1931* (London: SCM Press, 1962), p. 79.

that simply to deny the polarity of divine eternity and creaturely temporality does not yet yield a real theological eschatology. According to Moltmann, this can only be achieved if Jesus Christ himself is understood to have a genuine future, and if, indeed, God himself has "future as his essential nature."[33] In Moltmann's view, since for Barth the Christ-event is ontically complete and cannot be transcended, the supposedly "eschatological" aspect of his theology still refers only to the eternal presence of God in time, rather than to the true presence of time, and so of the eschatological future, through Christ in God.[34] This key criticism of Barth has wide repercussions in Moltmann's theology and relates, in the end, to their differing views of the relation of the economic and the immanent Trinity.

Although Moltmann's trinitarian theology has been cited briefly in connection with the idea of atonement in the previous section, by reason of his position as expressed in *The Crucified God,* his theology is best understood in connection with the problem of eschatology. The result differs remarkably from Jüngel's theology. In the latter, as we have seen, the inner-divine relation is understood to be defined by the event of the cross, and specifically by the relation between the Father and the crucified Son, in the Holy Spirit. The pneumatological result of this procedure is a doctrine of the Holy Spirit akin to that in the Western filioquist tradition. Moltmann himself develops such a view as a minor theme in *The Crucified God:*

> In the cross, Father and Son are most deeply separated in forsakenness and at the same time are most inwardly one in their surrender. What proceeds from this event between Father and Son is the Spirit which justifies the godless, fills the forsaken with love and brings the dead alive.[35]

In Moltmann's wider theology, however, the trinitarian event of the cross is to be understood, not as a self-contained event, but as

33. Moltmann, *Theology of Hope,* pp. 16, 50-58.
34. Moltmann, *Theology of Hope,* p. 57.
35. Moltmann, *The Crucified God,* p. 244.

opening up an entire eschatological, trinitarian process.[36] The cross is thus an event within the whole eschatological history of the Trinity, which is yet to be completed.

Along with Moltmann, Wolfhart Pannenberg is the theologian who has done most to introduce the notion of eschatology into trinitarian theology. In several works, Pannenberg sketches the trinitarian implications of his more developed doctrine of God, according to which God's being is historical and oriented toward his future kingdom.[37] Building on an analysis of the biblical idea of God's lordship, he begins with the argument that "God's being and existence cannot be conceived apart from his rule," that to have power over the creation is "intrinsic to God's nature," and that, in view of the fact that the kingdom of God belongs to the future, "God's being is still in the process of coming to be."[38] In his development of this theme, Pannenberg idiosyncratically gives ontological priority to the future over the past, so that what God will be is nevertheless in a retroactive sense what God is now.[39] William Hill has summarized Pannenberg's difficult position well: "God will reveal Himself at the end as always having been what He has become historically."[40] While what this means might be unclear, it is certain that at its heart is the key concept of eschatology.

36. Moltmann, *The Crucified God*, p. 249.

37. Wolfhart Pannenberg, "Der Gott der Geschichte," *Kerygma und Dogma* 23 (1977): 76-92; also in his *Grundfragen systematischer Theologie. Gesammelte Aufsätze 2* (Göttingen: Vandenhoeck, 1980), pp. 112-28, from which references here are taken; Pannenberg, "Die Subjektivität Gottes und die Trinitätslehre," in the same volume, pp. 96-111; Pannenberg, "Problems of a Trinitarian Doctrine of God"; and Pannenberg, *Systematische Theologie, Band I* (Göttingen: Vandenhoeck & Ruprecht, 1988). For a comparative treatment of Moltmann and Pannenberg, see Roger Olson, "Trinity and Eschatology: The Historical Being of God in Jürgen Moltmann and Wolfhart Pannenberg," *Scottish Journal of Theology* 36 (1983): 213-27; and for a critical assessment of Pannenberg's theology of the Trinity, see Roger Olson, "Wolfhart Pannenberg's Doctrine of the Trinity," *Scottish Journal of Theology* 43 (1990): 175-206.

38. Wolfhart Pannenberg, *Theology and the Kingdom of God* (Philadelphia: Westminster Press, 1969), pp. 55-56.

39. Pannenberg, *Theology and the Kingdom of God*, p. 63.

40. William J. Hill, "The Historicity of God," *Theological Studies* 45 (1984): 323.

I do not propose at this point to enter into a discussion of the coherence of Pannenberg's position, but only to survey briefly its trinitarian implications and then pass on to a more extensive treatment of Moltmann's theology, which has been much more influential. Nevertheless, Pannenberg's treatment of the doctrine of the Trinity precedes much of Moltmann's work and broadly anticipates many of its results.[41] For example, in an essay on God and history, Pannenberg argues that the older doctrine of the immanent Trinity, which developed for various understandable historical and theological reasons, actually threatens to make the realm of creation and of historical redemption theologically redundant.[42] The presupposed dualism of the older conception, by which the Trinity in itself is sharply differentiated from the Trinity of the economy of salvation — the former being complete in and of itself and the latter being the outworking of sheer grace — is obviously inconsistent with Pannenberg's view that God's intrinsic being is in some sense temporally incomplete, awaiting final realization in the coming kingdom. Pannenberg therefore argues that the traditional view is called into question by the biblical theme of the work of the trinitarian persons in salvation history, and in particular in the cross of Jesus. In *Jesus — God and Man,* Pannenberg had argued that the divinity of Jesus Christ is decided retroactively from the resurrection;[43] now he argues in a more fully trinitarian sense that the divinity of the Father, too, is likewise placed in question by the crucifixion, and only affirmed with the resurrection.[44] Therefore the divinity of the Father, as well as that of the Son, is mediated through the history of Jesus Christ (although at the same time it must also be said that the present is here determined by the future).[45] All of this, however, is the work of the Holy Spirit: The Spirit raises Jesus from death, and thus certifies the divinity of the Father and the Son as well as their unity in the self-differentiation

---

41. Pannenberg, "Problems of a Trinitarian Doctrine of God," p. 252.

42. Pannenberg, "Der Gott der Geschichte," pp. 86-87.

43. Pannenberg, *Jesus — God and Man,* trans. Lewis L. Wilkins and Duane A. Priebe (London: SCM Press, 1968), pp. 53-114, 133-37.

44. Pannenberg, "Der Gott der Geschichte," p. 88.

45. Olson, "Trinity and Eschatology," pp. 222-224, and Olson, "Wolfhart Pannenberg's Doctrine of the Trinity," pp. 199-202.

of the two in the cross.[46] For Pannenberg, therefore, the eternal divinity of the Father is dependent on the reality of his kingdom as realized economically through the work of the Son and Holy Spirit.[47]

Moltmann's trinitarian pneumatology is basically similar. According to Moltmann, "the whole eschatology of the history of Christ . . . can also be described as the history of the Spirit, a result of the workings and indwellings of the Spirit through which the future that is hoped for enters into history."[48] As with Pannenberg, so with Moltmann: Without the doctrine of the Holy Spirit, his future-oriented theology would be inconceivable. Consistent with this, pneumatology assumes enormous importance in Moltmann's theology as a whole and in his trinitarian theology in particular. Of key significance in this respect is what might be called Moltmann's pneumatological deepening of the Barthian doctrine of election. For Barth, the fact that God sent his Son into the world in the incarnation led to the idea of Jesus Christ as the eternally elect man; for Moltmann, the fact that God sent his Son and Spirit into the world, thus opening himself to it, means that God is in himself open to his creation, and allows himself to be determined by its continuing history (*Church*, 55). The freedom of God is central in both conceptions: For Barth, the divine decision to be God in Jesus Christ, and not to be God without humankind, leads to a free self-determination of God to be eternally who he is in himself in Jesus Christ; for Moltmann, God eternally and freely throws himself open to be determined by the pneumatological, eschatological history that springs from the cross (*Church*, 53-56). The openness to creation involved is not one born of deficiency, therefore; as for Barth, it is an openness that derives from the fullness of divine being, from the "self-communicating livingness of God which overcomes death" (*Church*, 56).

In this context, Moltmann argues that the work of the Holy

46. Pannenberg, "Der Gott der Geschichte," p. 88.
47. Pannenberg, "Der Gott der Geschichte," p. 89.
48. Jürgen Moltmann, *The Church in the Power of the Spirit,* trans. Margaret Kohl (London: SCM Press, 1977), p. 34. Subsequent references will be given parenthetically in the text using the abbreviation *Church*.

Spirit must be understood in terms of the lordship of God, his indwelling in everything and his glorification in the renewing of creation:

> The eschatological meaning of the messianic mission of Christ and the Spirit lies in the glorifying of God and the liberation of the world, in the sense that God is glorified through the liberation and healing of creation, and that he does not desire to be glorified without his liberated creation. (*Church*, 60)

What is said of the Spirit economically, however, is also true immanently: The unification of the creation with the Father and the Father's glorification through that saving work is at the same time, in other words, the role of the Spirit in the unification of God and the glorification of the Father within the immanent Trinity. Since God is *in himself* open to the creation, he can only be unified and glorified *together with* the creation. Hence the unity and final glory of God will only come about with the eschatological goal of salvation history — indeed, it *is* the eschatological goal of salvation history. Hence, too, the history of the kingdom of God is itself the history of the unification and glorification of the Trinity (*Church*, 57-62). For Moltmann, God is not simply God in Jesus Christ; rather, he is God in history, and not without history, in the precise sense that he has chosen not to be God apart from the ongoing historical process that has yet to be completed "in the power of the Holy Spirit."

Moltmann's main treatment of the doctrine of the Trinity appears in *The Trinity and the Kingdom of God*, which deals first of all with the threefoldness of the God of revelation and secondly with the question of the divine unity. Thus he begins his doctrine of the Trinity with the three divine persons revealed in the biblical narratives, and moves from this "Trinitarian history" to the unity of the three. In this way, the unity of the persons is again from the beginning made formally dependent upon their history, as Moltmann understands it, in the biblical witness, and comes to be seen explicitly in terms of "the eschatological question about the consummation of the Trinitarian history of God."[49]

---

49. Jürgen Moltmann, *The Trinity and the Kingdom of God*, trans. Margaret

In Moltmann's theology, then, God himself is understood to be so radically and continuingly involved in temporality that he himself has, not only a history of his own, but also a future. The locus of this involvement is not so much the Son, through whom God once entered into the darkness of death, as it is the Spirit, in whom God's presence is continuous and continuing. Moltmann does not mean simply that "God is with us" in the conventional sense, but that God himself *is* his presence in the world through the Spirit, and that for this reason the world, too, is involved in the very being of God. The relations between the Father, Son, and Spirit, therefore, change as the history of the world and of God's presence in it unfolds (*Trinity*, 61ff.).

What is of special pneumatological importance is the fact that Moltmann understands the openness of God to the world to include the Spirit's indwelling and renewing of creation, so that the Spirit's role in achieving what we might call the "completion" of the divine life in unification and glorification cannot be achieved without the involvement of creation: Creation effectively becomes a moment in the divine life. Because the Spirit is nowhere other than in the world, in other words, God himself can only be who he is, in his final glory and unity, together with the world. Hence, according to Moltmann, God himself depends for his own being on salvation history, for without it he is not who he is, nor can he be who he will be in his own future without the world as it will be in its eschatological future (*Church*, 53ff.). Thus, for Moltmann, God is not just God in Jesus Christ, but rather *God in history* in a more radical and thoroughgoing sense, in that he has chosen *not* to be God apart from the ongoing historical process that has yet to be realized "in the power of the Holy Spirit."

At one point (*Trinity*, 94-96), Moltmann summarizes his overall trinitarian position in the following terms. (1) The rule of Christ has a trinitarian structure. (2) The Father, Son, and Spirit do *not* work by only one pattern. (3) The doctrine of the Trinity must be drawn from Scripture and reflect it. Scripture reveals that there is more than one trinitarian structure in the relations between the Father, Son, and Spirit. Up to now, however, dogmatic theology

---

Kohl (London: SCM Press, 1981), p. 149. Subsequent references will be given parenthetically in the text using the abbreviation *Trinity*.

has predominantly worked with variations on only one such pattern, the ancient paradigm "from the Father, through the Son, in the Spirit." (4) The common denominator of the changing patterns is the rule of God. (5) This history of God is *open* to creation and inclusive of it. (6) The unity of the Trinity presupposes the three divine persons who are active in this history, so that a monadic unity of one substance or subject is excluded; the unity must therefore be a fellowship rather than an identity, or a union as opposed to a numerical unity.

The divine fellowship that is the unity of the Trinity, to which we now turn, is the second central theme in *The Trinity and the Kingdom of God*. Western theology, according to Moltmann, has attempted to secure the unity of the Trinity in a separate, special doctrine of the divine substance or in the idea of the divine subjectivity. Moltmann's argument is that no such separate, special doctrine is needed; rather, the unity "is already given with the fellowship of the Father, the Son and the Spirit" (*Trinity*, 150). The unity is social, in short, and grounded precisely in the threefoldness of God. Personal and social character are aspects of the same reality, so that, just as the three divine persons are distinguished by their character as persons, so their unity or at-oneness is secured by their character as persons.

Moltmann appeals at this point to the trinitarian doctrine of *perichoresis*, which holds that each of the divine persons interpenetrates and dwells in the other two (*Trinity*, 150, 174-76). What is distinctive about Moltmann's doctrine of the divine unity through *perichoresis*, however, is the fact that this unity is not static. Furthermore, because it is relational, a function of the mutuality of the three persons, it is also eschatological, or still to be realized in all its fullness. Moltmann wants to proceed from the biblical testimony to his doctrine of God, but the biblical testimony, in his view, speaks about a consummation of the trinitarian history of God. He writes:

> The unity of the Father, the Son and the Spirit is then the eschatological question about the consummation of the Trinitarian history of God. The unity of the three Persons of this history must consequently be understood as a communicable unity and as an *open, inviting unity, capable of integration*. (*Trinity*, 149)

The biblical testimony to the triune God speaks of a God who unites others with himself, who even sunders himself from himself in the cross in order to reconcile all things to himself. God is thus in himself open to creation in such a way that his own unity will only be complete when all things are united with him in the consummated trinitarian relations of Father, Son, and Spirit. The divine unity is therefore not only eschatological but also soterio-logical: eschatological, because it is integral with salvation history and the *parousia;* soteriological, because God has opened himself to his creation in the incarnation and the sending of the Spirit in order to draw creation itself into the fellowship of his own divine life.

Moltmann's pneumatology has several particular strengths. In the first place, through his understanding of the development of the trinitarian relations themselves through salvation history, Molt-mann is able to provide a trinitarian explanation for the fact that the Holy Spirit was not sent to the church until after the resurrec-tion of Jesus from the dead; until then, the Spirit was not in the strict sense the Spirit of the Son. Rather, it is through the trinitarian history of the Christ-event that the Spirit has *become* the Spirit of the risen Christ (*Trinity,* 122ff.). Room is thus found within the doctrine of the Trinity itself for the fact that Pentecost succeeds Easter and for the fact that the Spirit of the Father is also the Spirit, not just of the Son, but of the risen Jesus Christ.

Second, Moltmann is able to represent the Holy Spirit success-fully as a personal agent within the Trinity. Moltmann thus effec-tively overcomes the standard problem of traditional trinitarian pneumatology; he condemns, for example, its understanding of the Spirit's personal character as a function of the relation between the Father and the Son, or else as an "energy" by which the divine outreach to the world is effected, arguing that such an understand-ing prevents the recognition of the Spirit's equality with the Father and the Son (*Trinity,* 125-26, 142-43). In Moltmann's social Trin-ity, by contrast, the Spirit is not just something the Father and the Son share in common, or a power of God by which the creation is liberated (although the Spirit is both); rather, the Spirit is actually the agent of acts that affect the Father and the Son. The Spirit, for example, glorifies the Father and the Son by bringing the creation back to the Father through the Son and by unifying it with the Father and the Son. The Spirit therefore has a distinct role of his own to play in the divine life, at once economic and immanent, and appears as the glorifying and unifying God (*Trinity*, 125-26).

Third, Moltmann's social Trinity is pneumatologically significant also for the dogmatic problem of the relation between the Son and the Spirit. Moltmann's doctrine of the Trinity can accommodate New Testament material that places the Son within the overarching sphere of the power and presence of the Spirit, on the one hand, and the Spirit within the overarching sphere of the saving work of the Son, on the other. The Father, the Son, and the Holy Spirit have a history of mutual relations that are variable rather than eternally unchanging. But Moltmann is able to take us beyond this again in his treatment of the dogmatic and ecumenical problem of the *filioque* doctrine.[50] Because we know the Father concretely as the Father of Jesus Christ rather than as the Father in a general sense, and because that same Father is the one from whom the Spirit proceeds, we need to speak of the Spirit's procession from the Father *of the Son*. This helps to clarify the relation of the Son to the Spirit: The Spirit proceeds from the Father in the eternal presence of the Son. For Moltmann, this is bound up with the divine unity. The Father is not the cause of the other two Persons and hence the principle of the divine unity, for the divine unity is a concrete, inner-trinitarian matter of the relationships of the Persons (*Trinity*, 188-90). It is as the Father of the Son and not as the Father who is the patriarchal monarch of the Godhead that the Father breathes forth the Holy Spirit, while the Holy Spirit for his part is no longer conceived along Western lines as the modalistic bond of unity between the Father and the Son in the one divine substance. Rather, the Spirit proceeds from the Father, receives his "form" from the Father and the Son (*Trinity*, 185-87), presumably through the economy of salvation, and also glorifies the Father and the Son by drawing the redeemed creation into the life of God.

---

50. Moltmann, *The Trinity and the Kingdom of God*, pp. 178-87, and Moltmann, "Theological Proposals Towards the Resolution of the *Filioque* Controversy," in *Spirit of God, Spirit of Christ*, ed. Lukas Vischer, Faith and Order Paper no. 103 (Geneva: World Council of Churches; London: SPCK, 1981), pp. 164-73.

There are, however, a number of inherent weaknesses in Moltmann's position, the first and most obvious, perhaps, being the notion of eschatology underlying his doctrine of the Trinity. Moltmann presupposes that the development of thought in the modern era must be taken up into theological thinking as well, so that there can be no return to earlier modes of thought.[51] However, the question arises whether or not eschatological thinking also should be abandoned; for Albert Schweitzer, for example, the thoroughly eschatological message of Jesus that historical criticism recovered at the end of the nineteenth century means that Jesus is "a stranger to our time."[52] Leaving aside the question whether Schweitzer correctly understood the nature of Jesus' own eschatological thinking, or that of the primitive Christian communities that produced the New Testament,[53] there is still room to ask whether Moltmann's apparently rather literal understanding of the coming kingdom of God can be sustained.[54]

In practice, Moltmann employs two languages and two conceptualities concerning eschatology in his theology: first, that of a literal divinization of the creation in the Trinity itself at the *eschaton;* and second, the conceptuality of the freedom of men and women, which "corresponds to it," and into which it can be "translated."[55] Perhaps this is unavoidable, to the extent that the final consummation, our divinization and God's glorification and unification, is by

51. Moltmann, *The Crucified God,* p. 238; cf. William J. Hill, *The Three-Personed God* (Washington: Catholic University of America Press, 1982), p. 168.

52. Albert Schweitzer, *The Quest of the Historical Jesus,* trans. W. Montgomery, 3rd ed. (London: SCM Press, 1981), p. 399.

53. James P. Mackey, *Jesus the Man and the Myth* (London: SCM Press, 1979), pp. 39-40.

54. Moltmann's reference in *The Trinity and the Kingdom of God,* p. 213, to the kingdom as "the eschatological kingdom of glory in which people will finally, wholly and completely be gathered into the eternal life of the triune God and — as the early church put it — be 'deified' " leaves us in little doubt as to his intentions; indeed, a literal rather than metaphorical understanding of the coming of the kingdom of God and the final consummation is required by Moltmann's theology of the Trinity, since without it God in himself will be left incomplete.

55. Moltmann, *The Trinity and the Kingdom of God,* p. 213. Cf. also, more generally, pp. 191-222 in that volume; *The Church in the Power of the Spirit,* pp. 133-361; and *The Future of Creation,* pp. 97-148.

definition beyond our present experience. Good Friday, Easter, and Pentecost may well provide the vital clue to what will be in the end, but Moltmann is naturally unable to articulate the nature of the divinization to which he points in concrete terms. On the other hand, the present implications of his idea of the future glorification of the children of God are spelled out in considerable detail; here the constant impulse is to offer a utopian vision of human existence, indebted, perhaps, more to the various philosophical traditions on which he draws than to the biblical idea of the coming kingdom of God.[56] This distinction is important, inasmuch as it indicates that the concrete economic basis of his doctrine of the Trinity may be less well defined than Moltmann himself realizes.

Were the whole idea of eschatology in the original Christian proclamation to be understood as mythological, and accordingly "deontologized," it might be possible to argue that Moltmann would be left with a cipher for the utopianism he espouses, but it would also follow that he would be without a detailed economic basis for his elaborate trinitarian theology. This reflects perhaps the central problem in Moltmann's position, not so much because biblical eschatological categories belong to an age and religious culture that are long past and cannot be recovered as because they were never intended to bear the ontological sense they do in Moltmann's theology. If Moltmann's understanding of the nature and significance of Christian eschatology cannot be sustained, however, then the trinitarian superstructure erected upon it must also be abandoned.

According to Rudolf Bultmann, for example, "The real point of myth is not to give an objective world picture; what is expressed in it, rather, is how we human beings understand ourselves in our world."[57] Thus I have used the word *deontologized* above, as opposed to Bultmann's own *demythologized*, in order to criticize Moltmann's overly ontological reading of biblical eschatology.

---

56. On these sources, see M. Douglas Meeks, *Origins of the Theology of Hope* (Philadelphia: Fortress Press, 1974), pp. 15-19, 108-17.

57. Rudolf Bultmann, "New Testament and Mythology," in Rudolf Bultmann, *New Testament Mythology and Other Basic Writings*, ed. and trans. Schubert M. Ogden (London: SCM Press, 1984), p. 9.

Therefore, whereas Moltmann condemns patristic theology for developing the idea of the epiphany of the eternal in time, as opposed to the biblical, eschatological mode of thought, and therefore for corrupting the biblical message,[58] it is equally arguable, on precisely the same grounds, that in developing biblical eschatology into a theology of the divine being, Moltmann himself goes well beyond biblical categories and the original function of eschatological language.

The limitations of Moltmann's argument also appear when his underlying understanding of the relation between the immanent and the economic Trinity is considered. Moltmann's argument in *The Trinity and the Kingdom of God,* as in his earlier work, is that in the economy of salvation, the Trinity is revealed both to be open to the world and consequently to have a genuine history (*Trinity,* 126-27). In itself, therefore, the economy of salvation reveals that the Trinity spans the gap between the finite and the infinite falsely posited in the theological tradition; for Moltmann, God cannot be who he is in himself without the fellowship of his creation. At one point, Moltmann alleges that the older doctrine of the immanent Trinity is purely the product of metaphysical dualism, but as he examines neither the basis for this dualism in the philosophical and theological traditions nor the metaphysical presuppositions on which his own positive position rests, his argument at this point must be taken to be overly simplistic.[59]

If the philosophical basis of Moltmann's rejection of the traditional idea of the immanent Trinity is questionable, there remains the ostensibly nonmetaphysical basis for the distinction, developed in *The Trinity and the Kingdom of God,* based on the theological

---

58. Moltmann, *Theology of Hope,* pp. 40-41.

59. Moltmann, *The Trinity and the Kingdom of God,* p. 158. My judgment echoes those of Catherine M. LaCugna, "Philosophers and Theologians on the Trinity," *Modern Theology* 2, no. 3 (1986): 169-81; David Brown, *The Divine Trinity* (London: Duckworth, 1985), pp. 307-8; and Richard E. Creel, *Divine Impassibility* (Cambridge: Cambridge University Press, 1986), *passim,* who argue, albeit concerning the doctrine of the Trinity as such on the one hand and the contemporary theological debate concerning divine impassibility on the other, that the philosophical groundwork for much contemporary theological discussion, including Moltmann's, has not been adequately developed.

idea of grace (*Trinity*, 151). The idea of divine grace, it is often argued, requires a distinction between the immanent and economic Trinity in order to preserve the freedom of God in his saving activity in the economy. The underlying assumption here is that the notion of grace presupposes divine freedom. If God were in some sense bound by necessity to save humanity, then the category of grace would be inappropriate; as the gospel is the gospel of grace, however, the divine freedom must be maintained, and thus a distinction must be posited between God in his intrinsic freedom and God in his economic condescension. Moltmann, however, rejects this argument as ill founded. We do not, he argues, face the alternatives of the freedom of God on the one hand and necessity in God on the other; rather, a correct understanding is to be based on the evangelical truth that God *is* love (*Trinity,* 151). Moltmann's point is that, because the economy of salvation proceeds from the love that God is, the notion of an external necessity in some sense determining the action of God is inappropriate. It is out of himself, that is, out of the love that he himself is, that God loves the world, so that in loving the world God is being true precisely to himself. This notion does not introduce an element of determinism into the activity of God, Moltmann argues, but rather reveals God's freedom: He is true to himself, self-determined, so that, as such, his love is his freedom and his freedom is his love.[60]

This argument is of particular significance for the doctrine of the immanent Trinity, since it posits an identity between the love that God is in himself and the love by which he saves the world. The implication is that the immanent Trinity cannot be conceived apart from the love that communicates salvation. In a reversal of considerable interest, Moltmann argues that the older doctrine of the immanent Trinity, in differentiating God in himself too sharply from God as he is for us, in fact endangers the very concept of grace that, it would appear, it is intended to protect (*Trinity,* 151-52). The distinction, he argues, effectively makes

---

60. Moltmann, *The Trinity and the Kingdom of God,* p. 151. See also pp. 114-18 in that volume, where Moltmann argues that the incarnation is neither free nor necessary, but both free and necessary because it stems from the divine love.

God in himself unknown and his hidden nature potentially arbitrary, whereas in the Christian revelation God is love and is known in himself to be such.

Moltmann therefore rejects the classical metaphysical basis for the older distinction between the immanent and the economic Trinity on the one hand and its chief theological justification on the other. What he proposes instead is that we understand the immanent and the economic Trinity in terms of a continuity in which the two "merge into one another" (*Trinity*, 152). This does not mean, however, that Moltmann rejects all differentiation between the two. With his rejection of the classical distinction in *The Trinity and the Kingdom of God*, Moltmann proposes a new understanding: The immanent Trinity is to be understood in the context of doxology, in which the church praises God for what he is in himself, whereas the economic doctrine of the Trinity speaks of God soteriologically (*Trinity*, 151-54).

Once again, however, the idea of the doxological Trinity has serious shortcomings, not the least of which is that it fails to address the ontological question of divine transcendence. What is proposed is not in the first place an ontological distinction, but a nominal or linguistic one: It is based, not on the difference between the essential nature and the activity of God *ad extra*, but rather in the consciousness of the intending subject and in the nature of his or her linguistic acts. No direct attempt is made to investigate the possible ontological basis of this linguistic differentiation. In this way the distinction is minimized, to say the least, but it survives in its minimalist form — and even beyond it, as we shall see — and continues to shape the content of Moltmann's treatment in certain respects.

Here Moltmann's formal statement of his own mature position on the relationship between the immanent and the economic Trinity is important. What he proposes is a variation on Rahner's axiom as his own trinitarian principle:

> Statements about the immanent Trinity must not contradict statements about the economic Trinity. Statements about the economic Trinity must correspond to doxological statements about the immanent Trinity. (*Trinity*, 154, italics omitted)

The content of Moltmann's doctrine of the Trinity surveyed above helps us to understand what he means here. The ontological notion of God in himself is to be replaced by the praise of God for what he is in himself — for example, for his goodness rather than for his particular *opera ad extra* that are deemed good — while the content of the "doxological" doctrine of the Trinity, what God is praised *for*, is to be determined by the content of the economic doctrine.

It is, however, hard to see how the idea of praising God for what he is in himself can be coherent without a prior idea of God in himself. Does not the entire scheme in fact depend upon a presupposed, and perhaps hidden, ontological distinction underlying the linguistic distinction? Were Moltmann consistently to adopt the view that no *metaphysical* distinction can be proposed, there would be no basis on which it could be judged that God is anything else or other than, literally, his *opera ad extra:* The Trinity, in consequence, would be (to adopt a term from recent christology) entirely *functional* rather than ontological. Were this the case, there could be no possible basis for a real linguistic distinction, since the question of what lies behind the activity of God could not arise in the linguistic sense, or in any other for that matter, given that the possibility of that ontologically grounded linguistic step has been eliminated.

One therefore has to conclude that Moltmann's reformulation of Rahner's axiom, at least as stated, cannot be sustained, and that, insofar as he continues (as he does) to speak of an immanent or ontological Trinity, certain hidden metaphysical presuppositions are presupposed. Nor does this necessarily militate against Moltmann's wider theological enterprise; as Donald MacKinnon once said, there is something intellectually frivolous about any aversion to the concern with "what is" in the metaphysical sense, and so too in theology: "theology is ontological, or it is nothing."[61] It does, however, raise questions about the allegedly nonmetaphysical character of Moltmann's trinitarian theology, for it clearly indicates that a metaphysics of the immanent Trinity is implicitly in view.

61. Donald MacKinnon, "Some Reflections on Hans Urs von Balthasar's Christology with Special Reference to *Theodramatik* II/2, III and IV," in *The Analogy of Beauty*, ed. John Riches (Edinburgh: T. & T. Clark, 1986), p. 169.

The character of this metaphysics can best be seen through Moltmann's discussion of the idea that the economic and the immanent Trinity form a continuity in which the two merge into one another. As we have seen, Moltmann is highly critical in this context of the traditional distinction, according to which it can be said that the economic Trinity in some sense reflects or reveals the immanent. His main point, however, is not so much to do away with the idea of the revelation of the immanent Trinity in the economic as it is to introduce the more important idea, foreign to the tradition, that the economic Trinity also has a "retroactive effect" on the immanent Trinity (*Trinity*, 160). In rejecting the metaphysics of Western dualism and in arguing that the economy of salvation affects the immanent Trinity, Moltmann thus introduces the metaphysical possibility that the immanent Trinity can be conceived as at least a partial product of the historical events of salvation history. Moltmann's position, as such, echoes aspects of process philosophy, although it admittedly cannot be likened to it in philosophical subtlety.[62]

The basis of this retroactive effect of the economy on God in himself lies, of course, in Moltmann's God himself, who opens himself to the creation and wills not to be himself without the creation. It is, in other words, grounded in the twin ideas that God is free and that God is love. Thus, for example, in discussing the immanent Trinity, Moltmann argues that the immanent trinitarian love of the Father for the Son — that is, the Holy Spirit — reaches out beyond the Son himself and is only fulfilled with the return of the love of the Son and of those who are united with the Son (*Trinity*, 161-70). God thus freely makes himself dependent on the creation for his own fulfillment; he is not who he is without us.

This means, however, that historical events become determinative of the immanent, eternal being of God. This thesis is not, of course, peculiar to Moltmann, but it appears perhaps more clearly in his theology than in others because of his distinctive idea of the trinitarian history of God. It is therefore difficult, as we have already seen, to resist the conclusion that the doctrine of the Trinity in

62. Fiddes, *The Creative Suffering of God*, pp. 123-43.

Moltmann reduces God in himself to his particular acts *ad extra*. As one commentator writes:

> Although Moltmann does not wish it, one seems forced to picture the scheme outlined in his book as a linear one with a temporal process culminating teleologically in a future state which is entirely determined by the process's cumulative history.[63]

If the Trinity in the economy of salvation is in process, in other words, then by Moltmann's own trinitarian logic the immanent Trinity must also be in process, and as such will only come to completion at the *eschaton*. One thus has to ask whether or not Moltmann's theology threatens to reduce the immanent Trinity to the economic, and to make God in himself a product of the historical process. Moltmann's claim is that the concept of the immanent Trinity must be retained as the concept distinguishing the God who reveals himself from the revelation as such. If, however, it is really the case that the immanent Trinity is in process, and that it is a product of its successive historical determinations, then it is doubtful even that the concept of such a revealer underlying the revelation is coherent. The case is rather more likely the reverse, where the "revelation," as it were, underlies the "revealer," and the "interaction" between the immanent and the economic Trinity is in fact less an interaction than a one-way determination of the immanent by the economic Trinity.[64]

William J. Hill criticizes Moltmann's theology at this point more sharply. According to Hill, the idea of eschatology, in which the *eschaton* will one day be reached and God will be all in all (1 Cor. 15:28), is itself irreconcilable with Moltmann's view of God; referring primarily to Moltmann's trinitarian *theologia crucis*, he writes:

> The pronounced emphasis upon historicity as even the mode of divine being leaves unexplained why suddenly it all comes to an

---

63. Olson, "Trinity and Eschatology," p. 221.
64. Olson, "Trinity and Eschatology," p. 221.

end. . . . Again, if the content of divine history, as trinitarian, is death as a phenomenon within God (so that suffering is not in contradiction to love but its condition; and thus God is to be found in his opposite), then how does God any longer remain a God of love once suffering and death are overcome?[65]

The question Hill thus poses is whether or not Moltmann, within his understanding of the trinitarian history of God and his conception of the being of God as found in his opposite, is able to allow that the *eschaton* will ever come, since once it does the historical process in relation to which God is intrinsically defined will be brought to an end. Moltmann's trinitarianism may well be consistent with the idea of an eternally and infinitely unfolding process, but not, it would seem, with biblical eschatological ideas, in which the consummation will finally be realized.

65. Hill, *The Three-Personed God,* p. 175.

8. A Trinitarian Doctrine of the Holy Spirit

IT IS CLEAR from the argument of the previous chapter that the potential for growth in trinitarian theology in general and in pneumatology in particular that was mentioned at the outset has still to be realized, and that the claim of contemporary trinitarian theology to a more adequate pneumatological position than the older tradition can be exaggerated. The doctrine of the Trinity today remains a crucial area of theological controversy, and pneumatology is in many ways one of its weakest links.

What remains to be done is to outline the more positive results for trinitarian pneumatology that emerge from recent theological scholarship. In this chapter, I shall take up this question in three sections, the first two of which will be concerned with the basis for the development of a trinitarian theology, and the third with possible directions for our understanding of the Holy Spirit in the immanent Trinity, and an associated social doctrine of the Trinity.

The Problem of Economic Diversity

The most basic problem in contemporary trinitarian theology concerns the economic starting point from which particular systematic conceptions are developed. The positions that we have surveyed all presuppose some version of the general idea of economic-immanent trinitarian identity, and all claim to be grounded in the economy of salvation. The different resulting theologies, however, show how many paradigms in the economy are, in principle, available for development. This reflects a fundamental problem in trinitarian thought: the sheer diversity, not only of the possible trinitarian *interpretations* to which the economy of salvation is susceptible, but of the actual economic basis of trinitarian theology itself.

Such diversity can be enriching from the standpoint of Christian spirituality, but the range of economic themes in question presents a great challenge to those who attempt to formulate a systematic trinitarian conception. Thus it was that conflicting views of the trinitarian *taxis* emerged in the older theological tradition, finding support in different aspects of the economy of salvation.[1] In particular, much of the controversy surrounding the procession of the Holy Spirit in the history of theology derives from ambiguities inherent in the biblical witness, ambiguities reflected also in the wider spiritual and theological tradition. The various spiritual,

---

1. Three examples can be cited briefly. First, there is the trinitarian *taxis* of Father → Spirit → Son, which is indebted to the biblical, messianic tradition of the synoptic Gospels. Excluding the adoptionists, the chief theological representatives of this position include the Syrian fathers Aphraates and Ephrem (W. Cranmer, *Der Geist Gottes und des Menschen in frühsyrischer Theologie* [Münster: Aschendorff, 1979]), and, as recent ecumenical research has shown, the medieval Byzantine writers Gregory of Cyprus and Gregory Palamas (Dumitru Staniloae, "The Procession of the Holy Spirit from the Father and His Relation to the Son, as the Basis of Our Deification and Adoption," and Markos A. Orphanos, "The Procession of the Holy Spirit According to Certain of the Later Greek Fathers," in World Council of Churches, Commission on Faith and Order, *Spirit of God, Spirit of Christ*, ed. Lukas Vischer [Geneva: World Council of Churches; London: SPCK, 1981], pp. 174-86 and 21-45). Second, there is the more familiar trinitarian *taxis* of Father → Son → Spirit, which on the whole predominates in Eastern Christian theology and which also has important Western advocates. This derives in part from the Middle and Neoplatonic traditions, but also gains its chief support from those biblical texts which speak of the Son as mediator and giver of the Holy Spirit. The third paradigm is that of the Western filioquist tradition, which is more difficult to represent schematically, but in which the Father and the Son together breathe forth the Spirit as their common bond of love. Here the Augustinian psychological analogy is undoubtedly of fundamental importance, but the paradigm also depends on various New Testament texts that associate love and unity with the Holy Spirit.

liturgical, and theological traditions that appear in the wider history of the Christian church also represent different economic conceptions, and potentially different starting points for theologies of the Trinity.[2]

Because of the unity of the economic with the immanent Trinity affirmed in contemporary theology, however, the difficulties that must now arise from the diversity of the economic basis are greatly intensified. Clearly, if our doctrine of the Trinity depends on the idea that the Trinity in itself is none other than what it is economically, then the question of its economic basis obviously becomes of fundamental importance. As we have seen, the diversity here has yielded a number of mutually exclusive trinitarian positions in contemporary theology. Moreover, since the relations between Father, Son, and Holy Spirit as represented in the economy do clearly differ, it is difficult to see how, in principle, such a result can be avoided on the basis of the contemporary trinitarian thesis.

One of the basic questions that we have to address, therefore, is how the diversity of the economy can be reconciled with any systematic conception of the Trinity. Such a systematic conception must by definition be self-consistent over against the contrasting elements within its economic basis. The problem is thus one of reconciling the initial diversity with the required unity. Three responses to this problem suggest themselves, responses that can also be seen to emerge from the theologies encountered in earlier chapters. The first is the attempt to transcend the diversity of the economic data provided by the New Testament by positing a series of stages in an overall development. The second is simply to be selective: One does not grant equal importance to each of the differing themes of the biblical witness. The third option is to attempt to qualify the idea of the unity of the economic with the immanent Trinity itself in such a way that the diversity of the economic basis no longer poses a threat to the development of a

---

2. Recently Yves Congar, *I Believe in the Holy Spirit*, trans. David Smith (London: Geoffrey Chapman; New York: Seabury Press, 1983), vol. 1, pp. 65-173, and Louis Bouyer, *Le Consolateur* (Paris: Les Éditions du Cerf, 1980), pp. 61-336, have provided extensive surveys of the pneumatological tradition from this point of view.

systematic conception. This third approach, I shall argue, offers the most persuasive alternative.

The first approach, of course, is the one taken by Moltmann, while the second is typified by Jüngel. Of these two, the second is the only one worth taking very seriously, since the attempt to unify the economic data in themselves in a single development, as in Moltmann's theology, rests on very weak exegetical and theological foundations. While there is no doubt that such a procedure might be possible, *if* the facts in question were susceptible to such a synthesis, one decisive consideration counts against it. Historical-critical study has shown that, while some New Testament documents did directly influence the development of others (for example, the compilers of Matthew and Luke knew Mark), the broad traditions of thought in the New Testament were developed for the most part in isolation. For this reason, one has to understand the different streams of tradition as representing different theologies, since for the most part they were not written with the others in view. In a discussion of unity and diversity in the New Testament, Ernst Käsemann has written:

> We now have three results: (a) the variability of the New Testament kerygma; (b) the extraordinary wealth of theological positions in primitive Christianity (a phenomenon going beyond the horizon of the New Testament); (c) the incompatibility between some of these positions.[3]

Käsemann concludes that the New Testament canon constitutes a basis, not for theological unity, but rather for theological pluralism.

This has important implications. Not only must we say that the different New Testament traditions cannot be unified artificially in a single "trinitarian history of God," but we must also recognize that the attempt to do so does violence to their own character. It is, in fact, an *a priori* presupposition concerning the unity of the economic and the immanent Trinity, rather than the economic data

3. Ernst Käsemann, "The Canon of the New Testament and the Unity of the Church," in his *Essays on New Testament Themes,* trans. W. J. Montague (London: SCM Press, 1964), p. 103.

themselves, which has resulted in Moltmann's economic synthesis. In practice, therefore, the thesis that the economic Trinity is the immanent Trinity, and vice versa, appears in this case to militate against its original intention, which was to relate trinitarian theology directly to the economy and to allow the internal dynamic of the latter to shape the form and content of the former. Instead, in this approach to the diverse economic basis, quite the opposite occurs.

A stronger case can be made for the second approach, which can be said in general to arise from a theological assessment of the relative theological significance of different aspects of the broader economy of salvation, and an appropriation into trinitarian pneumatology of those deemed to be of central importance. Here, however, one must still pose the question on what grounds the choice of the central economic paradigm is made, and whether or not the resulting restriction of economic trinitarian *taxis* can be justified. The problem, as we have seen, is that the biblical economy represents the relations between Father, Son, and Holy Spirit in differing ways. Therefore, if we attempt in some sense to relativize this diversity, we appear to contradict the initial purpose of the turn to the economy, which was precisely to ground the doctrine of the Trinity more fully in God's acts in history.

In the theological tradition, the difficulties that arise from the diversity of the economy are not so severe. Since the idea of the unity of the economic and the immanent Trinity in the contemporary sense is not asserted, the problem of the diversity of the economic basis does not necessarily pose an immediate threat to the unity of the Trinity. Moreover, because the immanent Trinity is by definition hedged about with apophatic qualifications, the various concrete trinitarian theologies that appear in the tradition are arguably to be seen less as contradictory representations of the Trinity than as competing images of an ultimately hidden mystery.

More importantly, perhaps, the traditional understanding of the fundamental economic event of revelation in Jesus Christ, mediated through the Chalcedonian two natures doctrine, makes it possible to deny that every aspect of the economy needs to be taken up into trinitarian theology in the first place. On the basis of the two natures doctrine, for example, one can logically argue that Christ received the Spirit in his human nature, but that he gives the Spirit in his divine nature, just as he suffered on the cross as the incarnate Son of God, and therefore in his human nature, but was and is strictly impassible in his divine nature. The idea that one can thus begin with an economic distinction concerning what refers to the relation between the divine nature of Christ and the Holy Spirit, on the one hand, and between his human nature and the Spirit, on the other, can serve as a useful tool in resolving the theological problem of the diversity of* the economy. The problem here is a relative loss of the unity of Jesus Christ rather than of the doctrine of the Trinity, as the varied aspects of the economy are to be referred to the two natures of Christ rather than to the Trinity itself.

The latter strategy is employed at times by various recent trinitarian theologians, among them Karl Barth. Thus, in his treatment of the conception of Jesus by the Holy Spirit in *Church Dogmatics* I/2, Barth argues that just as it is only through the activity of the Spirit that men and women believe, so the work of the Spirit in the conception of Jesus is to be understood as miraculously enabling human nature to be assumed by the Word.[4] The role of the Holy Spirit in the conception of Jesus is to make it possible for the humanity to be there for the Word when the Word becomes flesh: The Word works in the work of the Spirit to unite the humanity with himself. In this sense, Barth writes, "The very possibility of human nature's being adopted into unity with the Son of God is the Holy Ghost. . . . Through the Spirit it becomes really possible for the creature, for man, to be there and to be free for God."[5] The role of the Holy Spirit as active in relation to Christ is thus restricted by Barth to the human nature assumed by the Word in the incarnation. In *Church Dogmatics* I/1, the same point is made even more clearly; Barth asks here, in connection with his defense of the *filioque,* if the fact that Jesus can be said in some sense to have received the Spirit at his conception, baptism, and resurrection indicates that an inner-trinitarian relation between the Holy Spirit and the Son, which is neither begetting nor pro-

4. Barth, *Church Dogmatics,* I/1–IV/4, ed. G. W. Bromiley and T. F. Torrance, trans. G. W. Bromiley et al. (Edinburgh: T. & T. Clark, 1936-69), I/2 (2nd ed., 1975), pp. 196-202.

5. Barth, *Church Dogmatics,* I/2, p. 199.

cession, should be postulated.[6] Barth's response is again that, because the Spirit's work here is related to the human nature of Christ and to its assumption by the Word, it is relevant only to our adoption as children of God, rather than being directly revelatory of an eternal work of the Spirit on the Son of God himself.

It is questionable, however, how far Barth's later doctrine of election, consistently thought through, can be reconciled with this earlier conception; the idea that there is no *Logos asarkos* ("discarnate" Word) seems to make any attempt to distinguish in this way between the human and divine natures of Christ virtually impossible. Barth himself, of course, did not formally abandon the two natures doctrine after developing his doctrine of election. On the contrary, as late as *Church Dogmatics* IV/2, he maintains that the Chalcedonian doctrine of the two natures of Christ must be affirmed: The divine and human natures are on the one hand without confusion or change and on the other without division or separation.[7] At the same time, however, though only with reference to the latter, he writes:

> We do not have here a divine and eternal and heavenly Christ who is not wholly of human essence, nor a human and temporal and earthly Jesus who is not wholly of divine. We do not have here a dual, but the one Jesus Christ, who is as such of both divine and human essence, and therefore the one Reconciler, Saviour and Lord. *He pre-existed as such in the divine counsel. He was born and lived and died as such.*[8]

Barth's reference to the doctrine of election here raises the question of how the divine and human natures can indeed be ultimately separated; if Jesus Christ is the eternal man in Barth's sense, then the human nature properly belongs to his divinity, according to the eternal divine choice, and is not simply an "extra" assumed externally. If this is the case, however, then it is difficult to see how the whole range of human experience, including his experience of the

6. Barth, *Church Dogmatics*, I/1, pp. 485-86.
7. Barth, *Church Dogmatics*, IV/2, pp. 62-64.
8. Barth, *Church Dogmatics*, IV/2, p. 64, italics added.

Spirit and finally his suffering and death, does not belong to his intrinsic being as the eternal Son of God, and so to the doctrine of the Trinity.

The issue in fact turns upon how one understands the unity of the economic with the immanent Trinity, which is, in a sense, what is at stake in the doctrine of election. In Barth's own theology, as we have seen, this is a somewhat controversial point, but in subsequent trinitarian theology the issue becomes very clear indeed. The fact is that the older form of christological dualism, represented by the two natures doctrine, is inconsistent with the idea of the unity of the economic with the immanent Trinity. The more the latter unity is emphasized, the less the former duality can be maintained.

In Rahner's theology, for example, the immediate christological extension of his trinitarian *Grundaxiom* is the affirmation of a "more essential and more intimate" relation between the divine and human natures of Christ than was previously posited in the tradition. According to Rahner,

> Human nature in general is a possible object of the creative power and knowledge of God, because and insofar as the Logos is by nature the one who is "utterable" (even into that which is not God); because he is the Father's Word, in which the Father can express himself, and, freely, empty himself into the non-divine; because, when this happens, that precisely is born which we call human nature. In other words, human nature is not a mask . . . assumed from without, from behind which the Logos hides to act things out in the world. From the start it is the constitutive, real symbol of the Logos himself. So that we may and should say, when we think our ontology through to the end: man is possible because the exteriorization of the Logos is possible.[9]

In subsequent theology, this thesis is developed further. According to Moltmann in *The Crucified God*, for example, a trinitarian theology of the cross must abandon the doctrine of the two natures

---

9. Rahner, *The Trinity*, trans. Joseph Donceel (London: Burns & Oates, 1970), pp. 32-33.

altogether in order to avoid emptying the cross of deity.[10] Moltmann understands the doctrine of the two natures as interpreted
in the context of the problem of the suffering of Jesus to be a
function of the doctrine of divine *apatheia*. If, however, we take
our concept of God from the event of the cross, the suffering of
God on the cross becomes essential to a trinitarian doctrine of God.
Thus, although one commentator argues that Moltmann rejects
the doctrine of the hypostatic union,[11] Moltmann's position is best
understood as a trinitarian intensification of the doctrine of the
hypostatic union: Because the economic Trinity "is" the immanent
Trinity, and vice versa, the human nature of Christ in some sense
"is" his divine nature, and vice versa. Moltmann's point is not to
deny the divinity but to affirm its unity with the humanity, on the
basis of his understanding of the unity of the economic and the
immanent Trinity.

The problematic character of the two natures doctrine in the
face of the idea of the unity of the economic with the immanent
Trinity means that another way must be found to reconcile the
diversity of the economic basis with the unity of the Trinity. One
could, for example, do so by effectively restricting consideration to
a single consistent economic trinitarian model. The one-sidedness
of Barth's Revealedness doctrine might even be mentioned in this
context, despite his adoption of the two natures doctrine, since in
Barth's theology the idea of the outpouring of the Spirit who bears
witness to Christ after the resurrection and ascension constitutes,
in the end, his total understanding of the work of the Spirit. A
clearer example, perhaps, is Jüngel's trinitarian pneumatology,
which is based on a procedure in which everything is made to rest
on the event of the cross.

In either case, the approach is to exclude certain aspects of
the wider potential economic basis of a trinitarian pneumatology
in favor of a single aspect, which is then taken to constitute the
economic foundation required for subsequent development. There

10. Jürgen Moltmann, *The Crucified God,* trans. R. A. Wilson and John
Bowden (London: SCM Press, 1974), p. 245.
11. William J. Hill, *The Three-Personed God* (Washington: Catholic University of America Press, 1982), pp. 169-70.

can be little doubt, of course, that, given the original economic restriction, a coherent view of the Trinity can thus be generated. This, however, is precisely the problem, for the fact that the various trinitarian positions that can thus be developed are equally dependent on the economy and at once in themselves complete and mutually exclusive means that the question of the basis of the original economic restriction must be raised.

Quite apart from the two natures doctrine, it is clear that there are both theological and, to a lesser extent, historical grounds for some such restriction of the relevant economic data. The first justification of such an approach is that it is possible to speak of an internal canon in the Scriptures themselves that raises certain theological themes to prominence.[12] The death of Christ can be said to be the center of the New Testament, as Jüngel maintains. This can be argued on grounds internal to Scripture — for example, on the basis of such Pauline texts as 1 Corinthians 1:18ff., which speaks of the centrality of the cross — or in keeping with a more general theological thesis concerning the atonement. Alternatively, either on the basis of John's Gospel or on various theological and philosophical grounds, the incarnation might be posited as the New Testament's central theme, the total economy of salvation being sustainable only if the incarnation is accepted as of primary significance. A number of other alternatives — such as the idea of the kingdom of God, as in classical liberal theology and in some contemporary liberation theology — are also conceivable.

The limitation of this approach is that the judgment as to what the center of the economy of salvation is can always be disputed; there is even an internal debate about this in Scripture itself. Clearly, certain definite conclusions can be reached, such as that the fact that Jesus might have slept or ate at such and such a time, or that he lived for so many years, is of no particular significance over against the fact that he was crucified under Pontius Pilate and the claim that he was raised from the dead. In the wider sense as well, some of the more searching passages from Paul or the parables of Jesus must be taken more seriously than,

12. James D. G. Dunn, *Unity and Diversity in the New Testament* (London: SCM Press, 1977), pp. 374-76.

let us say, the apocalyptic expectations peculiar to Jude. However, more weighty questions of biblical interpretation and Christian theology, such as how one reconciles the teaching of Jesus and of Paul, or the christologies of the synoptics and of John, are destined to be matters of permanent controversy. In this sense, the supposed simplicity of the turn to the economy that characterizes contemporary approaches to the doctrine of the Trinity appears merely superficial, particularly in view of the fact that, in its inception, the doctrine of the Trinity developed over a long period of time out of extraordinarily complex biblical, theological, and philosophical considerations.

A second possible justification for this approach would be the search for what is historically most primitive, on the grounds that what is closest to the original revelatory event should serve as the foundation for subsequent theology. Thus, for example, the search for the *ipsissima verba* of Jesus, or again for the "christology" of Jesus himself or of the earliest Christian community, could be conceived as a way out of the dilemma of economic diversity. It might be argued, therefore, that the Jesus of the synoptics, who is more the Jesus of living memory, rather than the Pauline or Johannine Jesus of theological interpretation, should serve as the foundation for christology, and thus, for example, that the original preaching of the kingdom is of primary theological importance. The weakness of this approach, however, is again obvious: What is later historically cannot be taken *a priori*, as it were, to be less adequate theologically, or even necessarily less accurate historically.

By way of summary of this point, let us take the case of the crucifixion of Jesus, where there is no doubt that we are concerned with something more theologically central and more historically certain than, for example, his conception by the Holy Spirit. On both grounds, it would be plausible to argue that as an economic basis for trinitarian theology, the crucifixion must take precedence over the conception. The problem, however, arises in connection with the idea of the unity of the economic with the immanent Trinity, on the basis of which one would apparently have to insist, not only that the economic basis be prioritized in this way, but that those economic paradigms which conflict with the one chosen be effectively *excluded* from consideration. This appears to be necessary for the simple reason that all the relevant economic paradigms, taken in themselves, are susceptible to trinitarian development — as we have seen, with mutually inconsistent results.

Such a restriction of the relevant economic material is certainly possible, but in practice the result of this procedure again appears to thwart the original purpose of the turn to the economy in contemporary trinitarian theology. Whereas the intention was to relate the content of the doctrine of the Trinity more explicitly and immediately to the economy of salvation, the cost of the methodology involved appears to be a selective focus on one aspect of the economy and an effective exclusion of the rest. This results in a rather arbitrary restriction of the economic material in relation to which the trinitarian theology in view was originally intended to be developed.

The only way that seems to offer an escape from this dilemma is the third possible approach mentioned at the outset, which represents a more minor tendency in contemporary trinitarian theology. This is to loosen the relation between the economic and the immanent Trinity by emphasizing the distinction of the two even in their unity. This tendency is particularly associated with the positions of such Catholic theologians as Walter Kasper, although it also appears, as we shall see, in the theology of Karl Barth (though undifferentiated from his doctrine of election), and cannot be taken to be foreign, in itself, to Protestant theology. With reference to Rahner's axiom as the rallying cry of contemporary trinitarian theologians, for example, one commentator has written:

> Interpreters . . . have tended to divide into two camps: those who believe in a strong identity of immanent and economic Trinity and those who would qualify that identity by positing a prior actuality of the immanent Trinity. Moltmann [and] Jüngel . . . seem to hold to the strong sense of the identity. That is, each in his own way represents the innertrinitarian life of God as a salvation-historical process. . . . Kasper holds to a weaker sense of the identity in *The God of Jesus Christ*. While agreeing that the economy of salvation must not be seen as merely a temporal manifestation of an eternal and immutable immanent

Trinity, he wishes to avoid the opposite misinterpretation which would dissolve the immanent Trinity in the economic Trinity.[13]

This passage recognizes a distinction between two basic senses in which the idea of the unity of the economic with the immanent Trinity has been affirmed, although perhaps the language of a "strong" versus a "weak" identity of the economic and the immanent Trinity is too imprecise.

What our third approach implies is that there is indeed a clear and close relation of identity between the economic and immanent Trinity, but a relation that is best understood as analogical, according to the traditional theological conception, and that thus lays emphasis upon their unity-in-*difference,* rather than as a radical sublation of distinction through the idea that the Trinity in itself is what it is in the economy as such. Analogy, in short, can be defined as a method of predication in which concepts relating to something known are referred to something relatively unknown, on the basis of some presupposed similarity between the two objects. In Hans Urs von Balthasar's theology, for example, an attempt is made to unite the economic and the immanent Trinity in their distinction, without at the same time relativizing that distinction, by positing the analogical principle of proportionality, or of proportional similarity, as the principle of their unity.[14]

From this point of view, Rahner's axiom could be understood to assert that the economic Trinity contains, in a mode appropriate to its representation in the created order, the reality of the heavenly, or immanent Trinity, and, in a corresponding sense, that the immanent Trinity is the reality contained in the economic. The idea of the unity of the economic and the immanent Trinity could thus be understood as an attempt to formulate the thesis that the divine mystery is indeed disclosed to us in Jesus, without at the same time minimizing the importance or the reality of the kenotic mode under which that mystery is given in Jesus. The mystery, in this case,

13. Roger Olson, "Wolfhart Pannenberg's Doctrine of the Trinity," *Scottish Journal of Theology* 43 (1990): 197-98.

14. Hans Urs von Balthasar, *Elucidations,* trans. John Riches (London: SPCK, 1975), pp. 18-25.

would be disclosed, but not *completely* disclosed. It would be for this reason, and only for this reason, that any particular aspect of the economy would not in and of itself have to contain the whole of the trinitarian mystery; not only do the separate moments of the economy not contain the whole of that mystery, but neither even does the economy as a whole.

This is clearly a fairly traditional view, which rests on the idea that the immanent Trinity is to be differentiated from the economic and yet is also a mystery that is disclosed to us — though only by way of *kenosis* — in the economic. It is notable — particularly in view of the virtually total silence of the commentators on the point — that Karl Barth adopted such a position in *Church Dogmatics* II/1 in his discussion of the "primary" and "secondary objectivity" of God.[15] This distinction arises in the course of a discussion of the reality of the church's knowledge of God in faith, which is, according to Barth, the presupposition of theological discourse. In the revelatory act of God on which faith (and, out of faith, Christian dogmatics) is based, God objectifies himself to us in such a way as to reveal himself as the loving God who demands the obedience of faith as our response to his self-revelation.

It is this presupposed reality of the knowledge of God in faith that raises the further theological question of the nature of the knowledge of God thus given. The problem Barth addresses is how the *mediate* knowledge of God, given through those finite events and objects in history by which God has chosen to reveal himself, represents a *true* knowledge of God.[16] It is here that the distinction between the "primary" and "secondary" divine objectivity is introduced. Barth maintains that God's givenness to us in revelation, his secondary objectivity, cannot be understood to be identical with God in himself because of the introduction of creaturely reality into his secondary objectivity in revelation:

We call this the primary objectivity of God, and distinguish it from the secondary, i.e., the objectivity which He has for us too

15. Barth, *Church Dogmatics,* II/1, pp. 16ff.
16. Barth, *Church Dogmatics,* II/1, p. 16.

in His revelation, in which He gives Himself to be known by us as He knows Himself. It is distinguished from the primary objectivity, not by a lesser degree of truth, but by its particular form suitable for us, the creature. God is objectively immediate to Himself, but to us He is objectively mediate. That is to say, He is not objective directly but indirectly, not in the naked sense but clothed under the sign and veil of other objects different from Himself.[17]

Nevertheless, as Barth says in the same place, "His secondary objectivity is fully true, for it has its correspondence and basis in His primary objectivity." He proceeds to argue that the principle of the "correspondence" in question here is a *sacramental* one: God gives himself to be known by men and women "in, with, and under" the finite objects that serve as the vehicles of his self-revelation.[18]

17. Barth, *Church Dogmatics*, II/1, p. 16.

18. Barth, *Church Dogmatics*, II/1, p. 52. Reference might also be made at this point to the idea of Christ as the "primordial sacrament" of God in recent theology: He is the "exegesis" (John 1:18) of the Father, in flesh, both as a visible sign of grace and as the reality of that grace itself (to which our own sacraments in the narrower sense point back). The word *sacramental*, as we have seen, is used in this sense by Barth, but it is Eduard Schillebeeckx, in *Christ the Sacrament of Encounter with God* (London and Melbourne: Sheed and Ward, 1963), pp. 15-16, who has perhaps stated the position most clearly:

> the saving activity of Jesus is *sacramental*. For a sacrament is a divine bestowal of salvation in an outwardly perceptible form which makes the bestowal manifest; a bestowal of salvation in historical visibility. The Son of God really did become true man. . . . The man Jesus, as the personal visible realization of the divine grace of redemption, is *the* sacrament, the primordial sacrament, because this man, the Son of God himself, is intended by the Father to be in his humanity the only way to the actuality of redemption. . . . Human encounter with Jesus is therefore the sacrament of the encounter with God.

Since limiting this conception of sacramentality to Jesus would appear to be a "christomonistic" restriction, however, a more comprehensive alternative might be justified, involving the idea that the whole of the saving work of the Father, Son, and Holy Spirit is the "sacrament" of the immanent Trinity, which is given in it in a manner appropriate to its accommodation to the creation in the economy. The term *sacrament* has the advantage that it connotes the specific events of Christian revelation with which we are necessarily concerned in trinitarian theol-

This sacramental correspondence is itself, for Barth, rooted in and based on the act of God in revealing himself. It is thus to God's gracious act of condescension in revelation that appeal must finally be made to find the real basis of our knowledge of God. God has graciously made himself accessible to sinful men and women, so that the knowledge of God given in faith has a divine and not an anthropological basis. Fundamentally, God is not in himself something other than what he is in revelation, precisely because it is God who has acted. It is God himself who is present in the creaturely signs, which for that reason serve as sacramental objects taken up and used by God for his own purpose:

> Revelation means the giving of signs. We can say quite simply that revelation means sacrament, i.e., the self-witness of God, the representation of His truth, and therefore of the truth in which He knows Himself, in the form of creaturely objectivity.[19]

It is this sacramental correspondence between God's objectivity *ad extra* and *ad intra* that, according to Barth, provides the possibility of a real knowledge of God. The fundamental sacramental reality in question is, of course, the man Jesus Christ, who is the Word made flesh. From this primary sacramental reality there stretches forward and backward in time a sacramental continuity in the existence of the church and of Israel. This christological basis introduces, finally, the knowledge of the Trinity as such:

> the heart of it all is that it is He Himself, the one, supreme and true Lord, who thus unveils Himself to us; that in revelation we have to do with His action as the triune God, and therefore with Himself in every creaturely work and sign that He uses. On this basis and only on this basis can there be real knowledge of God.[20]

---

ogy, whereas historically *analogy* has a long history as a technical term in the doctrine of God. *Analogy* as a technical term, however, cannot finally be abandoned, even in the context of the theology of the economic and the immanent Trinity, in particular because of its recognized logical status.

19. Barth, *Church Dogmatics*, II/1, p. 52.
20. Barth, *Church Dogmatics*, II/1, p. 51.

Within this conception, a sacramental correspondence obtains between the economic Trinity and the immanent Trinity, founded not on the ontological identification of the two but solely on the grace of revelation.

Barth also speaks here, significantly, of the "analogy of faith," finding such language unavoidable.[21] The argument is that as long as we allow God's revelation itself to dictate the terms of the proportionality involved in analogy, rather than the idea of an essential proportionality of being that can then be developed in a natural theology, analogy is a necessary and valuable tool for theological discourse. Barth's claim, however, is that the principle of the similarity between God's revelation and God in himself is not a general similarity of being, but purely God's truthfulness in his self-revelation.[22]

It is this aspect of Barth's theology that needs to be drawn out more clearly in contemporary trinitarian theology. The resulting approach could, in principle, constitute a *via media,* on the one hand between the theology that seeks to exclude all but one consistent economic trinitarian *taxis* from consideration and the theology that seeks to unify the diverse elements artificially, and on the other between the contemporary affirmation of the unity of the economic with the immanent Trinity and the older distinction between them. Such an approach would preclude the necessity of an arbitrary restriction of the economic data to a single aspect of the diverse economy as the basis of a trinitarian theology, so that the diversity of the economy could be maintained without the imposition of an artificial unity, and a doctrine of the Trinity could be developed from all the relevant economic data. This would allow a certain flexibility in the treatment of the economy. Because the unity of the economic and the immanent Trinity would be qualified

21. Barth, *Church Dogmatics,* II/1, pp. 225-28.
22. Evidently, if such a position were consistently maintained, then despite the christological doctrine of election and the idea of Christ as the eternal man, a basic distinction between the economic and the immanent Trinity would have to be maintained as well. Here, Barth's theology differs sharply from that of certain of his followers — and among those surveyed above, from Jüngel's and Moltmann's in particular. Curiously, Roman Catholic theologians such as Kasper appear closer to his thought at this point than do many Protestants.

analogically, not every aspect of the economy of salvation would need to be taken in itself to be of trinitarian significance. An adaptation of the two natures doctrine, for example, would still be possible on this view, while at the same time a christology in which the emphasis lay on the unity of Christ's person could still be developed, consistent with an integral trinitarian theology affirming the passivity and activity of Christ in relation to the Spirit.

The Reciprocity of Christ and the Spirit

Throughout this study, we have met with reasons for conceiving the economic basis for a trinitarian theology of the Holy Spirit in a pneumatology conceived in close connection with christology. The very attempt to develop a *trinitarian* pneumatology, of course, implies that such connections must at some point be drawn. This is not to say that the relation between the Spirit and the Father is to be excluded; indeed, this relation has traditionally been given ontological priority over the Spirit-Son relation, in view of the doctrine of the Father as the "first" person of the Trinity and as "source" of the other two persons. At the same time, however, the connection between the Spirit and Christ in the economy is of primary importance in the epistemological sense, since it is in the light of this that the Father-Spirit relation itself is truly known. Thus the relation of the Spirit to Christ can never be neglected in pneumatology.

A number of factors arising in recent theology, however, suggest that a specific relation of *reciprocity* might obtain between Christ and the Spirit. Modern biblical scholarship concerning the Spirit must be considered first of all, in particular the recognition among exegetes of the importance of both Spirit and Logos christology (to use the later terms) in New Testament thought. These not only appear to reflect the differing concerns of distinct New Testament theologies but also are to be found as parallel emphases within a single New Testament tradition: the Johannine. The connection between pneumatology and christology which thus appears in New Testament thought itself is already two-sided, involving apparent reversals of the line of dependence between the Spirit and

Christ, sometimes between different New Testament traditions and sometimes within the same traditions.[23]

Second, in the contemporary theological context, ecclesiological problems and ecumenism have brought the question of the relation between the Spirit and Christ to prominence. The pentecostal and charismatic movements, for example, challenge the domestication of the Spirit to institutional structures and the practical subordination of the Spirit to the Word. Similarly, ecumenical discussions of ecclesiology have also focused attention on the crucial importance of pneumatology for the theology of the church. A number of theologians have concluded that a recovery of the two-sidedness of the relation between the Spirit and Christ that appears in the New Testament would be an attractive theological option from the ecumenical point of view, since it provides a theological ground for the diversity of the different theological traditions. According to Yves Congar, for example, the central differences between the West and the East can be seen to be focused in eucharistic theology; in the West, the decisive role in the eucharist is accorded to the words of institution, the *verbum*, whereas in the East the invocation of the Holy Spirit, the *epiclesis*, is of central significance.[24] Congar maintains both that the two approaches are complementary and that for the good of the church they require integration. In the same way, but from the standpoint of Eastern Orthodoxy, John Zizioulas has argued that an adequate "synthesis" of christology and pneumatology is the prerequisite to a resolution of the ecumenical problems of ecclesiology.[25]

Third, the *filioque* doctrine has emerged as one of the key dogmatic problems of the ecumenical movement. One of the key

---

23. The work of Schweitzer, Hermann, Dunn, and others on the Pauline view of the Spirit has also been of particular importance in this respect, showing the extent to which even Paul, who was formerly understood to advocate an "incarnational" christology in the usual sense of the term, is able to adopt a version of Spirit christology as well. Cf. Rom. 1:3-4; 1 Cor. 15:45; 2 Cor. 3:17; and also Chapter 1 above. Elsewhere, the two-sidedness of the relation also appears: cf., e.g., Luke 3:22 vs. Acts 2:33; and John 1:32-34 vs. 20:22.

24. Congar, *I Believe in the Holy Spirit*, vol. 3, pp. 228-74.

25. John D. Zizioulas, *Being as Communion* (London: Darton, Longman and Todd, 1985), pp. 123-42.

suggestions made in recent years concerning the *filioque* has again been that an emphasis on the reciprocity between the Spirit and Christ is needed. Thus, for example, it has become clear that exaggerated attacks of West against East and East against West, to the effect that the one detaches pneumatology entirely from christological control and that the other completely subordinates pneumatology to christology, must be rejected, on the simple grounds that both traditions have clear theological mechanisms for avoiding such extremes. Despite the rather different conceptualities employed in the two traditions, therefore, the two are not as far apart as sometimes appears.[26] It is in keeping with this view that the Faith and Order Commission, in "The *Filioque* Clause in Ecumenical Perspective," formally recommends that the reciprocal relationship between the Spirit and Christ that obtains at the level of the economy of salvation in the New Testament witness be seen to be of central importance to the ecumenical enterprise and be formally taken up into the doctrine of the immanent Trinity.[27]

Finally, the issue of the relation between the Spirit and Christ is also clearly of central importance in contemporary trinitarian pneumatology, in the sense that the material differences between the positions encountered in the previous chapters derives from their different economic starting points, each of which involves a different view of that relation. The trinitarian pneumatology that is oriented to the problem of revelation and faith and that understands the Spirit as the Spirit who reveals Christ, for example, differs fundamentally from that drawn from the synoptic christology of anointing, and indeed contradicts it. The same could be said of the other theological models examined.

I have already argued that the material tensions in the economic basis upon which trinitarian theology rests ought to determine the

---

26. Congar, for example, argues that the pneumatological positions of the East and West must be understood to be complementary expressions of the one trinitarian faith, although admittedly in terms of their different, more basic overall trinitarian presuppositions. See, e.g., Congar's survey of recent developments in *I Believe in the Holy Spirit*, vol. 3, pp. 174ff., esp. 213-14.

27. World Council of Churches, Commission on Faith and Order, "The *Filioque* Clause in Ecumenical Perspective," §§III-V, in Vischer, ed., *Spirit of God, Spirit of Christ*.

formal limits of the argument that the economic Trinity is the immanent Trinity, and vice versa. The diversity of the economic basis itself, in short, *requires* us to qualify the idea of the unity of the two by a kenoticism regarding the economic Trinity and a recognition of the analogical character of all knowledge of the immanent Trinity. Otherwise the diversity of the economic basis leads to a series of premature restrictions of the relevant economic data and to a number of one-sided trinitarian positions, none of which can be reconciled with the rest. Since it is one and the same Christ who is anointed with the Spirit, who suffers on the cross, who sends the Spirit to the church after the resurrection, and who mediates the new creation and final glorification of the children of God, such contradictions cannot ultimately be sustained in systematic theology. The unity of the Christ-event itself therefore appears to demand that the one-sidedness of recent trinitarian pneumatologies be modified in such a way as to maintain the diversity of the economy, on the one hand, while preserving the unity of the Trinity, on the other.

Following the suggestions of the Faith and Order Commission noted above, therefore, and in keeping with the way in which the question of the doctrine of the Holy Spirit has been raised in contemporary theology, the possibility of bringing the idea of a reciprocity between the Spirit and Christ to formal expression in trinitarian theology can now be considered. The starting point for such a conception must obviously be the diversity of the biblical witness, which presents the mission of Christ as dependent upon the work of the Spirit but also presents the mission of the Spirit as dependent upon the work of Christ. More than this, however, what is required is a developed and integrated pneumatological christology and christological pneumatology that can be taken up in their reciprocity into trinitarian theology. Historically, the doctrine of the Trinity did not develop simply out of reflection on Scripture, or from a consideration of isolated biblical episodes, but out of the christological and pneumatological controversies of the first four centuries of Christian theology. The economic basis for the doctrine, in consequence, was an already highly "theologized" understanding of the events of the economy of salvation, expressed in patristic christology and pneumatology. Recent trinitarian theology has similarly relied upon a complex series of theological presuppositions concerning the economy of salvation. Barth's doctrine of divine self-communication, Jüngel's theology of the cross, and Moltmann's understanding of eschatology as a trinitarian history, together with the pneumatological "christology of ascent" developed by Mühlen and Kasper, are all essentially economic doctrines that ground their respective trinitarian theologies of the Spirit.

The implications of a theology of reciprocity between pneumatology and christology developed along these lines would be considerable, not just for trinitarian theology as such, but also for wider questions of the economy of salvation, as expressed, for example, in ecclesiology and spiritual theology, to which trinitarian theology is also implicitly and explicitly related. For instance, the practical subordination of the work of the Spirit to the Word in a theology such as Barth's can be justified to some extent from Scripture and has a systematic basis in his trinitarian theology of the Revealer, his Revelation, and its Revealedness, and thus in the priority Barth gives to christology over pneumatology. In Barth's theology, however, as in much Protestant theology, this has wider implications for ecclesiology and the spiritual life, which are thereby focused not only *by,* but also to a great extent *in,* the proclamation of the Word. The "ontic" role of the *Spiritus Creator,* together with the importance of religious experience of the Spirit, the role of the affective life in the approach to God through art and the senses, as well as the illuminative role of the mystic, can very easily be diminished in this way, while ecclesial life, the liturgy, and spirituality are thereby impoverished. On the other side, the one-sidedness of ecclesial life that can arise from a priority of pneumatology over christology is well documented in the excesses of the Montanists, for example, or of the radical reformation and the charismatic and pentecostal movements. Ecclesiology can be one-sided here as well, with even worse results.

If, however, a theology of the reciprocity of the Spirit and Christ in the economy and in the Trinity were to be developed, as the Commission on Faith and Order has suggested, it would follow that such one-sidedness in ecclesiology and spirituality could no longer be sustained systematically. In pneumatology, progress toward such a position is of the utmost importance. At the same time, an increasing encounter of the various traditions of ecclesiology and spirituality in the concrete life of the church is also important as the soil from which such systematic reflection will grow. Ecclesiology and spirituality are intimately related to trinitarian thought, for the doctrine of the Trinity has logical priority over the doctrines of the church and of the Christian life, but we should not for that reason neglect the importance of the ecclesial *praxis* and culture in which theology and theologians have their roots. An enrichment of the scope of pneumatology in this sense can be seen to be one of the practical promises held forth by ecumenism, while ecumenism, in turn, can be seen to be a focus of promise for the future of the doctrine of the Holy Spirit.

The Holy Spirit in the Immanent Trinity

We turn, therefore, to consider possible directions for the theology of the Holy Spirit in the immanent Trinity. Even if our main theological emphasis were to fall upon the doctrine of the economic Trinity, we could not ultimately avoid this question, since an adequate understanding of the economic Trinity requires a satisfactory doctrine of the immanent Trinity. The function of the doctrine of the Trinity since patristic times has been to ground the saving work of the triune God in the being of the triune God himself. In interpreting the economy in this way, however, trinitarian theology has to concern itself with the immanent Trinity, since otherwise it cannot, by definition, succeed in its desire to provide an absolute ground for salvation in the being of the triune God himself.

It is frequently said that the difficulties involved in developing a trinitarian theology of the Holy Spirit are greater than those we encounter in connection with the other two persons. The problem, in fact, is as basic as the very terms in which the doctrine of the Spirit is conceived. Even the name "Holy Spirit" itself, for example, unlike "Father" and "Son," is not a relative but an absolute term, which could in itself be used as appropriately of the divine essence, or even of the Father and Son, as of the Spirit himself in the trinitarian sense.[28]

---

28. Vladimir Lossky, "The Procession of the Holy Spirit in the Orthodox Triadology," trans. Edward Every, *The Eastern Churches Quarterly* 7, supplementary issue 2 (1948): 34-35; and Congar, *I Believe in the Holy Spirit*, vol. 3, p. 6.

Thomas Aquinas notes that the third person, unlike the Father and the Son, has no proper name.[29] In the same way, the terms *procession* and *spiration* do not possess the relative theological precision of corresponding terms such as *filiation* and *sonship*. The Father, in fact, cannot really be understood as the "Father" of the Holy Spirit, but rather only as his "Spirator," so that even the creedal phrase "who proceeds from the Father" is misleading. Even our most basic terminology here is problematic and has to be deliberately accommodated to the doctrine of the Holy Spirit.[30]

As Congar suggests, the limitations of language can be seen as something of an advantage as well as a disadvantage, in the sense that they keep us from presuming that our knowledge can extend too far into the mystery of the Trinity.[31] Terms such as *Spirit* and *spiration*, or *Father* and *Son*, or *filiation* and *sonship* are all ultimately analogous, so that an apophatic qualification is written into the very structure of our discourse. The terms used in pneumatology at this point, however, are particularly problematic, for the reasons indicated. To this extent, one of the primary difficulties to be overcome in a trinitarian theology of the Holy Spirit is the limitation inherent in the terminology we begin with — because of the limitation that attaches to all theological analogy, indeed, but also because of the particular weakness inherent in the analogies used in pneumatology.

It is at this point, however, that the contribution of contemporary trinitarian theology to the task of a future pneumatology could be most significant. The economic categories it works with

29. Thomas Aquinas, *Summa Theologiae*, 1a. 36, 1.

30. This problem appears to be less severe, however, in the East than it is in the West. Staniloae ("The Procession of the Holy Spirit from the Father," pp. 174-86) argues that one of the reasons why the East is unable to admit that the Spirit proceeds from the Son is that "spiration" is proper to the Father, so that accepting the doctrine of double procession would imply that the Son was a Father as well. Staniloae refers to a number of patristic sources for this argument and goes on to state: "It would be preferable to use the word 'procession' for the relation of the Spirit to the Father, and for his relation to the Son, the term 'goes out from' doubled with other terms like 'shines out from' or 'is manifested by,' terms which have been used by the eastern Fathers" (pp. 176-77). The East generally employs a more specific and differentiated terminology in its pneumatology than does the West.

31. Congar, *I Believe in the Holy Spirit*, vol. 3, p. 5.

provide a number of new conceptual models that take us well beyond the limitations of terms such as *procession*, or even *Spirit* itself. At the same time, they carry us back to the ultimate basis of trinitarian theology in the economy of salvation and serve as a check against a doctrine of the Trinity that is unrelated to it. At the center of Christian theology stands the conviction that the divine trinitarian life has truly been shared with us in Jesus Christ. In the salvation-historical events with which we have to do, a genuinely salvific trinitarian "history" has taken and is taking place. If trinitarian theology is not immediately oriented to salvation history in the interests of soteriology, therefore, it loses its proper theological function and becomes irrelevant to the primary concern of Christian theology, which is precisely the saving work of God. Once this happens, however, it also tends to fruitless speculation, since it is then no longer controlled by the economic events it is intended to interpret. As Rahner writes in the passage that is so often cited:

> The basic thesis which . . . presents the Trinity as a mystery of salvation (in its reality and not merely as a doctrine) might be formulated as follows: The "economic" Trinity is the "immanent" Trinity and the "immanent" Trinity is the "economic" Trinity.[32]

In the previous section, I suggested that the basic reciprocity that obtains between the Spirit and Christ at the economic level might profitably be taken up into the theology of the immanent Trinity. Now the possibility of a theology of immanent trinitarian reciprocity can be considered more fully. In fact, such a theology is able to claim a surprisingly rich inheritance from both Eastern and Western theologies. Three specific theological positions can be considered: (1) the idea of Spirit-Son reciprocity as taken up in Hans Urs von Balthasar's adaptation of the *filioque* doctrine; (2) the attempt by a number of Orthodox theologians to deal with the question of the inner-trinitarian relation between the Spirit and the Son in terms of reciprocity and the Orthodox doctrine of the divine *energeia;* and (3) the idea of *perichoresis* in trinitarian theology. I shall argue, however, that none of these is entirely adequate to the

32. Rahner, *The Trinity,* pp. 21-22, italics omitted.

notion of inner-trinitarian reciprocity, that the idea of reciprocity involves a broadly "social" understanding of the Trinity, and that, in this respect, recent trinitarian theology on the whole offers the possibility of a genuine advance beyond the achievement of traditional theology.

First of all, therefore, there is the option of a theology of reciprocity as developed in Balthasar's treatment of the *filioque* doctrine.[33] Balthasar develops a doctrine of what he calls "trinitarian inversion" in a direct attempt to deal with the problem of economic diversity. Balthasar's theology, like Barth's, is also of interest because his theology of trinitarian inversion demands an analogical qualification of the unity of the economic Trinity with the immanent Trinity. Balthasar's theology is deficient, however, in its understanding of the two-sidedness of the relation between the Spirit and Christ; according to Balthasar, the Spirit is given economically to the Son as the Spirit who proceeds from the Father, and given by the Son to the church as the Spirit who proceeds from the Son. The inversion of *taxis* is therefore economic only, inasmuch as the various moments with which we are concerned in the economy as a whole have their ultimate ground in different aspects of the inner-trinitarian life.

In Balthasar's theology, in short, the apparent reciprocity between the Spirit and Christ is understood in terms of the doctrine of double procession: On the one hand, the Spirit is the Spirit who proceeds from the Father and is bestowed on the Son; on the other hand, the Spirit is the Spirit who proceeds from the Son, that is, the response of the Son in love to the Father. It is thus that the Spirit can also be the Son's to give. Such an interpretation of the *filioque* has a great deal to be said for it. It might be argued, for example, and with some justification, that the "Fatherly" side of the procession of the Spirit has been underemphasized in the West, and that many of the deficiencies of Western pneumatology might be overcome if this side of the procession were to be given more

---

33. See my article, "The Anointing of Christ and the *Filioque* Doctrine," *Irish Theological Quarterly* 60 (1994): 241-58. The main sources are Hans Urs von Balthasar, *Theodramatik* (Einsiedeln: Johannes Verlag, 1978), II/2; and *Theologik* (Einsiedeln: Johannes Verlag, 1987), III.

sustained treatment. Nevertheless, the fundamental problem remains: The Holy Spirit does not truly appear as a trinitarian agent in his own right. What is in view is not so much the reciprocity of Spirit and Son as the relation between the Son and the Father. In terms of the economic problem of reciprocity as outlined above, therefore, Balthasar's approach appears to confuse the activity of the Spirit in relation to Christ with the Father-Son relation. A true theology of reciprocity, on the other hand, would allow the Spirit to be an inner-trinitarian agent in his own right, truly "of one substance" with the Father and the Son, whose agency in this sense has never been in doubt.

This assessment reflects an Eastern criticism of the doctrine of the Holy Spirit in Western theology that was outlined earlier in connection with the *filioque* dispute. If, however, one were to accept the Western view that the Spirit can truly be understood in his hypostatic quality as the relation of love subsisting between the Father and the Son, and admit the implied limitation of the personal agency of the Spirit, Balthasar's position could certainly be adopted. This wider implication of his position is, however, not one that I have been prepared to support, for the reasons specified.

Second, the Eastern doctrine of the trinitarian *energeia* can be considered as a possible *locus* of Spirit-Son reciprocity. This concept is of special importance for the Eastern theology of the Holy Spirit, inasmuch as the mainstream Eastern view is that the Spirit proceeds from the Father alone at the level of the divine essence, but "comes forth" from the Father and the Son at the level of the eternal divine energies. Dumitru Staniloae points out that in the medieval Byzantine tradition, after the *filioque* had become the official cause for schism with the West, the doctrine of divine *energeia* became the central focus of Eastern pneumatological development; in fact, it enabled the East to relate the Son and Spirit at the eternal, inner-trinitarian level without recourse to the *filioque*.[34] What is essential for Western theology to acknowledge is that in the Eastern tradition the divine *energeia* are as eternal and truly "inner-trinitarian" as the community of divine essence; the difference, according to East-

---

34. Staniloae, "The Procession of the Holy Spirit from the Father," pp. 178-84.

ern thought, is that the energies make God "participable," or communicable, whereas in the divine essence God is radically inaccessible.[35] Indeed, the medieval Byzantine theologian Gregory Palamas even employed a broadly Augustinian analogy of love *(eros)* on this basis.[36] According to Palamas, the Spirit can be understood as the love of the Father for the Word and of the Word for the Father, both immanently and economically, but only with reference to the eternal divine energies; in his *ousia,* the Spirit is the Spirit of the Father alone.

On the basis of the Eastern theology of the *energeia,* a number of modern Eastern theologians have advocated a theology of reciprocity in trinitarian pneumatology. Staniloae, for example, attempts to take this theme up from the point of view of a social doctrine of the Trinity, arguing that, while the Spirit receives his hypostatic existence from the Father alone, his personal character is constituted also by his network of relations with both the Father and the Son, a network that exists eternally in the divine *energeia.*[37] Staniloae writes:

35. Paul Evdokimov, *L'Esprit Saint dans la tradition orthodoxe* (Paris: Cerf, 1969), pp. 61-62. This is a point often missed in Western theology. Cf., however, Gregory Palamas, *Triad.* 3.2.5ff. (ET *The Triads,* ed. John Meyendorff, trans. Nicholas Gendle [New York: Paulist Press, 1983], pp. 93ff.); Vladimir Lossky, *The Vision of God,* trans. Asheleigh Moorhouse (Clayton, WI: Faith Press, 1963), pp. 124ff.; and Congar, *I Believe in the Holy Spirit,* vol. 3, pp. 61ff., who also provides an extensive bibliography.

36. Gregory Palamas, *Cap. Phys. Theol.* 36-37 (*PG* 150, 1144-45), referred to by Evdokimov, *L'Esprit Saint dans la tradition orthodoxe,* p. 59, and Orphanos, "The Procession of the Holy Spirit," p. 33.

37. Staniloae, "The Procession of the Holy Spirit from the Father," pp. 184-86. Staniloae here attempts to take up one side of Moltmann's suggestions in his essay "Theological Proposals Towards the Resolution of the Filioque Controversy," to the effect that the Spirit receives his existence from the Father but his "image" or "relational form" — that is, his personal character — from the Son (Moltmann, *The Crucified God,* pp. 164-73). Staniloae argues that Moltmann is right to posit a clearer distinction between the Father and the Son in their relations with the Spirit than is possible on the *filioque* paradigm, but wrong to distinguish between the existence and personal character of the Spirit in this way. The proper distinction, he argues, is between the trinitarian *ousia* and *energeia.*

There is a reciprocity of infinite richness in its complexity between the Three Persons of the Holy Trinity, and it is this which gives them their fully personal character. But there is a special reciprocity between the Son and the Spirit which is reflected in their contact with the world.[38]

Some version of the Eastern doctrine of the *energeia* is arguably what is required in Western theology in order to give substance to the theme of reciprocal trinitarian relationality. However, the problem of the foreign conceptuality remains, so that it is difficult to see how such an adaptation of the doctrine could ever be widely accepted in Western theology.

A third possibility from the tradition is closely related to the previous discussion and comes very near to what is meant by reciprocity: the doctrine of *perichoresis*. Etymologically, the term connotes mutual involvement or interchange; as such, its initial theological usage was in christology: Gregory Nazianzen and Maximos Confessor employed it in connection with the two natures doctrine.[39] It is, however, very rare before John Damascene, who took the term from Gregory and Maximos and reinterpreted it primarily in a trinitarian sense.[40] In his theology, *perichoresis* refers to the mutual interpenetration or eternal circulation of divine life among the persons. *Perichoresis* in this sense is of central importance in John Damascene's trinitarian thought — indeed, so much so that

---

38. Staniloae, "The Procession of the Holy Spirit from the Father," p. 186.

39. L. Prestige, "[*Perichoreo*] and [*Perichoresis*] in the Fathers," *Journal of Theological Studies* 29 (1928): 242-44; and A. Chollet, "Circuminsession, -cession," *Dictionnaire de théologie catholique*, ed. A. Vacant et al. (Paris: Libraire Letouzey et Ané, 1905), vol. 2, cols. 2527-32.

40. John Damascene, *De fide orth.*, 1.8; 1.14; 4.18; cited by Prestige in "[*Perichoreo*] and [*Perichoresis*] in the Fathers," pp. 242-44. The idea of mutual interchange between the persons, however, is certainly found earlier. It appears, for example, to be supported by scriptural texts such as John 10:38; 14:11; and 17:21 (vis-à-vis the Son and the Father) and perhaps 1 Cor. 2:10 (vis-à-vis the Spirit and the Father). The idea of mutual interchange is also particularly important in the trinitarian theology of the Cappadocians, with their strong pluralism, and in particular in Gregory of Nyssa (Prestige, "[*Perichoreo*] and [*Perichoresis*] in the Fathers," p. 244). It was John Damascene, however, who first used *perichoresis* as a technical term in trinitarian theology.

it is put on a level with the unity of the divine nature as the ground of divine unity.[41] As such, it is apparently intended as a measure against tritheism on the one hand and modalism on the other: The persons are indeed one in their hypostatic interpenetration, and yet three since this interpenetration presupposes a genuine plurality.

Through the influence of John Damascene, the doctrine of *perichoresis* came to be accepted *de fidei* in both Eastern and Western trinitarian theology. However, like other trinitarian doctrines, it is understood differently in the two traditions. In the East, where the primary data of trinitarian theology are the *hypostaseis* rather than the *ousia*, *perichoresis* remains, as in John Damascene, a doctrine of trinitarian unity. Eastern theology is much more dynamic than Western theology at this point; each *hypostasis* is drawn to the other two, while the three are one precisely because they are completely outward-looking in this sense. In Latin theology, on the other hand, the divine *substantia* is logically prior to the persons and serves as the fundamental ground of trinitarian unity. *Perichoresis (circumincession)* here is conceived as a function of substantial unity, since on this basis there is a perfect fusion of relational activity in the one divine life.[42]

Clearly, the idea of the reciprocity between the Spirit and Christ arising from our study of contemporary trinitarian pneumatology is closely related to the traditional doctrine of *perichoresis*, particularly in its Eastern expression. In this sense reciprocity leads to a broadly Eastern view of the Trinity, which begins with the three persons and their work and moves from there to the question of trinitarian unity. It is only when the priority of the persons is thus accepted, in other words, that the idea of reciprocity can be developed.

41. John Damascene, *Nat. comp.* 4. Prestige ("[*Perichoreo*] and [*Perichoresis*] in the Fathers," p. 249), having surveyed the use of the term *perichoresis* in John Damascene's thought, draws the following conclusions: "[*Perichoresis*] is not a consequence but an equivalent of unity. . . . It has drawn to itself the adjectives denying confusion, which in earlier writers were associated with [*henosis*]. . . . It represents an attempt to define the nature of this unity. . . . It is illustrated negatively by being treated as incompatible with separation in substance, in place, or time, in power, operation, or will."

42. Thomas Aquinas, *Summa Theologiae*, 1a. 42, 5. See also Chollet, "Circuminsession, -cession"; and A. M. Bermejo, "Circumincession," *New Catholic Encyclopedia* (New York: McGraw-Hill, 1967), vol. 3, p. 880.

In the social Trinity advocated by Eastern theologians such as Staniloae and Evdokimov, the idea of the perichoretic relations of the three persons at the level of the divine *energeia* is put forward as the way ahead for ecumenical reasons. We have also seen that Moltmann, who speaks of the mutual relations of the persons in a similar way, develops both a strong doctrine of the priority of the persons and a strong view of *perichoresis* in his trinitarian theology, relying on *perichoresis* as the *sole* principle of trinitarian unity. Moltmann thus attempts to avoid the obstructions that the priority of substance in Western theology and the monarchianism of Eastern theology present to his radical trinitarianism. According to Moltmann:

> The unity of the trinitarian Persons lies in the circulation of the divine life which they fulfil in their relations to one another. This means that the unity of the triune God cannot and must not be seen in a general concept of divine substance. That would abolish the personal differences. But if the contrary is true — if the very difference of the three Persons lies in their relational, perichoretically consummated life process — then the Persons cannot and must not be reduced to three modes of being of one and the same divine subject. The Persons themselves constitute both their differences and their unity. . . . [T]hrough the concept of perichoresis, all subordinationism in the doctrine of the Trinity is avoided. It is true that the Trinity is constituted with the Father as starting point, inasmuch as he is understood as being "the origin of the Godhead." But this "monarchy of the Father" only applies to the *constitution* of the Trinity. It has no validity within the eternal circulation of the divine life, and none in the perichoretic unity of the Trinity. Here the three Persons are equal; they live and are manifested in one another and through one another.[43]

43. Moltmann, *The Trinity and the Kingdom of God: The Doctrine of God*, trans. Margaret Kohl (London: SCM Press, 1981), p. 175. This, however, is a thesis that neither the West nor the East can strictly accept. The former point is obvious; on the latter, see, e.g., Evdokimov, *L'Esprit Saint dans la tradition orthodoxe*, pp. 48, 71-72, where he argues that the energetic *perichoresis* in the divine life involves a reciprocity between the Son and the Spirit, which, however, has its ultimate source and goal in the Father.

There is no doubt that the doctrine of *perichoresis* must assume new importance if the idea of inner-trinitarian reciprocity is to be developed, as in Moltmann's theology, into a broadly social doctrine of the Trinity. We can expect in this context both that the precedent of previous doctrines of *perichoresis* can and will be drawn upon and that the idea of *perichoresis* will be developed further. It is questionable, however, whether the doctrine of *perichoresis* itself can bear all the weight necessary for the development of the idea of reciprocity in the inner-trinitarian sense, since it was not originally developed with this problem in mind. The problem is that *perichoresis* is a derivative and secondary doctrine that, in its classical expression, could be deduced from other doctrines already developed, without any reference to the economy of salvation or even, strictly speaking, to the problem of trinitarian *taxis*. The mutual indwelling of the persons is in this sense a corollary of the idea that the three are one and the one three. The problem of reciprocity as defined here, on the other hand, involves the idea of the interpersonal trinitarian relations deriving from the economy, and, on this basis, genuine reversals of the economic trinitarian *taxis*, whereas the doctrine of *perichoresis*, even when affirmed strongly in particular theologies in the older tradition, was never taken to abrogate the (generally one-sided) doctrines of trinitarian *taxis* held. Thus the doctrine of *perichoresis* has never been understood either by Eastern or Western theologians to be capable of overcoming the differing view of the trinitarian *taxis* with respect to pneumatology that separates the two traditions.

The question that has to be faced in this context, therefore, has wider implications for the structure of trinitarian theology than can be expressed in a simple reaffirmation of the doctrine of *perichoresis*, reflecting not only the assumptions of the Eastern and Western trinitarian traditions but also those of contemporary trinitarian theology. One problem here, of course, is how *perichoresis* is to be defined, in the sense that it makes all the difference whether it is taken to occur, for example, as an expression of the unity of divine substance, or as a more genuine expression of interpersonality at the level of the *energeia*. We have seen from the doctrine of the divine *energeia* that Eastern theology is able to differentiate between the sense in which the Spirit is related to the Father alone as the "source" of the

Trinity and the sense in which he is eternally related both to Father and Son in a reciprocal relationship in the "energetic" life of the Trinity. This distinction makes a more sophisticated approach to the problem possible in Eastern than in Western theology. This points, however, to the fundamental question at stake, concerning the idea of the person or *hypostasis* itself and in particular concerning the nature of its hypostatic relations, which the doctrine of *perichoresis* as such presupposes. The question is whether or not it is possible to conceive of the persons in such a way that an inner-trinitarian relation that is not ultimately a procession is possible.

A great deal depends upon the answer given to this question. In Eastern theology, the energetic hypostatic relations are distinguished from the processions, making possible a doctrine of energetic trinitarian relationality; indeed, in Eastern theology, the processions themselves are not understood primarily in a relational sense, but rather as differing modes of origin *(tropoi hyparxeos)*.[44] In Eastern theology, according to Vladimir Lossky, the relations are held only to *express* the prior absolute diversity of the persons.[45] This does not mean, however, that the inner-trinitarian relations become purely secondary. Rather, in Eastern theology, as we have seen, the threefold relations of the persons are of enormous importance: not just the relations between the Father and the Son on the one hand and, on the other, between the Father and the Son as one principle and the Spirit, as in the Western-Augustinian tradition, but the relations between each person and the other two persons in distinction. According to Evdokimov, for example, the most important single factor contributing to a proper understanding of the trinitarian theology of the Christian East is the threefold character of the relations among the persons.[46] This is one of the reasons why the East is unable to adopt the Western view of the relations of opposition: One can really only *oppose* two principles, whereas the relations of the

---

44. Lossky, "The Procession of the Holy Spirit in the Orthodox Triadology," pp. 37-38.

45. Lossky, "The Procession of the Holy Spirit in the Orthodox Triadology," p. 38.

46. Evdokimov, *L'Esprit Saint dans la tradition orthodoxe*, pp. 42ff.

persons are triple; with regard to the Spirit and the Son, therefore, Eastern thought has it that the Spirit proceeds from the Father conjointly and together with the begetting of the Son upon whom he rests, while the Son is begotten by the Father conjointly and together with the procession of the Spirit who manifests him. Each has a relation of origin to the Father, a relation of procession, in other words, and a relation to the other person that is not of origin or procession. In the latter case, the relation is not causal, but one of interdependence within the perichoretic life of the three.

In the Western-Augustinian tradition, by contrast, all inner-trinitarian relations are understood as qualities logically consequent upon the actions of generation and spiration, while it is these relations which distinguish the persons. The doctrine of relations is thus immediately implied by the doctrine of the processions. According to Thomas Aquinas, for example, there are only four real relations in the Trinity: fatherhood, sonship, spiration, and procession, corresponding to the two acts of generation and spiration on their active and passive sides.[47]

The idea of a true inner-trinitarian reciprocity between the Spirit and the Son such as we have in view can, however, only be said to be possible if there are relations that are not immediately derivative of the processions in this sense. From the standpoint of the Western tradition, one could not, for example, maintain the *filioque* together with a parallel *"spirituque"* doctrine, affirming that the Son is begotten of the Father and the Spirit together. With the Western, semi-causal conceptuality of trinitarian procession, such a reversal of the natural order or *taxis* of the persons could never be contemplated. Within the terms of Western theology, therefore, if the Spirit and the Son are to be related at all in the inner-trinitarian life, it will have to be through either a *filioque* or a *spirituque* doctrine, but not through both, since in Western theology the processions are the sole grounds of the personal relations. Equally, however, within the terms of the Western view that the only real inner-trinitarian relations are rooted in the processions, the Eastern doctrine of the procession

47. Thomas Aquinas, *Summa Theologiae*, 1a. 28, 4.

of the Holy Spirit from the Father alone would mean that the Spirit has no relation to the Son, or vice versa. A distinction between the processions and some other inner-trinitarian relations is therefore an absolute prerequisite for a theology of inner-trinitarian reciprocity.

It is here that the social doctrine of the Trinity must begin, and not simply, as is sometimes alleged,[48] with a simple assertion of the priority of the plurality of the persons over the unity of the one God. (These are perhaps best seen as antinomies in all trinitarian theologies.) The social doctrine of the Trinity undoubtedly presupposes the irreducible plurality of the persons, but it is more immediately concerned with a rather different problem: not with plurality for its own sake, as it were, but rather with inner-trinitarian relationality. More specifically, the social doctrine of the Trinity begins with the idea of the Trinity as a *community* of Father, Son, and Holy Spirit, whose relations are conceived to be genuinely personal, in the nature of love, rather than relational in the more abstract, ontological sense of the "relations of opposition." In this sense, its economic basis in the concrete relations of the persons in the economy is strong — far stronger, for example, than the economic basis of the idea of self-communication underlying the trinitarian theologies of Barth and Rahner. The development of a trinitarianism grounded in the concrete relations of the persons in the Christ-event must in this sense be reckoned to be one of the major achievements of post-Barthian and post-Rahnerian trinitarian theology, even if the theologies that have thus emerged have rested on questionable appropriations of the relevant economic data.

The older Western trinitarian tradition, however, can also enrich our understanding at this point, and in particular the line of thought inaugurated in the twelfth century by Richard of St. Victor, which we have already encountered briefly. There are only two significant trinitarian traditions in Western medieval theology: the Augustinian, which is mediated by Anselm and Peter Lombard and which culminates in Thomas Aquinas, and that initiated by Richard of St. Victor, which continues in the Franciscan tradition in Alex-

48. So, e.g., Hill, *The Three-Personed God*, p. 217.

ander of Hales and Bonaventure.[49] In his *The Trinity* Richard sketches the outlines of an alternative to the prevailing Augustinian trinitarian theology of his day, adopting a much more conciliatory stance toward the East than the hard-line and unimaginative Augustinian approach taken a half-century earlier by Anselm in his *De Processione Sancti Spiritus.* One breathes a totally different air in Richard's theology — a fact not lost on Thomas Aquinas, whose feet were planted firmly in the Augustinian camp at this point, and who found it necessary, as we shall see, to oppose Richard root and branch.

Richard's trinitarian theology begins with the Johannine idea that God is love.[50] His argument is that God, who is love, is *necessarily*[51] a community of persons, and indeed a Trinity, since love cannot exist where there is only one, and is incomplete when it is not open to more than a selfish possession of a single other.[52] The analogy Richard employs is not one based on the soul, but one based on the social dynamic of human love, whether between friends or in the man-woman relationship of marriage. To be totally absorbed in love for the other, in short, without being open to more than such an "I-Thou" relationship, is, Richard argues, a sign of weakness, a kind of selfishness, and a sure mark of imperfection in love. Thus the love between friends or lovers is in fact debilitating,

---

49. Hill, "The Historicity of God," p. 226, with reference to Michael Schmaus, *Der liber propugnatorius des Thomas Angelicus und die Lehrunterschiede zwischen Thomas von Aquin und Duns Scotus,* vol. 2, *Die trinitärischen Lehrunterschiede* (Münster: Aschendorff, 1930).

50. Richard of St. Victor, *The Trinity,* 3.2, 6. The critical edition is Richard de Saint-Victor, *La Trinité* (Paris: Sources Chrétiennes, 1969). There is a partial translation of the work in *Richard of St. Victor: The Twelve Patriarchs, The Mystical Ark, Book Three of the Trinity* (London: SPCK, 1979).

51. Richard's theology is intended to provide "necessary reasons" for what faith believes (*The Trinity,* 1.5; 3.1); this does not mean, as Frederick Copleston, in *A History of Philosophy* (New York: Image Books, 1962), II/2, p. 179, points out, that we can discern the necessity fully, but only that there must be necessary reasons for what necessarily exists, so that, as God is necessarily a Trinity, there must be a necessary reason for this fact. The "necessary reasons" adduced, therefore, are not fully comprehended, but approached by way of the analogy of human love. See, e.g., Richard, *The Trinity,* 3.13.

52. Richard, *The Trinity,* 3, esp. 3.2, 11, 14, and 15.

an ugly thing, when it does not welcome others into its sphere; expanding on Richard's argument, one might say that friendship is somehow *meant* to be inclusive of others, and that sexual love is *meant* to bear fruit in the family. He writes:

> the best kind of love, and the fullness of goodness, is not possible where a defective will or faculty excludes a sharing of pleasure and joy. Therefore those who truly love should search with equal desire for someone to be mutually loved, in perfect concord. Thus you see how the consummation of love [in the Trinity] requires a Trinity of persons, without which that love is unable to exist in all its integrity.[53]

Such a vision of love is both remarkable and illuminating, in particular because of the way it can be seen to provide a theoretical basis for *agape* as both a natural and a supernatural love that seeks to share the self with others, not for gain, but simply because of what it is. In the trinitarian sense, furthermore, love is what God is; love is not to be appropriated technically to the Holy Spirit as the third person of the Trinity, as in Augustine, but is rather to be understood in terms of the divine being itself, so that it is from this that the distinctive logic of God as a Trinity of three persons flows. Because God is love, and specifically the perfection of love, God is necessarily a community of love, a Trinity.

The spirit of the Augustinian enterprise of believing in order to understand is evident in Richard's trinitarian theology, and his position can be said to offer a rational account of plurality and indeed of the triunity of God that is at least as persuasive as any other. In the practical sense, his trinitarian theology of love provides a basis for the Christian community, and the community of human beings generally. Richard's theology also shows that a doctrine of the Trinity that emphasizes the threeness of the Father, Son, and Spirit will not necessarily undermine their unity; indeed, his *The Trinity* begins with a treatment of the unity of the divine substance,[54] and his attention only then turns to the idea that there is

53. Richard, *The Trinity*, 3.11, my translation.
54. Richard, *The Trinity*, 1; 2.

"true plurality in that true and simple Divinity," since its highest perfection is love.[55]

Another important aspect of Richard's trinitarian thought, which again distinguishes it sharply from Augustine's, is the fact that he successfully sustains a discussion of the persons as related in love, without immediate reference to the doctrine of the processions. In the whole of book 3 of *The Trinity*, where Richard's main argument for the plurality of the persons in God appears, he does not once develop the Augustinian relational doctrine of the persons, nor does he use the (Anselmian) phrase "relations of opposition." Indeed, Richard goes so far in his alternative to the prevailing Augustinian orthodoxy as to develop his own doctrine of the person in book 4 of the same work: A person, he argues, differs from a substance precisely in its singularity, its incommunicability. A substance is indicated by the name "man," but a person by the name "Peter."[56] The difference is between *what* one is and *who* one is. A human person's distinctiveness is defined by being, origin, or both taken together; in God, there is no difference in being between the Father, Son, and Spirit, but there are different modes of origin, as Richard puts it.[57] One might say that the doctrine of the person Richard develops is a doctrine of individuality — an individuality that is not, however, atomistic, but instead is constituted precisely in social relationship. One exists as a human being and as an individual precisely in relation to others, and so it is also with the Father, Son, and Holy Spirit.[58]

Richard's theology, then, while bearing superficial similarity to Augustine's in the role given to relationality, follows a very different course. Thomas Aquinas himself notes this fact several times with reference to the theology of Richard (and his theological successors among Thomas's Franciscan contemporaries) in his discussion of the trinitarian relations in the *Summa Theologiae*.[59] In connection with his view that the persons are their relations, Thomas notes that a

55. Richard, *The Trinity*, 3.1.
56. Richard, *The Trinity*, 4.6.
57. Richard, *The Trinity*, 4.15.
58. Richard, *The Trinity*, 4.16-24.
59. Thomas Aquinas, *Summa Theologiae*, 1a. 40, 2; 40, 3. Thomas also disputes the Victorine view that the nature of love requires that God, being love, is a Trinity in 1a. 32, 1, ad 2.

different view has been taken, to the effect that the relations are merely a sign of personal distinction, which is itself based in the mode of origin, that is, begetting and spiration. His response essentially represents the Augustinian view that there are only three ways in which one might be able to distinguish the persons: according to either substance, accidents, or relations. Since the substance is identical and there are no accidents in God, we are left with the relations as the sole basis of personal distinction. These, furthermore, are simply logical expressions of the acts of filiation and spiration: fatherhood and sonship, on the one hand, and active and passive procession on the other.

Thomas's criticism, however, points to the limitations of his own position as much as to those of Richard's. William J. Hill's recent critique of Richard, which follows in the Thomist tradition, raises the problem well:

> [Richard's] emphasis seems to fall, not upon love as a dynamism giving rise to the Word and the *Pneuma,* but upon the very nature of love as presupposing an inner relationality that is personal in kind. This is his primal and dominating principle to which the doctrine of the processions is subordinate. The universal tradition on the invariant order among the Persons demanded that he give consideration to the processions. But there his system reaches an impasse, because while love may well require a plurality of persons as its condition, it does not explain the origin of such a plurality. If the processions also constitute a structure indigenous to love, then it is difficult to explain that the Father is without origin, that the Son arises from the Father alone, and that the Spirit's origin is from the Father and the Son (at least in the Western tradition that Richard represents). That is, it is difficult to maintain a distinct personal identity for each of the Three.[60]

This criticism can only be justified, however, so long as the only real trinitarian relations are the processions; Richard's position is not that there are no processions, to be sure, nor is it that there is

---

60. Hill, *The Three-Personed God,* pp. 230-31.

no trinitarian *taxis* flowing from the natural order of the procession. Rather, his position is akin to that of the East on this point: The three persons are constituted as distinct by origin, and not by relation; the relations only express the distinction.[61]

Richard's trinitarian theology offers a coherent alternative within Western theology to the predominant Augustinian position. Its crucial presupposition, however, is that relations in the Trinity need not necessarily be relations of origin or processions. On this basis, the Son and Spirit can indeed be eternally related while not having their eternal origin in one another. There can be little doubt that once the Augustinian theory of relational predication is relinquished, such a presupposition is perfectly intelligible. To use another social analogy, a natural brother and sister have the same origin, but the possibility of an interpersonal relationship between them is based not on this but on their own individual personalities. From the point of view of origin alone, an abstract relation could be established in an ontological or causal sense, while if the two had never met, their relation would be nonexistent from the standpoint of interpersonal reality. The trinitarian relations Richard has in view similarly depend upon whether or not the trinitarian persons as persons are capable, in themselves, of genuinely interpersonal relations of love. In the other main trinitarian tradition of the West, the persons are not strictly conceived as such; but for Richard they are, and in this respect his position is representative of the social doctrine of the Trinity.[62]

What Richard's theology does not do, however, is to develop this theory from the point of view of the economy of salvation. Instead, he regards the persons as abstract divine beings capable of loving relationships within the one substance of the God who is love, but beyond this he does not take us. There is in this sense a good case for the criticism that while Richard regards the immanent Trinity as an eternal life of relationality and love, the relations

61. Richard, *The Trinity*, 4.15, 20, 23-24.

62. According to Evdokimov, e.g., *L'Esprit Saint dans la tradition orthodoxe*, p. 48: "La relation entre le Fils et l'Esprit n'est pas causale, mais c'est une relation d'interdépendence et de *condition* car toute relation interdivine est toujours *triple* dans la circumincession éternelle de l'Amour divin."

themselves are really without any definite content. The very relationality of the trinitarian terms *Father* and *Son,* if not *Holy Spirit*
as well, is effectively lost in this way. The psychological analogy, by
contrast, which lies at the heart of the Augustinian tradition, speci-
fies the character of the two processions in terms of the characteristic
acts of a spiritual nature: memory, knowledge, and will.

We have seen, however, that the idea of reciprocity which
emerges from the economy itself cannot be reconciled with the
semi-causal view of the trinitarian relations that prevails in the
West, and that what is needed is a theology of inner-trinitarian
relationality beyond what is possible on the basis of the Western
relational understanding of the persons. This is what is provided
by the social doctrine of the Trinity, where the divinity of the three
persons is such that they are capable of genuine interpersonal
relationships. These relations do not simply follow the order of
the processions, for then genuine mutuality and reciprocity would
not be possible. The Eastern doctrine of the procession of the
Spirit from the Father *alone,* for example, would thus rule out *any*
relation between the Spirit and the Son, while in the West, no
genuinely *reciprocal* relation between the two would be possible,
because the relation following from the procession is one-sided.
For the social Trinity, however, both the Spirit and the Son must
be capable of being the subject of acts that relate each to the other.
Here, the idea of Spirit-Son reciprocity is secured. This means that
both the Spirit and the Son can be active and passive in relation
to the other in the immanent life of the Trinity, and not merely,
as in the older Western paradigm, active and passive in one direction only — that is, from Son to Spirit, in the immanent Trinity,
and the reverse only under the conditions of the incarnation,
namely, by virtue of the humanity assumed by the Son and the
improper mode of speech made possible by the doctrine of the
communicatio idiomatum.

If a theology of immanent trinitarian reciprocity is to be developed, however, it will have to meet the criticism that, like Richard's
social doctrine of the Trinity, it does not sufficiently differentiate the
relations of the persons. If this criticism holds, then to the extent that
the Spirit and the Son are asserted merely to be related reciprocally,
the relations are simply indistinguishable. The contribution of the

contemporary trinitarian tradition to the social doctrine of the Trinity is of real importance at this point, however, for the images of anointing, revealedness, atonement, and eschatological fulfillment provide a wealth of specifically relational content for trinitarian pneumatology, a content that has already been developed in a number of theologies in a systematic way. On the basis of the idea that the economic Trinity is the immanent Trinity, indeed, this concrete relationality has become a major, perhaps *the* major, theme of trinitarian theology, since the sending of the Son and Spirit and their salvation-historical relatedness as the "two hands of the Father" are constitutive of the economic Trinity. No trinitarian theology that presupposes the unity of the economic and the immanent Trinity, therefore, can ultimately avoid taking up these relations into the theology of the immanent Trinity. Thus the thematization in post-Barthian and post-Rahnerian trinitarian theology — in particular, of the obedience of the incarnate Son to the Father, the loving unity of the Father and the Son in the Spirit even in the event of the cross, the anointing of the Son with the Spirit, and so on — flows from this systematic starting point.[63] What we are concerned with here is not an abstract series of processions within the divine being by which its unity is differentiated in a threefold way, but rather the living, historical reciprocity of the trinitarian persons in the concrete events of the economy of salvation.

A theology of Spirit-Son reciprocity in a social doctrine of the Trinity must thus begin with the concrete, economic relationality between the Spirit and Christ, based on an analysis of the role of

---

63. In Barth and Rahner, of course, this starting point is combined with a particular thesis concerning the self-communication of God, so that the economic trinitarian relations tend to be assimilated to the self-communication paradigm. It is for this reason above all that both Barth, *Church Dogmatics,* I/1, pp. 355ff., and Rahner, *The Trinity,* pp. 103ff., criticize the terminology of trinitarian "persons" and opt instead for the term "modes of being." However, the deeper implication of the view that the Trinity in itself is known from what it is *ad extra* and that it "is" what it is *ad extra* in the sense of Rahner's axiom is that the relations of the Father, Son, and Spirit, which are more complex than that given in the self-communication paradigm, be taken up into discussion of the immanent Trinity. This is precisely what has happened in post-Barthian and post-Rahnerian theology. In this sense, the positions of Barth and Rahner, contrary to their expressed intentions, lead to a social doctrine of the Trinity.

the Holy Spirit in christology and of Christ in pneumatology. In the economy, however, what the Spirit "gives" to Christ and what Christ "gives" to the Spirit in their reciprocal economic relationship are not identical. It is possible, for example, to say on the basis of the anointing theme that Christ is filled with the Spirit, and thus that the Spirit is the "unction" of Christ; but one would have no basis for the converse statement that the Spirit is "filled" with Christ. What the Spirit receives from Christ is not an anointing but rather, as in the Johannine tradition, "what is Christ's" (John 16:14), that is, the particular christocentric form of his mission after Jesus' death and resurrection.

Abstracting from this in the direction of a theology of the immanent Trinity, it becomes possible, not only to say that the Spirit and the Son relate mutually to one another in the fellowship of the divine trinitarian life, but also to give these relations content. We know that in the economy the Spirit rests upon the Son, and that the Son gives the Spirit to those who believe. Each has active and passive relations to the other, so that within the trinitarian life a relation of reciprocity exists between the Spirit and the Son, not a relation that is identical on each side, but a relation of activity and passivity that is appropriate to each.

If, however, the active and passive mutual relations of the Spirit and the Son can be seen in this way, they can also be understood in terms of the relations each of the two has, not to the other, but also to the Father *in* their respective relations to the other. Richard's analogy of a community of love, involving three persons and not just two, for example, requires that a genuine reciprocity between the Spirit and the Son should involve the Father as well. Staniloae has developed a similar position from the standpoint of the Christian East:

> The Son sees the Father not only as he by whom he is begotten, but also as him from whom the other proceeds. . . . But in his link with his other other [i.e., the Spirit], or in the procession of this one from himself, the Father does not forget the Son as Son, but insofar as the Third Person also proceeds from him, all the complex richness of his relationship with the Son can be seen. . . . In his turn the Son knows in the light of his other, by

whom the Father lives in all the richness of his love for the Son — the Son knows his Father and his love towards him more fully. Not only does the Father by his link with the Spirit live his love towards the Son in its fullness, that is to say not only does the Son shine out brightly towards the Father in the light of the Spirit cast by the Father on the Son, but also the Spirit is fully realized from the Father by the Son.[64]

It becomes possible, in fact, to make the following fourfold distinction in the interpersonal relations between the Spirit and the Son: In the active relation of the Spirit to the Son, the Spirit is related to the Son as the Son of the Father; in the passive relation of the Son to the Spirit which corresponds to this, the Son is related to the Spirit as the Spirit of the Father; similarly, in the active relation of the Son to the Spirit, the Son is related to the Spirit as the Spirit of the Father; in the passive relation of the Spirit to the Son, finally, the Spirit is related to the Son as the Son of the Father. The distinctions thus made in the reciprocal relations between the Spirit and the Son are important from the point of view of the social doctrine of the Trinity, since on the basis of the social analogy, none of the persons is what he is except in relation to the other two. The persons as well as the relations, therefore, can be seen to be genuinely distinct.

Clearly, any trinitarian relation that is taken up from the economy into the theology of the immanent Trinity must be understood under a kenotic qualification, so that the apophatic character of the immanent Trinity is preserved. The task of developing a theology of the inner-trinitarian relations from the economy therefore has to reckon seriously with the paradox that an adequate doctrine of the immanent Trinity is only possible when an apophatic reticence about it is embraced. This does not mean, however, that nothing whatever can be said about the immanent Trinity. The kenotic character of the economic Trinity and the ultimately apophatic character of the immanent Trinity do not preclude all knowledge of the immanent Trinity; rather, these are the limits that

64. Staniloae, "The Procession of the Holy Spirit from the Father," pp. 185-86.

define the scope of our knowledge of the Trinity, and thus make it what it is. As we have seen, the terms *Father, Son,* and *Holy Spirit* themselves are analogies, as are the terms *filiation* and *spiration*. This does not, however, prevent us from abstracting from the usual finite sense of the terms in developing a trinitarian theology, or even in the most simple affirmation of trinitarian faith. The same can, in principle, be said of the concrete salvation-historical relations of the persons as the basis for a theology of inner-trinitarian relationality. A recognition of the finite, temporal character of these relations is clearly required, but this does not mean that this character cannot be transcended in developing a theology of the immanent Trinity.

In its emphasis on the economy, therefore, contemporary theology has pointed the way to a new understanding of the trinitarian life of God as relational. It shows us, if at times through its limitations, that it is necessary to move beyond the kenotic form of the economy to a proper level of abstraction in the theology of the immanent Trinity, and at the same time rightly focuses attention on the fact that our knowledge of the immanent Trinity comes only by way of the economy. Given these qualifications, however, it does seem that the doctrine of the Holy Spirit in the immanent Trinity can indeed be deepened by the new appraisal of the concrete relationality of the persons in the economy that has taken place in recent theology. Although critical questions arise, the reorientation of the doctrine of the Trinity to the concrete content of the economy of salvation undoubtedly provides a fruitful basis for theological reflection.

9. *Light of Truth and Fire of Love*

WE MUST NOW return by way of a conclusion to the realms of faith and life, which must be the central concern of the Christian doctrine of the Holy Spirit. However necessary the turn to trinitarian theology may be, the doctrine of the Holy Spirit is fundamentally concerned with something more important in the human sense. Christian theology, in short, itself exists only for the sake of religious life, and in religious life, the doctrine of the Spirit is absolutely central. "What is born of the flesh is flesh, and what is born of the Spirit is spirit" (John 3:6). "God is spirit, and those who worship him must worship in spirit and truth" (John 4:24). "It is the spirit that gives life" (John 6:63). The biblical texts could be multiplied almost indefinitely, and from a variety of sources.

At this point, however, we face one of the most fundamental problems of contemporary theology. The real theme of the doctrine of the Holy Spirit is that of human life and growth in relation to God, for by the power of the Spirit we are drawn into the fellowship of the Father and the Son. This, however, stands in sharp conflict with the central concerns of modern Western thought and culture, where the autonomy of human beings, their self-fulfilling potentiality and freedom, has become the normative concern. The dilemma we face at this point is that all talk of human existence in relation to God in the contemporary context has become deeply problematic, and yet it must be possible if theology, and in particular pneumatology, is to have any meaning at all.

The centrality of freedom in modern thought is well established. In fact, freedom has become the dominant issue in virtually all aspects of our lives. To be free in our relationships with nature through our technologies, with other people in political and social existence, and with ourselves in the psychological sense is the great ideal that grips the modern imagination and moves the modern will. Thus it is that practically all the major intellectual movements that have shaped the twentieth century have freedom as their central theme. Though competing claims are made concerning the real nature of the freedom sought, so that the concept itself is somewhat ambiguous, no theology in the world today can afford to neglect it. The nature of theology itself, its very viability and the status of its claims, is ultimately at stake.

In our older intellectual traditions, human spirituality was understood to be bound up with the awareness of the unconditional true and good, unconditional in the sense that it imposes itself upon us, whether as nature or as reason itself or, more often, as the work of God, the transcendent source. Theology, of course, has tended to adopt the latter view, developing along the way a range of philosophical perspectives that have highlighted the notion of transcendence. For the older theology, therefore, truth and value are in the ultimate sense derived from God, or are even seen as identical with God.

This remained true even in early modern and Enlightenment thought. The historical period spanning roughly the fifteenth to the eighteenth centuries, which comprises the eras of Renaissance, Rationalism, and Enlightenment, broadly preserved the idea of God as the source of truth and value intact. Enlightenment thought raised problems for the older forms of religious faith — in fact, as often as not it explicitly set out to do so — but belief in God as a positive requirement of human reason and will still figured in the thought and culture of this entire period. In Descartes's *Meditations on First Philosophy*, for example, God is the guarantor of the rationality of the universe, so that he is indispensable to the foundations of science. Similarly, in Kant's philosophy, any scientific role for God is dismissed in the *Critique of*

Pure Reason, but God reappears in the *Critique of Practical Reason* to lend intelligibility to the structures of morality. In both cases, God serves an integral function in the ordinary rational enterprise, so that human beings are what they are and are capable of doing what they do by virtue of their relation to him. Although often opposed to traditional forms of religious "superstition," therefore, Enlightenment thought is not strictly antireligious or inimical to the theological enterprise per se.

In the contemporary context, however, this crucial role for God in human affairs has disappeared, along with the view that truth and value are absolute and unconditional. It is difficult to overemphasize the importance of this observation in the contemporary theological context. The burden of the philosophy of the twentieth century is to establish that all that is distinctively human has a purely *human* foundation. This is basic to the modern doctrine of freedom. It begins with the assumption that freedom will only be real when all that is distinctively human — including human spirituality in all its concrete associations — is grounded in human existence rather than in something higher than ourselves. The intention is not, therefore, to empty human life of the spiritual, understood in its most general sense as the awareness of truth and value in individual and social life, but rather to *humanize* the spiritual, in order to make it consistent with *human* interests and goals. The supposition is that, if this can be achieved, human beings will be as spiritual as they ever were, but they will be so with eyes open to the fact that their spirituality is grounded in themselves. It is for this reason and in this sense that atheism dominates modern philosophy.

We can see this above all in one of the great expositions of the philosophy of individual freedom of the twentieth century, the philosopher Jean-Paul Sartre's seminal essay, *Existentialism and Humanism.* This is now something of a neglected masterpiece, but it raises more clearly than do most theologies what the real *theological* issue at stake in modernity really is. Sartre presupposes an ideal of individual freedom that lies at the heart of much of our culture and reasons that if there were a God, then no human being could be free in this sense, for a God would impose an order upon human life, an order that would so limit this radical freedom as to render it nonexistent.[1] In short, we would, as God's creatures, have a human nature, a nature that could not allow for the effectively infinite possibilities open to us, whether this be in our ethical choices or in any other sphere.

Sartre's argument is astonishing in its simplicity. It rests on the simple affirmation that he simply *is* radically free, that despite the temptation to social conformism, he has the capacity to constitute *himself* by means of his own decisions. God does not do this for him. Since God is on the side of the static human "essence" imposed artificially from outside, as he puts it, the whole idea of God stands opposed to the actual reality that, for Sartre, a human being is. There is no God, therefore, for the *real* idea of freedom destroys the *ideal* of God as *unfree* and therefore as *unreal*. The logic of the argument can be expressed succinctly: If there were a God, he (Sartre) would not be free; but since he is free, there is no God.

For Sartre, therefore, the doctrine of autonomous humanity requires that a link be made between freedom and atheism, and more particularly between freedom from God and the living of a truly human existence. Sartre's conclusions are drawn explicitly against the views of such contemporaries as Gabriel Marcel, who sought to develop a Catholic existentialism; but crucially, these conclusions are intended simply to be intellectually self-consistent. Existentialism, the modern doctrine of individual freedom, is "nothing else but an attempt to draw the full conclusions from a consistently atheistic position."[2] With Marcel, we may question on a theoretical level Sartre's conviction that any consistent and adequate doctrine of human freedom will be in principle atheistic, but there can be little doubt that his position rings true as far as much of our culture is concerned, where our presupposed freedom and a functional if not a theoretical atheism do go hand in hand.

Perhaps an alternative approach can shed further light on this question. We live in an age in which cultural and psychological relativism have so taken hold that one is considered neanderthal if,

---

1. Jean-Paul Sartre, *Existentialism and Humanism*, trans. Philip Mairet (London: Methuen, 1948), pp. 27ff.

2. Sartre, *Existentialism and Humanism*, p. 56.

in one's moral evaluations, for example, there is any claim to absoluteness. This is one of the basic characteristics of what has come to be known as the "postmodern" situation. The result of this relativism, however, is paradoxically and radically decentering. Beginning with the conviction that the human being is at the center of all things, it leads to the conclusion that as a result there can be nothing objectively true or good that imposes itself on the human mind or will, no real "center" upon which all can be agreed. Since truth and value are seen as the creations of culturally conditioned, psychologically fragile human beings, all claims to absoluteness are seen as amounting to a claim to have gotten outside the circle of social and psychological relativity that is the basic characteristic of the human condition.

The formal self-contradiction that lies in this ought not to escape our notice; those who "know," apparently with certainty, that there is no certainty simply fail to think coherently, and in the end this will bring down the whole postmodern edifice with a crash, just as it has brought down similar positions in the past (e.g., late medieval nominalism). The contradiction that lies in it was exposed long ago by, among others, Plato, who in the *Theaetetus* takes up the claim of Protagoras that "man is the measure of all things," arguing that we can only think coherently by seeing knowledge as penetrating to the heart of being rather than as existing merely in the perception of the knower.[3] One does not, however, have to know Plato to grasp the difficulty inherent in radical epistemological relativism. The problem is not so much one of admitting the fact that our knowledge is partial and expressed in terms of linguistic conventions, for this is undoubtedly the case; the problem arises when relativism is pressed to become the basic principle of human thought. At this point, relativism cannot be consistently maintained, for it is self-destroying in the sense that it turns against itself to empty itself, too, of certainty. Nevertheless, the failure to see the point persists widely.

This is scarcely the place to embark on a full-scale treatment of the philosophy of knowledge. Nevertheless, we need to recognize that what has happened in our time is that the realm of meaning, the sphere of truth and value that is basic to the spiritual life, has

3. Plato, *Theaetetus*, 152aff.

been "finitized" or taken out of the hands of God and made to dwell on the earth, and there alone. If the consciousness of truth and value can be taken to be a mark of human spirituality in its most general sense, what this means is that human spirituality, too, has been finitized, naturalized, as it were, and made to become something purely earthly. Thus the whole concept of transcendence is called into question. But once this view comes to be accepted, theology itself is no longer possible. This is the real source of the "death of God" in the modern world. The philosopher Nietzsche, who coined this phrase, accordingly speaks in his philosophy of the need to "translate man back into nature,"[4] which means, in his own terms, to overturn the tendency to otherworldliness in all thought and life and to comprehend humanity from a thoroughly this-worldly perspective.

Nietzsche himself is frequently taken to be *the* philosopher of our time, even though he died at the end of the last century, but he is more honest about the implications of his position than most. He recognizes the fundamental rupture that the death of God carries with it into the human spirit, for "God" in Nietzsche is a cipher for the whole question of the old absolute verities, and even for the ideal of reason as such. The great strength of Nietzsche's philosophy is that it reckons honestly with the revolutionary impli-cations of a purely finite humanity. All human thought and life — including Nietzsche's own — are reckoned to be the product of instinct rather than having some independent rational or spiritual status. There are only perspectives, Nietzsche tells us, including the Nietzschean perspective that there are only perspectives! His central argument is that the death of God means that there are only finite individuals in a finite world where they, and they alone, create their own truths and values — truths and values to suit themselves. The key to life is to have the *strength* to affirm this in practice. For Nietzsche, therefore, a truly human life is still possible — Nietzsche is no nihilist — but it is a life that only a few have the courage to live, for the implications of the death of God for life are too terrifying for the mass of humanity to accept.

4. Friedrich Nietzsche, *Beyond Good and Evil*, trans. Walter Kaufmann (New York: Vintage Books, 1966), §230.

This is not a philosophical position that Christian theology can work with, despite the fact that one can identify occasional theological flirtations with isolated themes from Nietzsche. The more realistic and sobering view is that not only the Nietzschean philosophy but the whole ideal of human freedom that characterizes our time presents the most fundamental of challenges to theology — and to a revitalized doctrine of the Holy Spirit. It might even be argued that the most basic problem we face in contemporary theology is to find a way to reconstruct an understanding of human nature in which the relation to God has central place. Without this, there is no theology worthy of the name in any case, and there is nothing left in our self-understanding to correspond to the biblical conception of the work of the Holy Spirit in the world.

The crucial point to recognize is this: If "God is dead" on a cultural level, then this is so, not so much for metaphysical reasons, but because a particular conception of what it is to be *human* has disappeared. This implies, however, that a renewed understanding of human life as complete, as "free" perhaps, only in relation to God might mean that God himself can live again. If it was in the name of a free humanity that God died, in other words, then perhaps it can be only in the name of free humanity that God will again return to the center of the life of the world.

This implies that one of the key foci of theology must be theological anthropology, but it is clear that theological anthropology today can be meaningful only if it is constructed in critical dialogue with the modern doctrine of freedom. Two factors are especially important at this point. The first is the extent to which the ideal of freedom embraced by the contemporary world has in fact been radically *dehumanizing* — that is, the extent to which the "death of God" and the "death of man" go together. The preachers of freedom, in short, have not delivered their promised utopia. Indeed, quite the reverse has occurred: The age of freedom has been the single greatest era of human barbarity in history, while all around us, in the more private sphere, crime, drug abuse, suicide, and despair are all on the increase. Given that religion has been condemned as anti-human in the cause of freedom, it is now high time that theology took courage to reverse the charge against its opponents.

The second factor is arguably even more theologically important than the first, and it relates to the connection between pneumatology and theological anthropology. I have assumed that the terms *Spirit* and *spiritual* are correlative, not only in the sense that they belong in the same sphere of discourse, but also in the sense that they are intrinsically connected in the nature of reality itself. Now a second step is necessary: If we assume also that the "spiritual" marks out the territory, as it were, of what is distinctively human, of what "humanizes" us — what makes us the image of God, to use a classical Christian conception — then it is essential that our understanding of the work of the Holy Spirit should also be *humanizing* in its basic thrust. Yet here we stumble upon one of the major weaknesses of much of the theology of the twentieth century, especially in the Protestant tradition, which has actively sought to dissociate the Holy Spirit from the spiritual generally in human life. Ernst Käsemann, for example, criticizes all interpretation of the Spirit in terms of the "spiritual life" of moral inwardness.[5] According to Käsemann, this interpretation is impossible, because "Spirit" in the New Testament means the divine energy of miracle and ecstasy. Along the same lines, his teacher Rudolf Bultmann distinguishes between "animistic" and "dynamistic" thinking in New Testament pneumatology: In animistic thinking, the Spirit is conceived as an independent power that can fall on a person unexpectedly, enabling supernatural manifestations of power; in dynamistic thinking, the Spirit is an impersonal force that fills a person like a fluid.[6] In neither case is there any connection between the Christian concept of Spirit and the spiritual life seen as a humanizing potentiality. In fact, the basic thrust of the argument is to affirm the opposite, that the work of the Spirit has nothing to do with the ordinary features of human existence, or with human dignity. One might even say that the primary implication of this theology of the work of the Spirit is that it tends toward *dehumanization*, that it detracts from human life, and therefore that it negates the theme of the Spirit as the "life-giver."

5. Ernst Käsemann, "The Spirit and the Letter," in Käsemann, *Perspectives on Paul,* trans. Margaret Köhl (London: SCM Press, 1971), p. 139.
6. Rudolf Bultmann, *Theology of the New Testament,* trans. Kendrick Grobel (London: SCM Press, 1952), vol. 1, p. 155.

What has happened here is similar to the fate of the "kingdom of God" in much twentieth-century theology. A view of that kingdom as basically continuous with ordinary moral ideals, though ultimately as transcending and transforming them, has been widely replaced by a view of the kingdom as something wholly other-worldly. Since it has its source in God as the *totaliter aliter*, the kingdom is seen as totally discontinuous with all human moral idealism. The argument has been that only thus can theology be true to itself and to the nature of its subject matter. The kingdom of God, it is alleged, is the judgment and in the end the annihilation of all purely human ethical or political kingdoms. In it, the elements will melt with the fervent heat, rather than be taken up, harnessed to the good purposes of God, and transformed into something more glorious.

The exegetical merits of the case are beyond the scope of this study, but the following observation is not: Such a view is actually destructive of theology, for it is destructive of religious life. First of all, the argument, whether used of the Spirit or of the kingdom, makes religious belief actively irrelevant to humanity. A spiritual life that is wholly unconnected with the ordinary sphere of human moral inwardness (the expression used by Käsemann) is simply of no use or interest to us; it becomes something *unreal*. Quite apart from the theological question of the lack of a doctrine of creation in this theology, one must ask why something that does so little for *religion* has been defended. What is most curious is not so much where the conviction originated — what its theological source could possibly have been — as why it has been such a pervasive influence in theology in the twentieth century. At this point, as at many others, there is a strong case for an informed reassessment of the achievement of classical liberal Protestantism.

One area that also remains to be explored in this connection is the significance of worldwide Christianity, for, as we have seen, it is no longer true to say that Christianity is a "Western" religion. For this very reason, the antireligious tendencies that prevail in modern Western thought are plainly irrelevant to the numerical majority within the Christian church, and this is a fact that we can affirm with some thankfulness. The theological question that will dominate the next century is not how to rescue Christian faith from decline but how to give voice to Christian faith in a non-Western milieu. Where Christian theology in the non-Western world is not still postcolonial, questions of practice, of political justice, and of overcoming poverty often predominate. With the explosive growth of Christianity in the Pacific rim, however, where the great concentrations of economic wealth in the next century will be found, the move from such practical concerns to a more theoretical approach is inevitable.

At this point, Asian spirituality is destined to prove decisively important. What one Asian theologian has termed the "transposition from the point-nosed to the flat-nosed Christ"[7] will certainly not bypass the great insights of Buddhist and Confucian culture, any more than the original transposition of the Hebraic gospel into Greek culture bypassed the special genius — including the religious and theological genius — of the latter. Asian thought offers many avenues for exploration here. "In the East, which is the home of half of humanity . . . Western eyes are still hardly in a position to distinguish well the heights and depths of the rich variety of Asian spirituality."[8] To date, most of these possibilities have gone unexplored, but we can be sure that the development of a genuinely *Asian* Christianity will bring with it a theological vision shaped in terms of the Asian religious ethos. Theology will be reconstructed in new ways, ways that are likely to have little to do with the Greek ideal of Logos, or with contemporary Western religious scepticism. The dominance of Western culture, whether in the form of the culture of antiquity, of the Middle Ages, or of the modern period, has now come to an end for theology, and we may confidently expect a theological renaissance to be the result. In this situation, Christian theology will have much to learn and to gain from new developments.

What might this study, and in particular its treatment of contemporary theology, offer to the task of breathing new life into the doctrine of the Holy Spirit? Perhaps the single most important

7. Choan-Seng Song, *The Compassionate God* (London: SCM Press, 1982), p. 3.

8. Theo Witvliet, *A Place in the Sun,* trans. John Bowden (London: SCM Press, 1985), p. 151.

claim made in all that has been said concerns the reciprocal relations of christology and pneumatology. This reciprocity, which emerges from the New Testament and which has been rediscovered across a range of recent theological writing, amounts to a total interpenetration of each by each, a *perichoresis* that has enormous implications for how Christian faith is to be understood.

On the christological level, the reciprocity of Christ and the Spirit means that there can be no conception of Christ that does not encompass an understanding of the Christ-event as thoroughly pneumatological *in itself*. There can, therefore, be no adequate christology that is not oriented to pneumatology, as something leading onward from itself to the gift of the Spirit and so to the church. But equally, one must affirm the converse: There can be no adequate pneumatology where the centrality of Jesus is lost from sight, and therefore no theology of the Spirit or of the spiritual life in which the historical context and content of the central Christian story as presented in the New Testament is relinquished. In particular, as we might learn from the Fourth Gospel as well as from Paul, there is no *Christian* doctrine of the Holy Spirit that does not perceive the significance of the cross as the focal point of the Bible and as the source from which the gift of the Spirit flows. If there is a theology of glory, therefore, in our account of the Spirit, it is a glory that has its roots in lowly obedience, and finally in the suffering of the crucified one, in his total self-giving to the Father for the sake of the world. "The Spirit was not," in the *Christian* sense, until Jesus had been "glorified" (John 7:39) — a glorification that in the New Testament is inseparable from the passion.

This conclusion is important for a number of reasons. First of all, it represents something of an ecumenical consensus. Jürgen Moltmann, in a way that is particularly appropriate to the Reformation tradition, speaks of the need for theology to balance a pneumatological christology against a christological pneumatology, in order to avoid one-sidedness on either side.[9] But the same thesis can be found in the Roman Catholic theologian Yves Congar, while he himself can be said to be following an insight from the Orthodox

---

9. Moltmann, *The Spirit of Life*, trans. Margaret Kohl (London: SCM Press, 1992), pp. 71ff.

tradition in speaking in his theology of the "Pneumatised Christ."[10] It is this insight that has lain at the center of ecumenical discussions of the *filioque* in recent years, and that offers the prospect of an advance beyond the millennium-long stalemate over this question.

There is a great deal to gain from such an approach. The classical forms of Logos christology deriving from the patristic era are now religiously unsustainable, for example, both because of developments in Western intellectual culture and because of the sheer numbers of non-Western Christians in the world today. It may be, however, that the idea of the mutual interpenetration of christology and pneumatology will offer resources upon which new christologies may draw. In particular, the idea of the interpenetration of christology and pneumatology offers a way beyond the Logos-centered theology of the West, and the possibility for a new appreciation of the coinherence of the ideals of rationality on the one side and community on the other — or of truth and love, as the title of this chapter suggests.

Another of the implications of this is that it opens up possibilities for christology by which the humanity of Jesus may come to the fore. Since it is precisely a common humanity that all cultures share and that all human beings share with Jesus, it may well be the humanity of Jesus that offers the best prospect for addressing the new situation in which Christian theology in its global context is found today. We cannot seriously regard Logos christology as capable of providing the basis needed for theological renewal. The ideal of *logos,* or rationality, especially in its patristic-hellenistic adaptation, is no longer easily sustainable even in Western culture and is quite alien to much of the rest of the world. If, then, Jesus Christ is indeed the Word of God, it is *Jesus Christ,* in short, who is that Word — Jesus Christ as he lived the human existence common to all people, Jesus Christ who shared human frailty, who stood with "the poor" in the biblical sense, Jesus Christ whose human life is the perfect image of God. Whatever we say of his status as the Word from eternity to eternity cannot be allowed to detract from that.

10. Congar, *The Word and the Spirit,* trans. David Smith (London: Geoffrey Chapman, 1986), pp. 101ff.

An important factor related to these developments is that the new Christianity emerging in much of the non-Western world — but also, significantly, in the West itself — is highly pneumatic in character. In a recent book entitled *The Hallelujah Revolution,* Ian Cotton has highlighted the significance of this.[11] Even if we have grown accustomed to the idea that, despite its decline in the West, Christianity on the world scale is presently undergoing its fastest-ever period of expansion, what we are frequently less prepared to accept is that this is an expansion fuelled overwhelmingly by evangelical faith, and evangelical faith that more often than not is broadly charismatic in character. Signs and wonders are apparently the normal expectation of vast numbers of contemporary Christians. Cotton's thesis is at once controversial and illuminating: "if the essence of Western culture can be defined as a combination of scepticism, and faith in step-by-step rationality, then assuredly the Decline of the West — at this late-twentieth-century moment of Western 'triumph' — is already fact."[12] Cotton's argument is that it is an age of uncertainty that creates the conditions for religious revival, and that the wholesale decline in Western certainties, not least on questions of truth and value, makes our day ripe for religious phenomena such as this.

The reciprocity of christology and pneumatology, which has proven helpful in ecumenical theology and which offers an escape route for Christians worldwide from Western rationalism, provides us with resources to take up the challenge of charismatic Christianity as well. Here, too, we can begin to see how a renewed emphasis on the Holy Spirit might deepen our christology. The charismatic theologian Thomas Smail, for example, argues in his book *The Giving Gift* that there are christological grounds for a new emphasis on the Spirit. Working from the baptism narratives of the synoptic Gospels, he posits a pneumatic christology side by side with the traditional incarnational understanding: "The Son is Son, not solely because he shares the divine nature, but because he is in constant interaction with his Father receiving and giving the

11. Ian Cotton, *The Hallelujah Revolution* (London: Little, Brown, 1995), pp. 1-13.

12. Cotton, *The Hallelujah Revolution,* p. 4.

Spirit."[13] Smail's contention, developed from the heart of charismatic theology itself, sounds familiar. The central point is that the *static* unity of substance between Father, Son, and Spirit needs to be "fleshed out," in keeping with the logic of the incarnation itself, in terms of a *living* unity of initiative and response, love and obedience, development and depth. The claim is that only in this way can we do justice to that most basic of modern theological claims, that whatever else he was, Jesus was fully human, and so lived an ordinary (yet extraordinary!) life in relation to the Father, in faith, hope, and love. Thus it is "in the Spirit" as much as by unity of substance that Jesus is to be conceived as Son of God.

We have seen from the theologies of Heribert Mühlen and Walter Kasper that Spirit christology need not be seen as a rival to Logos christology, and, in fact, that the two can complement one another to considerable theological advantage. Their contention that Spirit christology is capable of dealing meaningfully with the historicity of Jesus' human existence, his human growth "in wisdom, and in stature, and in favour with God and man" (Luke 2:52, KJV), is of special importance. A location is thus found in christology for the development of Jesus' body and mind, of his sense of vocation, and for his human struggle to love and obey the Father, while at the same time the theological importance of the Spirit itself is highlighted. Rather than being an extra third category added only after all that is essential has been stated in theology, the Spirit is at the center of the whole divine drama, from its eternal origins through its outworking in history, and onward in time to the present and the eschatological future. The integration of christology, soteriology, and trinitarian theology in these theologies is an impressive achievement, the significance of which is far-reaching, and the import of which will certainly survive beyond our own generation in future Christian thought.

Two more observations can be added. First, if, as Logos, Jesus is to be seen as the eternal Son and hence as the revealer of God — or even as the Revelation itself, as Karl Barth maintains — then as the one anointed by the Spirit who loves to the end and who so fulfills his calling, Jesus is something more. It is as such that he is our brother,

---

13. Tom Smail, *The Giving Gift* (London: Hodder & Stoughton, 1988), p. 97.

meeting us from within our humanity and our history as the one with and in whom we share the life and love of God and neighbor. The descending movement by which God reaches out to the world through Word and Spirit thus reaches its goal in the point of return, or ascent, in which the creature raises its face to God and responds to his voice and calling. The first implies the second, as ever, and the second is grounded in the first, but in Jesus Christ the two are one in a single human life and in a single story: God's outreach in love here *becomes* the human response of love. In other words, christology is no exception to the general rule we have followed and discovered at other points in our explorations, that the Spirit is the point of terminus of the descending movement by which God comes to us, just as the Spirit is the point of the initiation of the journey back to the source. This structural principle, I believe, helps to locate the relation between christology and pneumatology in a wider systematic framework. Christologically, it means that the work of the Son is wholly geared to that of the Spirit, to spiritualization, as we might call it; pneumatologically, it implies that the work of the Spirit in and through the Son is directed to the goal of making others sons and daughters of God.

A second point follows from this. While it is true that the christology of the Logos can read as if it represented an exclusive claim to revelation, of access to God, and of salvation, a Logos christology that leads on to and implies such a conception of the Spirit need not be read in such a narrowly exclusive way. Unless one is prepared to focus the entire energies of God in salvation on the Word and to exclude the work of the Spirit, or to relegate the Spirit to a purely subordinate role, it is possible to see all human love, all human obedience to the moral law, and all those expressions of human dignity and of the potentiality for goodness as sharing something in common with Jesus, as touched by the same source of light and life. In fact, to say anything else would be to deny something central, not just to the doctrine of the Spirit, but also to the doctrine of Christ itself, for christology has within itself the moment of Spirit as fundamental to the whole, thus revealing it as something inescapable for Christian faith.

The idea of a reciprocity between Christ and the Spirit also has important theological implications beyond christology, in particular for the doctrine of the church. This is not only because the idea has immediate consequences for the church as a society in which privileges and responsibilities are shared, and in which human relationships are thus of central significance. It is also a point that relates to the theological foundations of ecclesiology and to the nature of the church as a theological entity. For if the Word and the Spirit are reciprocally related, such that each is what he is only in and under the other, then the church is both the "creature of the Word" and the "community of the Spirit" at one and the same time. There is no subordination of one to the other, but a thorough-going interchange of faith and fellowship, of truth and love — of orthodoxy and orthopraxis — in its life.

At this point we reach the "heart" of the doctrine of the Holy Spirit, and of the Christian life, which exists between these two poles of truth and love. In fact, either one of these abstracted from the other is partial and fragmented — something incapable even of being what it is itself. A stubborn adherence to doctrinal certainty without regard for ordinary charity in daily living or for the communion of saints is something far less than what it claims to be, for the truth in Christian theology must be essentially oriented to love. It is in love that it reaches fulfillment. The Christian life is one of "doing the truth" in love; only so can we grow into spiritual maturity and find the wholeness promised by the gospel (Eph. 4:15). In the same way, however, love without the discernment provided by an awareness of what is true, and Christian love practiced without reference to Christian teaching, is at best one-sided and at worst ridiculous. Love may be the greatest of all (1 Cor. 13:13), as Paul teaches, so that faith and hope without it are nothing, but one may say equally that, without the great vision of faith and hope, love leads astray.

This has implications also beyond the spiritual life. In much recent theology, for example, the ideals of justice and community have been opposed to the ideal of orthodoxy through the contemporary preference for "orthopraxy." The main criticism of this tendency that is occasionally heard is that love is oriented to truth, and therefore practice is oriented to doctrine.[14] Yet surely such a

14. E.g., Sacred Congregation for the Doctrine of the Faith, *Instruction on Certain Aspects of the Theology of Liberation* (London: Catholic Truth Society, 1984).

criticism represents only half the story, for truth is equally oriented to love, and equally at its service. What the idea of the reciprocity of truth and love allows us to say is that much of the debate about orthodoxy on the one hand and orthopraxis on the other is fundamentally flawed. If Christ and the Spirit are reciprocally related, if their relation is not hierarchical but wholly mutual, then the ideals of *logos* and *caritas,* too, must be seen to be mutually related. Each is open toward the other. At this point we need to move beyond the sterility of modern thought, and much modern theological thought, which tends to antithesize truth and value, and instead find a way in theology to hold them together. In doing so, theology might also render service to the wider sphere of contemporary intellectual culture — to science, for example — by showing that neither the true without the good nor the good without the true can sustain the human spirit.

Truth and love constitute the real "fundamentals" of the Christian life, and for this very reason they must always be the core concerns of pneumatology. They are equally the theological "source" and "goal": the source, because it is from the proclamation of the "Word of truth" and from the fellowship of the church that new life in the Spirit is born; the goal, because truth and love are of ultimately infinite content, so that they can never be realized in their transcendent fullness. One is always "on the way" toward them. There is much more that could be said at this point, of course, but it must be said by others, for here the task of systematic theology ends. Theology must now pass over into religious life, for in the same way that theology is rooted in the existence of the church, so its whole thrust must be toward the church and the lives of its members. And here all its complex concepts and arguments give way to a greater wisdom of childlike simplicity, to poverty of spirit, to seeking and finding, to the kingdom of God as the small seed that grows into something tall. Here the one thing needful is God himself, and the encounter with him in truth and love.

Bibliography

Aldenhoven, Herwig. "The Question of the Procession of the Holy Spirit and Its Connection with the Life of the Church." In World Council of Churches, Commission on Faith and Order, *Spirit of God, Spirit of Christ*, pp. 121-132. Edited by Lukas Vischer. Geneva: World Council of Churches; London: SPCK, 1981.

Altaner, Berthold. *Patrology*. Translated by Hilda C. Graef. New York: Herder and Herder, 1961.

Althaus, P. "Kenosis." In *Die Religion in Geschichte und Gegenwart*, vol. 3, cols. 1244-46. Edited by H. F. von Campenhausen et al. 3rd ed. Tübingen: J. C. B. Mohr, 1956-65.

Altizer, Thomas J. J. *The Gospel of Christian Atheism*. London: Collins, 1967.

Ambrose. *On the Holy Spirit*. Translated by Roy J. Deferrari. Washington: Catholic University of America Press, 1963.

———. *Sancti Ambrosii Opera*. Edited by Otto Faller. *Corpus Scriptorum Ecclesiasticorum Latinorum*, vol. 79/9. Vienna: Hölder-Pichler-Tempsky, 1964.

Anselm. *On the Procession of the Holy Spirit*. In Anselm of Canterbury, *Trinity, Incarnation, and Redemption: Theological Treatises*, pp. 81-134. Edited and translated by Jasper Hopkins and Herbert W. Richardson. New York: Harper & Row, 1970.

Athanasius. *The Letters of Saint Athanasius Concerning the Holy Spirit*. Translated, with introduction and notes, by C. R. B. Shapland. London: Epworth Press, 1951.

Augustine. *Oeuvres de Saint Augustin*. Paris: Desclée, De Brouwer et Cie, 1941- .

———. *The Trinity*. Translated by Stephen McKenna. Washington: Catholic University of America Press, 1963.

274

Badcock, Gary D. "Divine Freedom in Hegel." *Irish Theological Quarterly* 61 (1995): 265-71.

———. "The Anointing of Christ and the *Filioque* Doctrine." *Irish Theological Quarterly* 60 (1994): 241-58.

Baillie, D. M. *God Was in Christ: An Essay on Incarnation and Atonement.* London: Faber and Faber, 1948.

Balentine, Samuel E. *The Hidden God.* Oxford: Oxford University Press, 1983.

Balthasar, Hans Urs von. *Elucidations.* Translated by John Riches. London: SPCK, 1975.

———. *Klarstellungen.* 4th ed. Einsiedeln: Johannes Verlag, 1978.

———. *Man in History: A Theological Study.* Translated by William Glen-Doepel. London and Sydney: Sheed and Ward, 1968.

———. *Pneuma und Institution.* Einsiedeln: Johannes Verlag, 1974.

———. *Prayer.* Translated by Graham Harrison. San Francisco: Ignatius Press, 1986.

———. *Spiritus Creator.* Einsiedeln: Johannes Verlag, 1967.

———. *The Glory of the Lord: A Theological Aesthetics.* VII. Edited by John Riches and translated by Brian McNeil. Edinburgh: T. & T. Clark, 1989.

———. *The Theology of Karl Barth.* Translated by John Drury. New York: Holt, Rinehart and Winston, 1971.

———. *The von Balthasar Reader.* Edited by Medard Kehl and Werner Löser. Translated by Robert J. Daly and Fred Lawrence. Edinburgh: T. & T. Clark, 1982.

———. *Theodramatik.* II/2. Einsiedeln: Johannes Verlag, 1978.

———. *Theologik.* III. Einsiedeln: Johannes Verlag, 1987.

Banawiratma, J. B. *Der Heilige Geist in der Theologie von Heribert Mühlen.* Frankfurt-Bern: Verlag Peter D. Lang, 1981.

Barrett, C. K. *A Commentary on the Second Epistle to the Corinthians.* London: Adam & Charles Black, 1973.

———. *The Holy Spirit and the Gospel Tradition.* 2nd ed. London: SPCK, 1966.

———. "The Holy Spirit in the Fourth Gospel." *Journal of Theological Studies,* new series, 1 (1950): 1-15.

Barth, Karl. *Anselm: Fides Quaerens Intellectum.* Translated by Ian W. Robertson. London: SCM Press, 1960.

———. *Church Dogmatics.* I/1–IV/4. Edited by G. W. Bromiley and T. F. Torrance. Translated by G. W. Bromiley et al. Edinburgh: T. & T. Clark, 1936-69; 2nd ed. of I/1, 1975.

———. "Concluding Unscientific Postscript on Schleiermacher." In Barth, *The Theology of Schleiermacher,* pp. 261-79. Edited by Dietrich Ritschl. Translated by Geoffrey W. Bromiley. Edinburgh: T. & T. Clark, 1982.

———. *Fides quaerens intellectum.* München: Christian Kaiser Verlag, 1931.

———. "Hegel." In Barth, *Protestant Theology in the Nineteenth Century,* pp.

384-421. Translated by Brian Cozens and John Bowden. London: SCM Press, 1972.

―――. "The Gift of Freedom." In Barth, *The Humanity of God,* pp. 67-96. Translated by John Newton Thomas and Thomas Wieser. London: Collins, 1961.

―――. "The Humanity of God," in Barth, *The Humanity of God,* pp. 35-65. Translated by John Newton Thomas and Thomas Wieser. London: Collins, 1961.

Barth, Markus. *Ephesians 1–3.* Garden City, NY: Doubleday, 1974.

Bauckham, Richard. "Moltmann's Eschatology of the Cross." *Scottish Journal of Theology* 30 (1977): 301-11.

―――. *Moltmann: Messianic Theology in the Making.* Basingstoke: Marshall Pickering, 1987.

―――. " 'Only the Suffering God Can Help': Divine Passibility in Modern Theology." *Themelios* 9 (1984): 6-12.

Beardsworth, Timothy. *A Sense of Presence.* Oxford: Religious Experience Research Unit, 1977.

Berkhof, Hendrikus. *The Doctrine of the Holy Spirit.* London: Epworth Press, 1965.

Berkowitz, Luci, and Karl A. Squitier. *Thesaurus Linguae Graece Canon of Greek Authors and Works.* 3rd ed. New York and Oxford: Oxford University Press, 1990.

Bermejo, A. "Circumincession." *New Catholic Encyclopedia,* vol. 3, p. 880. New York: McGraw-Hill, 1967.

Biggar, Nigel. *Reckoning with Barth.* London and Oxford: Mowbray, 1988.

Bittlinger, Arnold, ed. *The Church Is Charismatic.* Geneva: World Council of Churches, 1981.

Bobrinskoy, Boris. "The *Filioque* Yesterday and Today." In World Council of Churches, Commission on Faith and Order, *Spirit of God, Spirit of Christ,* pp. 133-48. Edited by Lukas Vischer. Geneva: World Council of Churches; London: SPCK, 1981.

―――. "The Holy Spirit — in the Bible and the Church." *The Ecumenical Review* 41 (1989): 357-62.

―――. "The Indwelling of the Spirit in Christ: 'Pneumatic Christology' in the Cappadocian Fathers," *St. Vladimir Theological Quarterly* 28 (1984): 49-65.

Bolgiani, Franco. "La théologie de l'Esprit Saint. De la fin du 1er siècle au Concile de Constantinople (381)." In *Dieu révélé dans l'Esprit,* pp. 33-72. Edited by Bolgiani et al. Vol. 9 of *Les quatre fleuves: Cahiers de recherche et de réflexion religieuses.* Paris: Beauchesne, 1979.

Bolotov, B. "Thèses sur le «Filioque»," *Istina* 17 (1972): 261-89.

Bonaventure. *Bonaventure: The Soul's Journey into God, The Tree of Life, The Life of St. Francis.* Translated by Ewert Cousins. London: SPCK, 1978.

Bondi, Roberta C. "Apophatic Theology." In *A New Dictionary of Christian Theology*, p. 32. Edited by Alan Richardson and John Bowden. London: SCM Press Ltd, 1983.

Bosc, Jean. *The Kingly Office of the Lord Jesus Christ.* Translated by A. K. S. Reid [*sic*]. Edinburgh: Oliver and Boyd, 1959.

Bouillard, Henri. *Karl Barth.* 3 vols. Paris: Aubier, 1957.

Bouillard, Henri. *The Knowledge of God.* Translated by Samuel D. Femiano. London: Burns & Oates, 1969.

Bouyer, Louis. *Le Consolateur. Esprit Saint et vie de grâce.* Paris: Les Éditions du Cerf, 1980.

Braaten, C. E. "The Trinity Today." *Dialog* 26 (1987): 245-75.

Bracken, Joseph A. "Process Philosophy and Trinitarian Theology." *Process Studies* 8 (1978): 217-30.

―――. "Process Philosophy and Trinitarian Theology — II," *Process Studies* 11 (1981): 83-96.

Bradshaw, T. "Karl Barth on the Trinity: A Family Resemblance." *Scottish Journal of Theology* 39 (1986): 145-64.

Breck, John. " 'The Lord Is the Spirit': An Essay in Christological Pneumatology." *The Ecumenical Review* 42 (1990): 114-21.

Brown, David. *The Divine Trinity.* London: Duckworth, 1985.

―――. "Wittgenstein Against the Wittgensteinians: A Reply to Kenneth Surin on *The Divine Trinity*." *Modern Theology* 2 (1986): 257-76.

Brown, Raymond E. *Biblical Exegesis and Church Doctrine.* New York: Paulist Press, 1985.

―――. *The Birth of the Messiah.* London: Geoffrey Chapman, 1977.

Brown, Robert F. "On God's Ontic and Noetic Absoluteness: A Critique of Barth." *Scottish Journal of Theology* 33 (1980): 533-49.

Brunner, Emil. *Man in Revolt.* Translated by Olive Wyon. London: Lutterworth Press, 1939.

―――. *The Christian Doctrine of God.* Translated by Olive Wyon. London: Lutterworth Press, 1949.

Bulgakov, Sergius. *The Wisdom of God.* Translated by Patrick Thompson et al. London: Williams and Norgate, 1937.

Bultmann, Rudolf. *New Testament Mythology and Other Basic Writings.* Edited and translated by Schubert M. Ogden. London: SCM Press, 1984.

―――. *The Gospel of John.* Edited by R. W. N. Hoare and J. K. Riches. Translated by G. R. Beasley-Murray. Oxford: Basil Blackwell, 1971.

―――. *The History of the Synoptic Tradition.* Translated by John Marsh. Oxford: Basil Blackwell, 1972.

―――. *Theology of the New Testament.* Translated by Kendrick Grobel. 2 vols. London: SCM Press, 1952, 1955.

Burgess, Stanley M. *The Spirit and the Church: Antiquity.* Peabody, MA: Hendrickson Publishers, 1984.

Busch, Eberhard. *Karl Barth*. Translated by John Bowden. London: SCM Press, 1976.

Calvin, John. *Institutes of the Christian Religion*. Edited by John T. McNeill. Translated by Ford Lewis Battles. 2 vols. Philadelphia: Westminster Press, 1960.

Carr, Wesley. "Towards a Contemporary Doctrine of the Holy Spirit." *Scottish Journal of Theology* 28 (1975): 501-16.

Chollet, A. "Circuminsession, -cession." *Dictionnaire de théologie catholique*, vol. 2, cols. 2527-32. Edited by A. Vacant et al. Paris: Libraire Letouzey et Ané, 1905.

Clapsis, Emmanuel. "The Holy Spirit in the Church." *The Ecumenical Review* 41 (1989): 339-47.

Clements, Keith, ed. *Friedrich Schleiermacher: Pioneer of Modern Theology*. Edinburgh: T. & T. Clark, 1987.

Coakley, Sarah. "Can God Be Experienced as Trinity?" *Modern Churchman* 28 (1986): 11-23.

Coffey, David M. "A Proper Mission of the Holy Spirit." *Theological Studies* 47 (1986): 227-50.

————. *Grace: The Gift of the Holy Spirit*. Sydney: Catholic Institute of Sydney, 1979.

————. "The Gift of the Holy Spirit." *Irish Theological Quarterly* 38 (1971): 202-23.

————. "The Holy Spirit as the Mutual Love of the Father and the Son." *Theological Studies* 51 (1990): 193-229.

————. "The 'Incarnation' of the Holy Spirit in Christ." *Theological Studies* 45 (1984): 466-80.

Collins, Alice. "Barth's Relationship to Schleiermacher: A Reassessment." *Studies in Religion* 17 (1988): 213-24.

Colwell, John E. *Actuality and Provisionality: Eternity and Election in the Theology of Karl Barth*. Edinburgh: Rutherford House Books, 1989.

Congar, Yves. *I Believe in the Holy Spirit*. Translated by David Smith. 3 vols. London: Geoffrey Chapman; New York: Seabury Press, 1983.

————. *The Word and the Spirit*. Translated by David Smith. London: Geoffrey Chapman, 1986.

Copleston, Frederick. *A History of Philosophy*, vol. 2. New York: Image Books, 1962.

Cotton, Ian. *The Hallelujah Revolution*. London: Little, Brown, 1995.

Cowburn, John. *Love and the Person*. London: Geoffrey Chapman, 1967.

Cranfield, C. "The Baptism of Our Lord: A Study of St Mark 1,9-11." *Scottish Journal of Theology* 8 (1955): 53-63.

Cranmer, W. *Der Geist Gottes und des Menschen in frühsyrischer Theologie*. Münster: Aschendorff, 1979.

Creel, Richard E. *Divine Impassibility*. Cambridge: Cambridge University Press, 1986.

Crouzel, Henri. *Origen*. Translated by A. S. Worrall. Edinburgh: T. & T. Clark, 1989.

Daniélou, J. *The Theology of Jewish Christianity*. Translated and edited by J. A. Baker. London: Darton, Longman & Todd; Chicago: Henry Regnery, 1964.

de Halleux, André. "Towards an Ecumenical Agreement on the Procession of the Holy Spirit and the Addition of the *Filioque* to the Creed." In World Council of Churches, Commission on Faith and Order, *Spirit of God, Spirit of Christ*, pp. 69-84. Edited by Lukas Vischer. Geneva: World Council of Churches; London: SPCK, 1981.

de la Potterie, I. "L'Onction du Christ." *Nouvelle Revue Theologique* 80 (1958): 225-52.

de Regnon, Théodore. *Études du théologie positive sur la Sainte Trinité*. 4 vols. Paris: Retaux, 1892-98.

Dodd, C. H. *Historical Tradition in the Fourth Gospel*. Cambridge: Cambridge University Press, 1963.

du Roy, Olivier. *L'Intelligence de la Foi en la Trinité selon Saint Augustin*. Paris: Études Augustiniennes, 1966.

Dulles, Avery. *The Assurance of Things Hoped For*. New York and Oxford: Oxford University Press, 1994.

Dunn, James D. G. *Baptism in the Holy Spirit*. London: SCM Press, 1970.

———. *Christology in the Making*. London: SCM Press, 1980.

———. *Jesus and the Spirit*. London: SCM Press, 1975.

———. "Rediscovering the Spirit." *Expository Times* 84 (1972-73): 7-12.

———. *Unity and Diversity in the New Testament: An Inquiry into the Character of Earliest Christianity*. London: SCM Press, 1977.

———, and James P. Mackey. *New Testament Theology in Dialogue*. London: SPCK, 1987.

Dunne, Tad. "Trinity and History." *Theological Studies* 45 (1984): 139-52.

Duquoc, C. "Les Conditions d'une pensée de Dieu selon E. Jüngel." *Revue des sciences philosophiques et théologique* 65 (1981): 417-32.

During, Lisabeth. "Hegel, Barth and the Rationality of the Trinity." *King's Theological Review* 2 (1979): 69-81.

Durrant, M. *Theology and Intelligibility: An Examination of the Doctrine that God Is the Last End of Rational Creatures and the Doctrine that God Is Three Persons in One Substance: "The Doctrine of the Holy Trinity."* London: Routledge & Kegan Paul, 1973.

Durwell, F.-X. *l'Esprit Saint de Dieu*. 2nd ed. Paris: Les Éditions du Cerf, 1985.

Eichrodt, Walther. *Theology of the Old Testament*. Translated by John Baker. 2 vols. London: SCM Press, 1961, 1967.

Eunomius. *Eunomius: The Extant Works.* Edited and translated by Richard Paul Vaggione. Oxford: Clarendon, 1987.

Evdokimov, Paul. *L'Esprit Saint dans la tradition orthodoxe.* Paris: Les Éditions du Cerf, 1969.

Fackenheim, Emil. *The Religious Dimension in Hegel's Thought.* Bloomington: Indiana University Press, 1967.

Faller, Otto, ed. *Sancti Ambrosii Opera.* In *Corpus Scriptorum Ecclesiasticorum Latinorum,* 79/9. Vienna, 1964.

Feuerbach, Ludwig. *The Essence of Christianity.* Translated by George Eliot. New York: Harper Torchbooks, 1957.

Fiddes, Paul S. *The Creative Suffering of God.* Oxford: Clarendon Press, 1988.

Fitzmyer, Joseph A. *The Gospel According to Luke (I–IX).* Garden City, NY: Doubleday, 1981.

Ford, Lewis S. *The Lure of God: A Biblical Background for Process Theism.* Philadelphia: Fortress Press, 1978.

Fortman, Edmund. *The Triune God: A Historical Study of the Doctrine of the Trinity.* Philadelphia: Westminster Press, 1972.

Foster, M. B. "The Christian Doctrine of Creation and the Rise of Modern Natural Science." *Mind* 43 (1934): 446-68; 44 (1935): 439-66; 45 (1936): 1-27.

Franks, R. S. *The Doctrine of the Trinity.* London: Gerald Duckworth, 1953.

Freyer, T. *Pneumatologie als Strukturprinzip der Dogmatik. Überlegungen an die Lehre der 'Geisttaufe' bei Karl Barth.* Paderborn: Ferdinand Schöningh, 1982.

Fulton, W. "Trinity." In *Encyclopaedia of Religion and Ethics,* vol. 12, pp. 458-62. Edited by James Hastings. Edinburgh: T. & T. Clark, 1921.

Gabnebin, Laurent. "*De Trinitate:* Questions de méthode." *Études théologiques et religieuses* 61 (1986): 63-73.

Galloway, Allan D. "The New Hegelians." *Religious Studies* 8 (1972): 367-71.

Garrigues, J. M. *L'Esprit qui dit «Pere!» et le problem du filioque.* Paris: Téqui, 1981.

Garrigues, Juan-Miguel. "Procession et ekporèse du Saint Esprit." *Istina* 17 (1972): 345-66.

Gass, W. "Das patristische Wort OIKONOMIA." *Zeitschrift für Wissenschaftliche Theologie* 17 (1874): 465-504.

Gelpi, Donald L. *The Divine Mother: A Trinitarian Theology of the Holy Spirit.* Lanham: University Press of America, 1984.

Gollwitzer, Helmut. *An Introduction to Protestant Theology.* Translated by David Cairns. Philadelphia: Westminster Press, 1982.

Gollwitzer, Helmut. *The Existence of God as Confessed by Faith.* Translated by James W. Leitch. London: SCM Press, 1965.

Green, Clifford, ed. *Karl Barth: Theologian of Freedom.* London: Collins, 1979.

Green, F. W. "The Later Development of the Doctrine of the Trinity." In

Essays on the Trinity and the Incarnation, pp. 239-300. Edited by A. E. J. Rawlinson. New York: Longmans, Green, 1928.

Green, G. "The Mystery of Eberhard Jüngel: A Review of His Theological Programme." *Religious Studies Review* 5 (1979): 34-40.

Gregg, Robert C., and Dennis E. Groh. *Early Arianism.* London: SCM Press, 1981.

Gregory of Nazianzus. *Three Poems.* Translated by Denis Molaise Mehan. Washington, DC: Catholic University of America Press, 1987.

Gregory Palamas. *The Triads.* Edited by John Meyendorff. Translated by Nicholas Gendle. New York: Paulist Press, 1983.

Grumel, V. "S. Thomas et la doctrine des Grecs sur la procession de Saint-Esprit." *Echos d'Orient* 25 (1926): 257-80.

Gunkel, Hermann. *The Influence of the Holy Spirit: The Popular View of the Apostolic Age and the Teaching of the Apostle Paul.* Translated by Roy A. Harris and Philip A. Quanbeck II. Philadelphia: Fortress Press, 1979.

Gunton, Colin E. "Barth, the Trinity, and Human Freedom." *Theology Today* 43 (1986): 316-30.

———. *Becoming and Being: The Doctrine of God in Charles Hartshorne and Karl Barth.* Oxford: Clarendon Press, 1978.

———. "Transcendence, Metaphor, and the Knowability of God." *Journal of Theological Studies* 31 (1980): 501-16.

Guttiérrez, Gustavo. *A Theology of Liberation.* Translated and edited by Cadidad Inda and John Eagleson. London: SCM Press, 1974.

Hahn, Ferdinand. *The Titles of Jesus in Christology.* Translated by Harold Knight and George Ogg. London: Lutterworth Press, 1969.

Hamilton, Neill Q. *The Holy Spirit and Eschatology in Paul.* Edinburgh: Oliver and Boyd, 1957.

Hankey, W. J. *God in Himself: Aquinas' Doctrine of God as Expounded in the "Summa Theologiae."* Oxford: Oxford University Press, 1987.

———. "The Place of the Psychological Image of the Trinity in the Arguments of Augustine's *De Trinitate,* Anselm's *Monologion,* and Aquinas' *Summa Theologiae.*" *Dionysus* 3 (1979): 99-110.

Hanson, Anthony Tyrrell. *Grace and Truth: A Study in the Doctrine of the Incarnation.* London: SPCK, 1975.

Hanson, R. P. C. *The Attractiveness of God.* London: SPCK, 1973.

———. *The Search for the Christian Doctrine of God.* Edinburgh: T. & T. Clark, 1988.

Hardy, Edward Rochie, and Cyril C. Richardson, eds. *Christology of the Later Fathers.* Philadelphia: Westminster Press, 1954.

Harnack, Adolf von. *History of Dogma.* Translated by Neil Buchanan. 7 vols. London: Williams & Norgate, 1894-99.

———. *The Mission and Expansion of Christianity in the First Three Centuries.*

Edited and translated by James Moffatt. 2nd ed. London: Williams and Norgate, 1908.

Hay, David. *Exploring Inner Space*. Oxford: Mowbray, 1987.

Hegel, G. W. F. *Lectures on the Philosophy of Religion*. Edited by Peter C. Hodgson. Translated by R. F. Brown et al. 3 vols. Berkeley and Los Angeles: University of California Press, 1984-85.

Heitmann, C., and H. Mühlen, eds. *Erfahrung und Theologie des Heiligen Geistes*. Hamburg: Agentur des Rauhen Hauses and München: Kösel-Verlag, 1974.

Helm, Paul. *Eternal God: A Study of God Without Time*. Oxford: Clarendon Press, 1988.

Hendry, George S. "The Freedom of God in the Theology of Karl Barth." *Scottish Journal of Theology* 31 (1978): 229-44.

————. *The Holy Spirit in Christian Theology*. Philadelphia: Westminster Press, 1956.

————. *Theology of Nature*. Philadelphia: Westminster Press, 1980.

————. "The Transcendental Method in the Theology of Karl Barth." *Scottish Journal of Theology* 37 (1984): 213-27.

Hermann, Ingo. *Kurios und Pneuma*. München: Kösel-Verlag, 1961.

Heron, Alasdair. *A Century of Protestant Theology*. Guildford and London: Lutterworth Press, 1980.

————. *The Holy Spirit*. London: Marshall Morgan & Scott, 1983.

————. " 'Who Proceedeth from the Father and the Son': The Problem of the Filioque." *Scottish Journal of Theology* 24 (1971): 149-66.

Hill, Edmund. "Our Knowledge of the Trinity." *Scottish Journal of Theology* 27 (1974): 1-11.

Hill, William J. "The Historicity of God." *Theological Studies* 45 (1984): 320-33.

————. *The Three-Personed God: The Trinity as a Mystery of Salvation*. Washington: Catholic University of America Press, 1982.

————. "Uncreated Grace — A Critique of Karl Rahner." *Thomist* 26 (1963): 333-56.

Hodgson, L. *The Doctrine of the Trinity*. New York: Charles Scribner & Sons, 1944.

Hollenweger, Walter J. *The Pentecostals*. Translated by R. A. Wilson. London: SCM Press, 1972.

Hoyle, R. Birch. "Spirit (Holy), Spirit of God." In *Encyclopaedia of Religion and Ethics*, vol. 11, pp. 784-803. Edited by James Hastings et al. Edinburgh: T. & T. Clark, 1920.

Hübner, Hans. "The Holy Spirit in Holy Scripture." *The Ecumenical Review* 41 (1989): 324-38.

Irénée de Lyon. *Contra les hérésies*. Edited by Adelin Rousseau et al. Paris: Cerf, 1965- .

Isaacs, Marie E. *The Concept of Spirit: A Study of Pneuma in Hellenistic Judaism and Its Bearing on the New Testament*. London: Heythrop Monographs, 1976.

Jenson, Robert W. "The Logic of the Doctrine of the Trinity." *Dialog* 26 (1987): 245-49.

―――. *God after God: The God of the Past and the God of the Future, Seen in the Work of Karl Barth*. Indianapolis and New York: Bobbs-Merrill, 1969.

Jeremias, Joachim. *The Sermon on the Mount*. Translated by Norman Perrin. London: Athlone Press, 1961.

Jüngel, Eberhard. "Das Verhältnis von 'okonomischer' und 'immanenter' Trinität." *Zeitschrift für Theologie und Kirche* 72 (1975): 353-64.

―――. *God as the Mystery of the World*. Translated by Darrell L. Guder. Edinburgh: T. & T. Clark, 1983.

―――. ". . . keine Menschenlosigkeit Gottes . . . ." *Evangelische Theologie* 31 (1971): 371-90.

―――. *The Doctrine of the Trinity*. Translated by Horton Harris. Edinburgh: Scottish Academic Press, 1976.

―――. "Zur Lehre vom Heiligen Geist: Thesen." In *Die Mitte des Neuen Testaments,* pp. 97-118. Edited by Ulrich Luz and Hans Weder. Göttingen: Vandenhoeck & Ruprecht, 1983.

Kaiser, Christopher. "The Ontological Trinity in the Context of Historical Religions." *Scottish Journal of Theology* 29 (1976): 301-10.

Kalin, E. R. "Inspired Community: A Glance at Canon History." *Concordia Theological Monthly* 43 (1971): 541-49.

Kant, Immanuel. *Critique of Judgement*. Translated by James Creed Meredith. Oxford: Clarendon, 1928.

―――. *Critique of Practical Reason*. Translated by T. K. Abbott. London: Longmans, 1909.

―――. *Critique of Pure Reason*. Edited and translated by Norman Kemp Smith. New York: St. Martin's Press, 1965.

Karsavine, L. P. "L'Orient, l'Occident et l'Idée russe." Translated by S. Arminjon and M.-J. Guillou. *Istina* 17 (1972): 311-44.

Käsemann, Ernst. "Geist und Geistgaben im NT." In *Die Religion in Geschichte und Gegenwart,* vol. 2, cols. 1272-78. Edited by H. F. von Campenhausen et al. 3rd ed. Tübingen: J. C. B. Mohr (Paul Siebeck), 1958.

―――. "The Canon of the New Testament and the Unity of the Church." In Käsemann, *Essays on New Testament Themes,* pp. 95-107. Translated by W. J. Montague. London: SCM Press, 1964.

―――. "The Spirit and the Letter." In Käsemann, *Perspectives on Paul,* pp. 138-66. Translated by Margaret Kohl. London: SCM Press, 1971.

Kasper, Walter. *Jesus the Christ*. Translated by V. Green. London: Burns & Oates, 1977.

————. *The God of Jesus Christ*. Translated by Matthew O'Connell. London: SCM Press, 1984.

————. *Theology and Church*. Translated by Margaret Kohl. London: SCM Press, 1989.

Kelly, J. N. D. *Early Christian Creeds*. 3rd ed. London: Longman, 1972.

————. *Early Christian Doctrines*. 5th ed. London: Adam & Charles Black, 1977.

Kent, John H. S. "Christian Theology in the Eighteenth to the Twentieth Centuries." In *A History of Christian Doctrine*, pp. 461-591. Edited by Hubert Cunliffe-Jones. Edinburgh: T. & T. Clark, 1978.

Keruvilla, Abraham. "The Holy Spirit in the Mar Thoma Tradition." *The Ecumenical Review* 41 (1989): 436-45.

Kilian, Sabbas J. "The Holy Spirit in Christ and Christians." *American Benedictine Review* 20 (1969): 99-121.

Kilmartin, Edward J. "The Active Role of Christ and the Holy Spirit in the Sanctification of the Eucharistic Elements." *Theological Studies* 45 (1984): 225-53.

Klappert, Bertold. "Die Gottverlassenheit Jesu und der gekreuzigte Gott." *Verkündigung und Forschung* 20 (1975): 35-53.

————. "Tendenzen der Gotteslehre in der Gegenwart." *Evangelische Theologie* 35 (1975): 189-208.

Knight, G. A. F. *A Biblical Approach to the Doctrine of the Trinity*. Edinburgh: Oliver and Boyd, 1953.

Koch, Robert. *Geist und Messias*. Vienna: Verlag Herder, 1950.

König, A. "Le Dieu crucifié. Peut-on parler du Dieu crucifié? (Moltmann et Jüngel)." *Hokhma* 17 (1981): 73-95.

Kümmel, W. G. *Theology of the New Testament*. Translated by John E. Steely. London: SCM Press, 1974.

Küng, Hans. *The Incarnation of God: An Introduction to Hegel's Theological Thought as Prolegomena to a Future Christology*. Translated by J. R. Stephenson. Edinburgh: T. & T. Clark, 1987.

————, and Jürgen Moltmann, eds. *Conflicts about the Holy Spirit*. New York: Seabury Press, 1979.

LaCugna, Catherine Mowry. *God With Us*. San Francisco: Harper, 1991.

————. "Philosophers and Theologians on the Trinity." *Modern Theology* 2, no. 3 (1986): 169-81.

Lafont, Ghislain. *Peut-on connaître Dieu en Jésus Christ?* Paris: Les Éditions du Cerf, 1969.

Lake, Kirsopp, ed. *The Apostolic Fathers*. 2 vols. London: William Heinemann; New York: Macmillan, 1912-13.

Lampe, G. W. H. "The Holy Spirit and the Person of Christ." In *Christ, Faith and History*, pp. 111-30. Edited by S. W. Sykes and J. P. Clayton. Cambridge: Cambridge University Press, 1972.

————. *God as Spirit*. Oxford: Clarendon Press, 1977.

————, ed. *A Patristic Greek Lexicon*. Oxford: Clarendon Press, 1961.

Lash, Nicholas. "Considering the Trinity." *Modern Theology* 2 (1986): 183-96.

Lauer, Quentin. *Hegel's Concept of God*. Albany: State University of New York Press, 1982.

Le Guillou, M.-J. "La critique du Filioque de L. P. Karsavine." *Istina* 17 (1972): 293-310.

Lemopoulos, George. "Come, Holy Spirit." *The Ecumenical Review* 41 (1989): 461-67.

Lindbeck, George A. *The Nature of Doctrine: Religion and Theology in a Postliberal Age*. London: SPCK, 1984.

Loeschen, John R. *The Divine Community*. Kirksville, MO: Sixteenth Century Journal Publishers, 1981.

Loewenich, Walther von. *Luther's Theology of the Cross*. Translated by Herbert J. A. Bouman. Belfast: Christian Journals, 1976.

Lonergan, Bernard. *Method in Theology*. New York: Herder and Herder, 1972.

————. "Theology in Its New Context." In Lonergan, *A Second Collection*, pp. 55-67. Philadelphia: Westminster, 1974.

————. *The Way to Nicea*. Translated by Conn O'Donovan. London: Darton, Longman & Todd, 1976.

Long, J. Bruce. "Life." In *The Encyclopedia of Religion*, pp. 541-47. Edited by Mircea Eliade. New York: Macmillan, 1987.

Lossky, Vladimir. *The Mystical Theology of the Eastern Church*. Translated by members of the Fellowship of St. Alban and St. Sergius. Cambridge: James Clarke & Co., 1957.

————. "The Procession of the Holy Spirit in the Orthodox Triadology." Translated by Edward Every. *The Eastern Churches Quarterly* 7, supplementary issue 2 (1948): 31-53.

————. *The Vision of God*. Translated by Asheleigh Moorhouse. Clayton, WI: Faith Press, 1963.

Lovelace, Richard. "Pneumatological Issues in American Presbyterianism." *The Greek Orthodox Theological Review* 31 (1986): 335-50.

Löwith, Karl. *From Hegel to Nietzsche*. Translated by David E. Green. London: Constable, 1965.

Luther, Martin. *Luther's Works*. Edited by Jaroslav Pelikan and Helmut T. Lehmann. 55 vols. Philadelphia: Fortress Press, 1955- .

————. *Reformation Writings of Martin Luther*. Translated by Bertram Lee Wolff. 2 vols. London: Lutterworth Press, 1952.

Lyttkens, Hampus. *The Analogy Between God and the World: An Investigation of Its Background and Interpretation of Its Use by Thomas of Aquino*. Uppsala: A.-B. Lundequistska Bokhandeln; Wiesbaden: Otto Harrassowitz, 1953.

Macdonald, A. J. *The Holy Spirit*. London: SPCK, 1927.

Mackey, James P. *Jesus the Man and the Myth*. London: SCM Press, 1979.

————. *Modern Theology: A Sense of Direction*. Oxford: Oxford University Press, 1987.

————. *The Christian Experience of God as Trinity*. London: SCM Press, 1983.

MacKinnon, Donald. "Some Reflections on Hans Urs von Balthasar's Christology with Special Reference to *Theodramatik* II/2, III and IV." In *The Analogy of Beauty*, pp. 164-79. Edited by John Riches. Edinburgh: T. & T. Clark, 1986.

Macquarrie, John. *In Search of Deity: An Essay in Dialectical Theism*. London: SCM Press, 1984.

————. *Twentieth Century Religious Thought: The Frontiers of Philosophy and Theology, 1900-1960*. New York: Harper & Row, 1963.

Markus, R. A. "Trinitarian Theology and the Economy." *Journal of Theological Studies* 9 (1958): 89-102.

Mascall, E. L. *Whatever Happened to the Human Mind?* London: SPCK, 1980.

Matsoukas, Nikos. "The Economy of the Holy Spirit: the Standpoint of Orthodox Theology." *The Ecumenical Review* 41 (1989): 398-405.

Maxwell, Meg, and Verena Tschudin. *Seeing the Invisible*. London: Arkana, 1990.

McDonnell, Kilian. "A Trinitarian Doctrine of the Holy Spirit." *Theological Studies* 46 (1985): 191-227.

————. "Does Origen Have a Trinitarian Doctrine of the Holy Spirit?" *Gregorianum* 75 (1994): 23-38.

————. "The Determinative Doctrine of the Holy Spirit." *Theology Today* 39 (1982): 142-61.

McGrath, Alister E. *Iustitia Dei*. 2 vols. Cambridge: Cambridge University Press, 1986.

————. *The Making of Modern German Christology: From the Enlightenment to Pannenberg*. Oxford: Basil Blackwell, 1986.

McIntyre, John. *The Shape of Soteriology*. Edinburgh: T. & T. Clark, 1992.

McLellan, David, ed. *Karl Marx*. Oxford: Oxford University Press, 1977.

Meeks, M. Douglas. *Origins of the Theology of Hope*. Philadelphia: Fortress Press, 1974.

Melanchthon, Philipp. *Melanchthon on Christian Doctrine*. Edited and translated by Clyde L. Manschrenck. New York: Oxford University Press, 1965.

Michel, A. "Jésus-Christ." In *Dictionnaire de théologie catholique*, vol. 8, cols. 1108-1411. Edited by A. Vacant et al. Paris: Librairie Letouzey et Ané, 1924.

————. "Trinité (Missions et Habitations de la)." In *Dictionnaire de théologie catholique*, vol. 15, cols. 1831-32. Edited by A. Vacant et al. Paris: Librairie Letouzey et Ané, 1946.

Michel, Otto. "OIKONOMIA." In *Theological Dictionary of the New Testament*, vol. 5, pp. 151-53. Edited by Gerhard Friedrich. Translated by

Geoffrey W. Bromiley. Grand Rapids: Wm. B. Eerdmans Publishing Company, 1968.

Milbank, John. "The Second Difference: For a Trinitarianism Without Reserve." *Modern Theology* 2 (1986): 213-34.

Min, Anselm K. "Hegel's Absolute: Transcendent or Immanent?" *Journal of Religion* 56 (1976): 61-87.

————. "Hegel's Retention of Mystery as a Theological Category." *Clio* 12 (1983): 333-53.

————. "The Trinity and the Incarnation: Hegel and Classical Approaches." *The Journal of Religion* 66 (1986): 173-93.

Moltmann, Jürgen. *The Church in the Power of the Spirit: A Contribution to Messianic Ecclesiology.* Translated by Margaret Kohl. London: SCM Press, 1977.

————. *The Crucified God: The Cross of Jesus Christ as the Foundation and Criticism of Christian Theology.* Translated by R. A. Wilson and John Bowden. London: SCM Press, 1974.

————. *The Future of Creation.* Translated by Margaret Kohl. London: SCM Press, 1979.

————. "Theological Proposals Towards the Resolution of the *Filioque* Controversy." In World Council of Churches, Commission on Faith and Order, *Spirit of God, Spirit of Christ,* pp. 164-73. Edited by Lukas Vischer. Geneva: World Council of Churches; London: SPCK, 1981.

————. *Theology of Hope: On the Ground and Implications of a Christian Eschatology.* Translated by James W. Leitch. London: SCM Press, 1967.

————. *The Spirit of Life.* Translated by Margaret Kohl. London: SCM Press, 1992.

————. *The Trinity and the Kingdom of God: The Doctrine of God.* Translated by Margaret Kohl. London: SCM Press, 1981.

————. *The Way of Jesus Christ: Christology in Messianic Dimensions.* Translated by Margaret Kohl. London: SCM Press, 1990.

Mondin, Battista. *The Principle of Analogy in Protestant and Catholic Thought.* The Hague: Martinus Nijhoff, 1963.

Montague, George T. *The Holy Spirit: Growth of a Biblical Tradition.* New York: Paulist Press, 1976. Reprint Peabody, MA: Hendrickson, 1994.

Morris, Thomas V. *The Logic of God Incarnate.* Ithaca and London: Cornell University Press, 1986.

Moule, C. F. D. *The Holy Spirit.* Oxford: Mowbray, 1978.

Mühlen, Heribert. "Das Christusereignis als Tat des Heiligen Geistes." In *Mysterium Salutis,* III/2, pp. 513-45. Edited by Johannes Feiner and Magnus Löhrer. Einsiedeln: Benziger Verlag, 1969.

————. *Der Heilige Geist als Person in der Trinität bei der Inkarnation und im Gnadenbund: Ich — Du — Wir.* 5th ed. Münster: Aschendorff, 1988.

————. *Der Veränderlichkeit Gottes als Horizont einer zukünftigen Christologie: Auf dem Wege zu einer Kreuzestheologie in Auseinandersetzung mit der altkirchlichen Christologie.* Münster: Aschendorf, 1969.

————. *Una Mystica Persona. Eine Person in vielen Personnen.* 2nd ed. Paderborn: Verlag Schöningh, 1967.

Muller, R. A. "Incarnation, Immutability, and the Case for Classical Theism." *Westminster Theological Journal* 45 (1983): 22-40.

Neuner, J., and J. Dupuis, eds. *The Christian Faith.* Rev. ed. New York: Alba House, 1982.

Newman, Paul W. *A Spirit Christology: Rediscovering the Biblical Paradigm of Christian Faith.* Lanham, NY, and London: University Press of America, 1987.

Nietzsche, Friedrich. *Beyond Good and Evil.* Translated by Walter Kaufmann. New York: Vintage Books, 1966.

Nissiotis, N. A. *Die Theologie der Ostkirche im ökumenischen Dialog.* Stuttgart: Evangelische Verlagswerk, 1968.

Nissiotis, Nikos A. "Pneumatological Christology as a Presupposition of Ecclesiology." In *Oecumenica: Jahrbuch für ökumenische Forschung 1967,* pp. 235-52. Gütersloh: Gerd Mohn; Minneapolis: Augsburg Publishing House; Neuchâtel: Éditions Delachaux et Niestlé, 1967.

O'Donnell, John J. "In Him and Over Him: The Holy Spirit in the Life of Jesus." *Gregorianum* 70 (1989): 25-45.

————. *The Mystery of the Triune God.* London: Sheed & Ward, 1988.

————. *Trinity and Temporality: The Christian Doctrine of God in the Light of Process Theology and the Theology of Hope.* Oxford: Oxford University Press, 1983.

O'Donoghue, Noel Dermot. *Heaven in Ordinarie.* Edinburgh: T. & T. Clark, 1979.

————. "Mystical Imagination." In *Religious Imagination,* pp. 186-205. Edited by James P. Mackey. Edinburgh: T. & T. Clark, 1986.

————. *The Holy Mountain.* Dublin: Dominican Publications, 1983.

O'Donovan, L. J. "The Mystery of God as a History of Love: Eberhard Jüngel's Doctrine of God." *Theological Studies* 42 (1981): 251-71.

Oates, Wayne E. *The Holy Spirit and Contemporary Man.* Grand Rapids: Baker Book House, 1968.

Ogden, Schubert M. "On the Trinity." *Theology* 83 (1980): 97-102.

Olson, Roger. "Trinity and Eschatology: The Historical Being of God in Jürgen Moltmann and Wolfhart Pannenberg." *Scottish Journal of Theology* 36 (1983): 213-27.

————. "Wolfhart Pannenberg's Doctrine of the Trinity." *Scottish Journal of Theology* 43 (1990): 175-206.

Opsahl, Paul D., ed. *The Holy Spirit in the Life of the Church: From Biblical Times to the Present.* Minneapolis: Augsburg Publishing House, 1978.

Orphanos, Markos A. "The Procession of the Holy Spirit According to Certain of the Later Greek Fathers." In World Council of Churches, Commission on Faith and Order, *Spirit of God, Spirit of Christ,* pp. 21-45. Edited by Lukas Vischer. Geneva: World Council of Churches; London: SPCK, 1981.

Osei-Bonsu, Joseph. "The Spirit as Agent of Renewal: The New Testament Testimony." *The Ecumenical Review* 41 (1989): 454-60.

Outler, Albert C. "Pneumatology as an Ecumenical Frontier." *The Ecumenical Review* 41 (1989): 363-74.

Pailin, David A. *God and the Processes of Reality: Foundations of a Credible Theism.* London and New York: Routledge, 1989.

―――. "Process Theology." In *A New Dictionary of Christian Theology,* pp. 467-70. Edited by Alan Richardson and John Bowden. London: SCM Press, 1983.

Pannenberg, Wolfhart. "Der Gott der Geschichte." In Pannenberg, *Grundfragen systematischer Theologie. Gesammelte Aufsätze 2,* pp. 112-28. Göttingen: Vandenhoeck, 1980.

―――. "Die Subjectivität Gottes und die Trinitätslehre." In Pannenberg, *Grundfragen systematischer Theologie. Gesammelte Aufsätze 2,* pp. 96-111. Göttingen: Vandenhoeck, 1980.

―――. *Jesus — God and Man.* Translated by Lewis L. Wilkins and Duane A. Priebe. London: SCM Press, 1968.

―――. "Problems of a Trinitarian Doctrine of God." *Dialog* 26 (1987): 250-57.

―――. *Systematische Theologie, Band I.* Göttingen: Vandenhoeck & Ruprecht, 1988.

―――. "The Appropriation of the Philosophical Concept of God as a Dogmatic Problem of Early Christian Theology." In Pannenberg, *Basic Questions in Theology,* vol. 2, pp. 119-83. Translated by George H. Kehm. London: SCM Press, 1971.

―――. *Theology and the Kingdom of God.* Philadelphia: Westminster Press, 1969.

―――. "What Is Truth?" In Pannenberg, *Basic Questions in Theology,* vol. 2, pp. 1-27. Translated by George H. Kehm. London: SCM Press, 1971.

Parratt, John, ed. *A Reader in African Theology.* London: SPCK, 1987.

Pelikan, Jaroslav. "Montanism and Its Trinitarian Significance." *Church History* 25 (1956): 99-109.

―――. *The Christian Tradition.* 5 vols. Chicago and London: University of Chicago Press, 1971-89.

―――. "The Doctrine of the Filioque in Thomas Aquinas and Its Patristic Antecedents: An Analysis of *Summa Theologiae* I, q. 36." In *St. Thomas Aquinas 1274-1974,* vol. 1, pp. 315-36. Edited by E. Gilson et al. Toronto: Pontifical Institute of Medieval Studies, 1974.

Pietri, Charles. "Personne, analogie de l'âme humaine et théologie de l'Esprit. Brèves remarques sur Augustin, Mühlen et Rahner." In *Dieu révélé dans l'Esprit,* pp. 111-24. Edited by Franco Bolgiani et al. Paris: Éditions Beauchesne, 1979.

Pinnock, Clark. "The Need for a Scriptural, and Therefore a Neo-Classical Theism." In *Perspectives on Evangelical Theology,* pp. 37-42. Edited by Kenneth Kantzer and Stanley Gundry. Grand Rapids: Baker, 1979.

Pittenger, Norman. *The Holy Spirit.* Philadelphia: United Church Press, 1974.

Pollard, T. E. *Fullness of Humanity: Christ's Humanness and Ours.* Sheffield: Almond Press, 1982.

Prenter, R. "Heiliger Geist, dogmatisch." In *Die Religion in Geschichte und Gegenwart,* vol. 2, cols. 1283-86. Edited by H. F. von Campenhausen et al. 3rd ed. Tübingen: J. C. B. Mohr (Paul Siebeck), 1958.

Prestige, G. L. *God in Patristic Thought.* 2nd ed. London: SPCK, 1952.

————. "[*Perichoreo*] and [*Perichoresis*] in the Fathers." *Journal of Theological Studies* 29 (1928): 242-52.

Primavesi, Anne, and Jennifer Henderson. "The Witness of the Holy Spirit." *The Ecumenical Review* 41 (1989): 426-35.

Przywara, E. "Analogia entis (Analogie)." In *Lexikon für Theologie und Kirche,* vol. 1, cols. 468-73. Edited by Joseph Höfer and Karl Rahner. 2nd ed. Freiburg: Verlag Herder, 1957.

————. "Analogia fidei." In *Lexikon für Theologie und Kirche,* vol. 1, cols. 473-76. Edited by Joseph Höfer and Karl Rahner. 2nd ed. Freiburg: Verlag Herder, 1957.

Quasten, J. *Patrology.* 4 vols. Westminster, MD: Christian Classics, 1984.

Rahner, Karl. "Anonymous Christianity and the Missionary Task of the Church." In Rahner, *Theological Investigations,* vol. 12, pp. 161-78. Translated by David Bourke. London: Darton, Longman and Todd, 1974.

————. "Anonymous Christians." In Rahner, *Theological Investigations,* vol. 6, pp. 390-98. Translated by K. H. and B. Kruger. London: Darton, Longman and Todd, 1969.

————. "Current Problems in Christology." In Rahner, *Theological Investigations,* vol. 1, pp. 149-200. Translated by Cornelius Ernst. 2nd ed. London: Darton, Longman & Todd, 1965.

————. *Foundations of Christian Faith.* Translated by William V. Dych. London: Darton, Longman and Todd, 1978.

————. "Observations on the Doctrine of God in Catholic Dogmatics." In Rahner, *Theological Investigations,* vol. 9, pp. 127-44. Translated by Graham Harrison. London: Darton, Longman & Todd, 1972.

————. "On the Theology of the Incarnation." In Rahner, *Theological Investigations,* vol. 4, pp. 105-20. Edited and translated by Kevin Smyth. Baltimore: Helicon Press; London: Darton, Longman & Todd, 1966.

————. "Remarks on the Dogmatic Treatise 'De Trinitate.'" In Rahner, *Theological Investigations*, vol. 4, pp. 77-102. Edited and translated by Kevin Smyth. Baltimore: Helicon Press; London: Darton, Longman & Todd, 1966.

————. *Spirit in the World*. Translated by W. Dyck. New York: Herder and Herder, 1968.

————. "The Concept of Mystery in Catholic Theology." In Rahner, *Theological Investigations*, vol. 4, pp. 36-73. Edited and translated by Kevin Smyth. Baltimore: Helicon Press; London: Darton, Longman & Todd, 1966.

————. "The Theology of the Symbol." In Rahner, *Theological Investigations*, vol. 4, pp. 221-52. Edited and translated by Kevin Smyth. Baltimore: Helicon Press; London: Darton, Longman & Todd, 1966.

————. *The Trinity*. Translated by Joseph Donceel. London: Burns & Oates, 1970.

————. "Trinity, Divine." In *Sacramentum Mundi*, vol. 4, pp. 295-303. Edited by Rahner et al. London: Burns & Oates, 1970.

————. "Trinity in Theology." In *Sacramentum Mundi*, vol. 4, pp. 303-8. Edited by Rahner et al. London: Burns & Oates, 1970.

————, and Wilhelm Thüsing. *A New Christology*. Translated by David Smith and Verdant Green. London: Burns & Oates, 1980.

Raiser, Konrad. "The Holy Spirit in Modern Ecumenical Thought." *The Ecumenical Review* 41 (1989): 375-87.

Ramsey, Michael. *Holy Spirit*. London: SPCK, 1977.

Raven, Charles E. *The Creator Spirit*. London: Martin Hopkinson & Co., 1928.

Reardon, Bernard M. G. *Hegel's Philosophy of Religion*. London: MacMillan, 1977.

Rhodes, J. Stephen. "Christ and the Spirit: Filioque Reconsidered." *Biblical Theology Bulletin* 18 (1988): 91-95.

Richard de Saint-Victor. *La Trinité*. Paris: Sources Chrétiennes, 1969.

Richard of St. Victor. *Richard of St. Victor: The Twelve Patriarchs, The Mystical Ark, Book Three of the Trinity*. London: SPCK, 1979.

Richardson, Cyril. *The Doctrine of the Trinity*. New York: Abingdon Press, 1958.

Riches, John, ed. *The Analogy of Beauty: The Theology of Hans Urs von Balthasar*. Edinburgh: T. & T. Clark, 1986.

Rilliet, Jean. *Karl Barth — théologien existentialiste?* Neûchatel: H. Messeiller, 1952.

Ringgren, Helmer. *Israelite Religion*. Translated by David Green. London: SPCK, 1969.

Ritschl, Albrecht. *Theology and Metaphysics*. In Ritschl, *Three Essays*, pp. 149-217. Translated and with an introduction by Philip Hefner. Philadelphia: Fortress Press, 1972.

————. *The Theology of Albrecht Ritschl.* Edited by A. T. Swing. Translated by A. M. Swing. New York: Longmans, Green, 1901.

Roberts, Richard. "Karl Barth." In *One God in Trinity,* pp. 78-93. Edited by Peter Toon and James D. Spiceland. London: Samuel Bagster, 1980.

Robinson, H. Wheeler. *The Christian Experience of the Holy Spirit.* London: Nisbet & Co., 1928.

Rosato, Philip J. "Holy Spirit." In *A New Dictionary of Christian Theology,* pp. 262-69. Edited by Alan Richardson and John Bowden. London: SCM Press, 1983.

————. "Spirit-Christology: Ambiguity and Promise." *Theological Studies* 38 (1977): 423-49.

————. "The Mission of the Spirit Within and Beyond the Church." *The Ecumenical Review* 41 (1989): 388-97.

————. *The Spirit as Lord.* Edinburgh: T. & T. Clark, 1981.

Rupp, Gordon. "Word and Spirit in the First Years of the Reformation." *Archiv für Reformationsgeschichte* 49 (1958): 1-13.

Ryder, Andrew. *The Spirituality of the Trinity.* Dublin: Carmelite Centre of Spirituality, 1985.

Sacred Congregation for the Doctrine of the Faith. *Instruction on Certain Aspects of the Theology of Liberation.* Translated by Vatican Polyglot Press. London: Catholic Truth Society, 1984.

Sanders, E. P. *Paul and Palestinian Judaism.* London: SCM Press, 1977.

Sartre, Jean-Paul. *Existentialism and Humanism.* Translated by Philip Mairet. London: Methuen, 1948.

Scharlemann, Robert P. "Hegel and Theology Today." *Dialog* 23 (1984): 257-62.

Schillebeeckx, Eduard. *Christ the Sacrament of Encounter with God.* London and Melbourne: Sheed and Ward, 1963.

Schleiermacher, Friedrich. *The Christian Faith.* Edited by H. R. Mackintosh. Translated by James S. Stewart. Edinburgh: T. & T. Clark, 1928.

Schmaus, Michael. *Der liber propugnatorius des Thomas Angelicus und die Lehrunterschiede zwischen Thomas von Aquin und Duns Scotus.* Vol. 2 of Schmaus, *Die trinitärischen Lehrunterschiede.* Münster: Aschendorff, 1930.

————. *Die psychologische Trinitätslehre des Hl. Augustinus.* Münster: Aschendorffsche Verlagsbuch-handlung, 1927.

Schmemann, Alexander. *The Historical Road of Eastern Orthodoxy.* Translated by Lydia W. Kesich. London: Harvill Press, 1963.

Schmidt, M. A. "Heiliger Geist, dogmengeschichtlich." In *Die Religion in Geschichte und Gegenwart,* vol. 2, cols. 1279-83. Edited by H. F. von Campenhausen et al. 3rd ed. Tübingen: J. C. B. Mohr (Paul Siebeck), 1958.

Schmitt, H. C. "Prophetie und Tradition." *Zeitschrift für Theologie und Kirche* 74 (1977): 255-72.

Schoeps, Hans-Joachim. *Jewish Christianity: Factional Disputes in the Early Church.* Translated by Douglas R. A. Hare. Philadelphia: Fortress Press, 1969.

Schönborn, Christoph von. "Immanente und ökonomische Trinität: Zur Frage des Funktionsverlustes der Trinitätslehre in der östlichen und westlichen Theologie." *Freiburger Zeitschrift für Philosophie und Theologie* 27 (1980): 247-64.

Schoonenberg, Piet. *The Christ.* Translated by Della Couling. London: Sheed & Ward, 1969.

Schweitzer, Albert. *The Mysticism of Paul the Apostle.* Translated by W. Montgomery. London: A. & C. Black, 1931.

———. *The Quest of the Historical Jesus.* Translated by W. Montgomery. 3rd ed. London: SCM Press, 1981. (3rd English edition first published 1954.)

Schweizer, Eduard. "On Distinguishing Between Spirits." *The Ecumenical Review* 41 (1989): 406-15.

———. "[*Pneuma, Pneumatikos*]." In *Theological Dictionary of the New Testament,* vol. 6, pp. 332-451. Edited by Gerhard Friedrich. Translated by Geoffrey W. Bromiley. Grand Rapids: Wm. B. Eerdmans Publishing Co., 1968.

———. *Spirit of God.* New York: Harper & Row, 1960.

———. *The Holy Spirit.* Translated by Reginald H. Fuller and Ilse Fuller. Philadelphia: Fortress Press, 1980.

Segundo, Juan Luis. *Our Idea of God.* Dublin: Gill and MacMillan, 1980.

Sellers, R. V. *The Council of Chalcedon.* London: SPCK, 1961.

Smail, Thomas. *Reflected Glory.* London: Hodder & Stoughton, 1975.

———. *The Giving Gift.* London: Hodder & Stoughton, 1988.

Smeaton, George. *The Doctrine of the Holy Spirit.* 2nd ed. Edinburgh: T. & T. Clark, 1889.

Smith, John E. "Hegel's Reinterpretation of the Doctrine of Spirit and the Religious Community." In *Hegel and the Philosophy of Religion,* pp. 157-77. Edited by Darrel E. Christensen. The Hague: Martinus Nijhoff, 1970.

Smith, Mark S. *The Early History of God: Yahweh and the Other Deities in Ancient Israel.* San Francisco: Harper & Row, 1990.

Sobrino, Jon. *Christology at the Crossroads.* Translated by John Drury. London: SCM Press, 1978.

Song, Choan-Seng. *The Compassionate God.* London: SCM Press, 1982.

Stadler, Kurt. "The Filioque Clause in the Old Catholic Churches: The Chief Phases of Theological Reflection and Church Pronouncements." In World Council of Churches, Commission on Faith and Order, *Spirit of*

God, Spirit of Christ, pp. 97-109. Edited by Lukas Vischer. Geneva: World Council of Churches; London: SPCK, 1981.

Staniloae, Dumitru. "The Procession of the Holy Spirit from the Father and His Relation to the Son, as the Basis of Our Deification and Adoption." In World Council of Churches, Commission on Faith and Order, *Spirit of God, Spirit of Christ*, pp. 174-86. Edited by Lukas Vischer. Geneva: World Council of Churches; London: SPCK, 1981.

Stead, Christopher. *Divine Substance*. Oxford: Clarendon Press, 1977.

Stylianopoulos, Theodore. "The Filioque: Dogma, Theologoumenon or Error?" *The Greek Theological Review* 31 (1984): 255-88.

Suenens, Léon Joseph. *A New Pentecost?* Translated by Francis Martin. London: Fount Paperbacks, 1977.

Surin, Kenneth. "The Trinity and Philosophical Reflection: A Study of David Brown's *The Divine Trinity*." *Modern Theology* 2 (1986): 235-56.

Swete, H. B. *On the History of the Doctrine of the Procession of the Holy Spirit, from the Apostolic Age to the Death of Charlemagne*. Cambridge: Deighton, Bell, and Co., 1876.

————. *The Holy Spirit in the Ancient Church: A Study of Christian Teaching in the Age of the Fathers*. London: MacMillan, 1912.

Swinbourne, Richard. *The Coherence of Theism*. Oxford: Clarendon Press, 1977.

Sykes, S. W. "The Theology of the Humanity of Christ." In *Christ, Faith and History*, pp. 53-71. Edited by S. W. Sykes and J. P. Clayton. Cambridge: Cambridge University Press, 1972.

————, ed. *Karl Barth — Studies of His Theological Method*. Oxford: Clarendon Press, 1979.

Taylor, John V. *The Go-Between God: The Holy Spirit and the Christian Mission*. London: SCM Press, 1972.

————. *The Primal Vision*. London: SCM Press, 1963.

Tempels, Placide. *La philosophie bantoue*. Paris: Éditions Africaines, 1949.

Thielicke, Helmut. *The Evangelical Faith*. 3 vols. Translated and edited by Geoffrey W. Bromiley. Grand Rapids: Wm. B. Eerdmans Publishing Co., 1974-82.

Thomas Aquinas. *Summa Contra Gentiles. Book One: God*. Translated, with an introduction and notes, by Anton C. Pegis. Notre Dame and London: University of Notre Dame Press, 1975.

————. *Summa Theologiae*. Translated, with an introduction and notes, by Thomas Gilby et al. 61 vols. London: Eyre & Spottiswoode; New York: McGraw-Hill, 1964-81.

Thurmer, John A. "The Analogy of the Trinity." *Scottish Journal of Theology* 34 (1981): 509-15.

Tillich, Paul. *Systematic Theology*. 3 vols. London: SCM Press, 1978.

Toon, Peter. *Justification and Sanctification*. London: Marshall Morgan & Scott, 1983.

————, and James D. Spiceland, eds. *One God in Trinity*. London: Samuel Bagster, 1980.

Torrance, Thomas F. "Karl Barth and the Latin Heresy." *Scottish Journal of Theology* 39 (1986): 461-82.

————. *Karl Barth: An Introduction to His Early Theology, 1910-1931*. London: SCM Press, 1962.

————. "The Legacy of Karl Barth (1886-1986)." *Scottish Journal of Theology* 39 (1986): 289-308.

————. *The Trinitarian Faith: The Evangelical Theology of the Ancient Catholic Church*. Edinburgh: T. & T. Clark, 1988.

————. "Towards an Ecumenical Consensus on the Trinity." *Theologische Zeitschrift* 31 (1975): 337-50.

Toynbee, Philip. *Towards the Holy Spirit*. London: SCM Press, 1982.

Track, Joachim. "Analogie." In *Theologische Realenzyklopädie*, vol. 2, pp. 625-50. Edited by Horst Robert Balz et al. Berlin and New York: Walter de Gruyter, 1978.

Upkong, Justin S. "Pluralism and the Problem of the Discernment of Spirits." *The Ecumenical Review* 41 (1989): 416-25.

Vaggione, Richard Paul, ed. *Eunomius: The Extant Works*. Oxford: Clarendon Press, 1987.

Walker, William Lowe. *The Spirit and the Incarnation: In the Light of Scripture, Science and Practical Need*. 2nd ed. Edinburgh: T. & T. Clark, 1901.

Ward, Keith. *Rational Theology and the Creativity of God*. Oxford: Basil Blackwell, 1982.

Watkin-Jones, Howard. *The Holy Spirit in the Mediaeval Church*. London: Epworth Press, 1922.

Webster, John B. *Eberhard Jüngel: An Introduction to His Theology*. Cambridge: Cambridge University Press, 1986.

————. "The Identity of the Holy Spirit: A Problem in Trinitarian Theology." *Themelios* 9 (1983): 4-7.

Welch, Claude. *In This Name: The Doctrine of the Trinity in Contemporary Theology*. New York: Charles Scribner & Sons, 1952.

————. "The Holy Spirit and the Trinity." *Theology Today* 8 (1951): 29-40.

————, ed. and trans. *God and Incarnation in Mid-Nineteenth Century German Theology: G. Thomasius, I. A. Dorner, A. E. Biederman*. New York: Oxford University Press, 1965.

Wesley, John. *The Works of John Wesley*. 3rd ed. Grand Rapids: Baker, 1986.

Wiles, Maurice. "Some Reflections on the Origins of the Doctrine of the Trinity." In Wiles, *Working Papers in Doctrine*, pp. 1-17. London: SCM Press, 1976.

————. "The Holy Spirit in Christian Theology." In Wiles, *Explorations in Theology 4*, pp. 67-72. London: SCM Press, 1979.

Williams, George Huntston. *The Radical Reformation*. 3rd ed. Kirksville, MO: Sixteenth Century Journal Publishers, 1992.

Williams, R. D. "Barth on the Triune God." In *Karl Barth — Studies of His Theological Method*, pp. 147-93. Edited by S. W. Sykes. Oxford: Clarendon Press, 1979.

————. "Trinity and Revelation." *Modern Theology* 2 (1986): 197-212.

Wingren, Gustaf. *Theology in Conflict: Nygren, Barth, Bultmann*. Translated by Eric H. Wahlstrom. Edinburgh and London: Oliver and Boyd, 1958.

Witvliet, Theo. *A Place in the Sun*. Translated by John Bowden. London: SCM Press, 1985.

World Council of Churches, Commission on Faith and Order. *Apostolic Faith Today*. Edited by Hans-Georg Link. Geneva: World Council of Churches, 1985.

————. *Confessing One Faith*. Geneva: World Council of Churches, 1987.

————. *Louvain 1971*. Geneva: World Council of Churches, 1971.

————. *Spirit of God, Spirit of Christ*. Edited by Lukas Vischer. London: SPCK; Geneva: World Council of Churches, 1981.

————. *The Church: Report of a Theological Commission on Faith and Order, 1951*. London: SCM Press, 1951.

————. "The *Filioque* Clause in Ecumenical Perspective." In World Council of Churches, Commission on Faith and Order, *Spirit of God, Spirit of Christ*, pp. 3-18. Edited by Lukas Vischer. Geneva: World Council of Churches; London: SPCK, 1981.

————. *The Report of the Third World Conference at Lund, Sweeden, August 15-28, 1952*. London: SCM Press, 1952.

————. *The Uppsala Report 1968*. Edited by Norman Goodall. Geneva: World Council of Churches, 1971.

————. "Towards the Common Expression of the Apostolic Faith Today." In *Towards Visible Unity: Commission on Faith and Order, Lima, 1982. Vol. II: Study Papers and Reports*, pp. 29-46. Edited by Michael Kinnamon. Geneva: World Council of Churches, 1982.

Wright, David F. " 'Incidentalism' in Theology — Or a Theology for Thirty-Year-Olds." *Themelios* 11 (1986): 88-90.

Zahrnt, Heinz. *The Question of God: Protestant Theology in the Twentieth Century*. Translated by R. A. Wilson. London: Collins, 1969.

Zizioulas, John D. *Being as Communion: Studies in Personhood and the Church*. London: Darton, Longman and Todd, 1985.

Name and Subject Index

Index of Scripture References